Official Rules
of Card Games

Official Rules of Card Games

Albert H. Morehead, Editor

FAWCETT CREST • NEW YORK

INDEX

CHOICE OF GAMES

In selecting a game, the hostess has to weigh several questions: How many will want to play? How many know the games I have in mind? How difficult will it be to teach these games to persons who don't know them? Do my guests want to play studiously, for the sake of the game, or do they want to play socially, as an accompaniment to small talk?

The following guide is designed to help in selection. The games are first grouped according to the number that can play at one table. Many games can be played in one form or another by any number of players from two or three to seven. Such games are not entered under every head, but only under the numbers for which they are best. No game is listed more than twice (although many could in justice be listed three or four times).

Under each head the games are divided roughly into *hilarious*, *social* and *studious*. Obviously this division is rather arbitrary. It is not intended to indicate the mood in which a game *must* be played, but that in which it *can* be played. Hilarious games can be played to the accompaniment of juvenile rowdiness or adult small talk. Serious games either require close attention or give particular opportunity for skill or both. Social games are likewise contests of skill, but are less disrupted by irrelevant conversation.

The games that are easiest to teach to newcomers in a brief time are marked with asterisks (*).

Games for children are described on pages 11-13.

For TWO players

HILARIOUS
Eights*
Concentration°

SOCIAL
Canasta
Cassino
Cribbage
Forty-Five

Honeymoon Bridge
Piquet
Rummy*
Samba

STUDIOUS
Belotte
Bezique

California Jack
Domino Hearts*
Gin Rummy
Klaberjass
Knock Rummy
Pinochle
Russian Bank
Sixty-Six

For THREE players

HILARIOUS

Eights*
Concentration*

SOCIAL

Canasta
Cassino
Cribbage
Cutthroat Bridge

Cutthroat Euchre
Hearts
Rummy*
Seven Up

STUDIOUS

Auction Pinochle
Continental Rummy
Domino Hearts*

Five Hundred
Five Hundred Rum
Knock Rummy
Schafskopf
Six-Bid Solo
Skat
Towie
Trio

For FOUR players

HILARIOUS

Blackout*
Fan Tan*
I Doubt it*
Michigan*
Napoleon*
Pig*
Red Dog*
Snip Snap Snorem*

SOCIAL

Canasta
Euchre

Forty-Five
Hearts*
Pitch*
Poker Squares
Rummy
Seven Up*
Spoil Five

STUDIOUS

Auction Bridge
Auction Hearts
Auction Pinochle
Auction Sheepshead
Cinch

Continental Rum
Contract Bridge
Double-Pack Pinochle
Five Hundred
Liverpool Rum
Omnibus Hearts
Partnership 500 Rum
Partnership Pinochle
Persian Rum
Poker
Sixty-Six
Skat
Solo (Ombre)
Whist

For FIVE OR MORE players

HILARIOUS

Blackout*
Cancellation Hearts*
Fan Tan*
I Doubt It*
Michigan*
Napoleon*
Pounce*
Red Dog*

SOCIAL

Auction Euchre
Black Jack*
Double-Ace Euchre
Double Rum*
Five Hundred
Knock Poker
Oklahoma
Pitch

Spoil Five

STUDIOUS

Auction Hearts
Bridge
Liverpool Rum
Panguingue
Poker
Poker Squares

BANKING GAMES

Baccarat
Black Jack

Faro
Monte Bank

Chemin de Fer
Stuss

RECOMMENDED GAMES

The following games are not widely played but arouse great enthusiasm among those who play them and are therefore recommended to players interested in learning new games. Games marked (*) are especially easy to learn.

Panguingue
*Blackout (three to seven players)
Poker Squares (any number of players)

*Calculation (Solitaire)
Six-pack Bezique (two players)
Knock Poker

TEACHING CARD GAMES TO CHILDREN

Familiarity with playing cards and card games can be of tremendous educational and psychological benefit to children, and offers them immediate pleasure as well as lasting advantages. Child psychologists recognize the importance of bringing parents and children together on terms of equality, and this is most easily accomplished when they play card games together. An interest in playing cards stimulates a child's recognition of letters, forms and numbers, and later helps teach him to count. Children who have learned to amuse themselves with card games become more self-sufficient. In later years, of course, this same familiarity with card games will be a social asset to them.

Children are naturally attracted to the bright colors and pretty designs on playing cards. That adults, too, like to play with the cards is a gratifying discovery: it gives the child a sense of maturity. Card games are the foremost indoor recreation where parents and children can meet on a common ground of interest, without a feeling on the part of the children that parents are merely pretending interest in the juvenile toys. Many parents have found that card games, with their rules and their etiquette, are a powerful force in weaning children away from the "Me first!" and "That's mine!" and "I want it all!" of infancy.

A child is ready to play simple card games at the age of six. But at the age of four he should start learning the pack. Give a four-year-old a pack of cards; emphasize that it is his own, just as much as any other of his toys. At first he will throw the cards about, and delight in seeing them fall. He will soil them, tear them, deface them. Presently he will discover that there are two kinds, red and black, and will make a game of sorting them out. Then he will find that each color in turn is of two kinds; he will ask what they are called; and one day he will proudly ask, "Want to see me pick out all the diamonds?" He will ask the names of the picture cards; he will discover that the other cards are numbered, and will learn to arrange them in sequence and to sort them in groups.

On seeing adults play games with the cards, he will want to play too. Start him on Slapjack—good riotous fun. Next try him on Fish, and when he asks for more—he surely will —take up Stealing Bundles. This is the same as Cassino with building omitted. Each card is won by another of the same rank. But cards won must be stacked face up, and you can steal your opponent's bundle if you can match its top card. Later, when he is learning simple addition, take up fullfledged Royal Cassino—no happier introduction to arithmetic was ever devised!

With children who show marked powers of attention and memory, try Concentration. Many a seven-year-old is able to beat his parents at this game, despite their most honest efforts to win!

In teaching a child a new game, do not commence with a broadside of information about the rules. Put out the cards and start playing the game at once, telling him what to do at each juncture. Give him the rules little by little, as each necessity arises. After he feels at home in the game, a situation may arise for which he has had no instruction. If it is a matter of judgment, discuss it with him and advise his course. If it is a matter of law, be most careful to preface your dictum with "The rule is . . ." It is important to avoid creating any impression that rules are formulated on the spot to suit the case. Rules are rules, and have to be followed even if small fry thereby loses.

These games are ideal for children:

Ages 6—9

Slapjack

Stealing Bundles. Follow the rules of Cassino (page 269) except that there is no building and nothing counts but getting the most cards. When cards are taken in they are stacked face up, and if a player can match the top card of another player's stack, he can steal the entire stack.

Go Fish	Pig
Old Maid	Eights

War

Ages 10—12

Cassino	Concentration
Rummy	Auction Pitch
Go Boom	Authors

Ages 13—15

Hearts	Fan Tan
Michigan	I Doubt It

It must be emphasized that children in the younger age groups often enjoy playing games listed for older age groups, and vice versa; and that children often play many other games not listed here. It may also be noted that many of these games are also played seriously by adults. The list given is intended only to select some of the ideal games, and not to characterize all such games as children's games or to exclude other games which are equally suitable to play by children.

GENERAL RULES

Applying to All Card Games

Certain customs of card play are so well established that it is unnecessary to repeat them as part of the rules for each and every game. The following rules can be assumed to apply to any game, in the absence of any law expressly stating a different rule.

THE PACK—The standard pack of 52 cards contains four suits, each identified by its symbol, or pip: spades (♠), hearts (♡), diamonds (♢), clubs (♣); and thirteen cards of each suit: ace (A), king (K), queen (Q), jack (J), 10, 9, 8, 7, 6, 5, 4, 3, 2. Wherever the pack used for a game is stated to be "52 cards," reference is to this standard pack.

Packs of less than 52 cards are usually formed by stripping cards out of the standard pack; the first cards to be removed are the 2s, then the 3s, and so on in ascending sequence. The various depleted packs may then be defined by the total of cards remaining, e.g.,

> 36 cards (6 is the lowest remaining rank)
> 32 cards (7 low)
> 24 cards (9 low)

A fifty-third card—the *joker*—and a fifty-fourth card, which may be used as an extra joker, are usually packed with the standard 52-card pack and may become part of the pack if the rules of the game require it.

A *double pack* is formed by mixing two 52-card packs together, and so has 104 cards (plus jokers, in some games). A *Pinochle pack* of 48 cards is two 24-card packs mixed together, with two each of the A to the 9 in each suit; there is also a 64-card Pinochle pack formed by mixing together two 32-card packs. In assembling any of these double packs it is usually desirable to use cards of identical back design and color.

A pack of 63 cards is available for use in such games as require it; it includes, in addition to the usual 52 cards and joker, an 11 of each suit, a 12 of each suit, and a 13 of each of two suits.

THE DRAW—Several methods are in use for determination of partnerships, seats at the table, right to deal first, etc. The most common method is: The pack is shuffled and then spread face downward on the table, with the cards over-lapping. Each candidate draws one card. None of the four cards at each end of the pack may be drawn. The rank of cards so drawn determines partnerships, etc. This method is used in every game where no different method is specifically stated.

ROTATION—The right to deal, the turn to bid, the turn to play, all rotate clockwise, that is, from each player to his left-hand neighbor.

THE SHUFFLE—Any player at the table has the right to shuffle the pack (and as a matter of common law this right remains even where special rules of a game designate one player responsible for shuffling). In most games, the dealer has the right to shuffle last, and this is the rule when no different provision is stated.

THE CUT—Cutting is the act of dividing the pack into two packets and transposing the bottom packet to the top. Custom is for the dealer to present the pack, after shuffling, to his right-hand neighbor, who lifts a packet from the top and sets it down beside the bottom packet. Dealer completes the cut by placing the bottom packet on top of the other.

Each packet of the cut must contain a minimum of cards, which varies in different games, but usually is four or five.

ELDEST HAND—Means the left-hand neighbor of the dealer. Although this term is not used in all games, and other equivalent terms are encountered (*the age, senior, major*), the player in this position bids first and plays first in most games. The term *eldest hand* is therefore used throughout the rules for clarity.

THE DEAL—In most games, the first card dealt goes to the eldest hand, and the cards are distributed in clockwise rota-tion. There is variance in the number of cards dealt at one time, so that this number is expressly stated in connection with every game. The rule may be "one at a time," or "two at a time," or more at a time, but the same number of cards is dealt to every player in any one *round*. Sometimes the quota varies from round to round; e.g., the rule to "deal 3-2" means, to deal a round of three cards at a time, then a round of two cards at a time.

Unless otherwise noted, all cards must be dealt face down so that no player can see the face of a card dealt to another. The finding of a card face up in the pack is usually a valid cause for declaring a misdeal.

MISDEALING—It is a universal rule that on demand of any player there must be a new deal by the same dealer if the customary or prescribed rules of shuffling, cutting, and dealing are breached in any way. Usually the demand may no longer be made by a player who has looked at any of the cards dealt him, or by any player after the last card has been dealt (or the prescribed deal has been completed).

IMPERFECT PACK—A pack is incorrect if it does not comprise exactly the number, rank and suits of cards prescribed by the rules of the particular game. A pack may be incorrect by reason of the fact that some cards have been dropped on the floor, or have been gathered up in another pack, or by reason of the fact that it contains some cards belonging to another pack. The term *imperfect* is used in a narrower sense, to mean an incorrect pack which cannot be rectified by the simple act of removing foreign cards or restoring to it cards which originally were included in it. The only frequent imperfection is that the cards have become so worn and defaced that some are identifiable from the back.

When it is discovered that the pack is incorrect (and presumably was incorrect at the beginning of the current deal), the current deal is at once abandoned, even though it may have progressed through various stages of bidding or play. All scores made before that deal, however, stand without change. When it is discovered that a pack is imperfect, but only through having an identifiable card, the current deal usually stands if dealing has been completed, but the pack is then replaced.

CONDONEMENT OF AN IRREGULARITY—The laws of different games vary widely in the penalties applied to irregularities and in the extent to which they may be rectified to allow play to continue. But in all there is limitation of the time during which an allegation of error and claim to a penalty is valid. Thereafter, the failure to draw attention to the error is deemed to have condoned it, to have accepted it as regular.

Custom has fortified at least the following "statute of limitations":

Procedural error in shuffling, cutting, or dealing (not resulting in wrong numbers of cards in any hand): Stands after all players look at their hands. If a hand has too many or too few cards, a misdeal may be called until the cards have been mixed together; thereafter the deal and the score for it stand.

Error in bidding, declaring, making trump, etc.: Stands after the opening lead of the play.

Error in playing out the hands: Stands after the score for the deal is agreed upon.

Error in recording scores or in arithmetical computations: Stands after payment has been offered and accepted in settlement of the score.

Many games place a greater limitation upon the time available for penalization (and rectification) of an irregularity. But none extends the time beyond this "natural statute," which may therefore be accepted as the law in any case for which the rules of a game do not make specific provision.

Card-Playing Etiquette

An ability to play Bridge, Canasta, Poker and other popular card games is a social asset. To make the most of this asset one must be popular at the card table, and this depends even more upon good manners than upon skill as a player.

Observance of the following principles will increase one's popularity as a card player.

1. Sit erect at the table, maintain a quiet bearing, avoid nervous habits. When someone else is dealing it is best to sit back and wait until the deal is fully completed before picking up one's hand.

2. Practice handling the deck of cards. An appearance of clumsiness in shuffling and dealing gives a bad impression of one's ability to play the game: People associate awkwardness of one sort with awkwardness or ineptness of other sorts.

How to Shuffle—Learn to cut the cards, complete the cut, and shuffle the pack in the manner of the best players. Here is how the riffle-shuffle is done:

Divide the pack, face down, into two piles of roughly the same size. Place them both on the table and bring together the corners only. Holding down each portion with your fingers, bend up the corners with your thumbs. Slide the two portions a little closer together so that they interlock. Let the cards riffle downwards. They will fit together as though meshed, and the cards will be mixed. Now relax the pressure of your fingers on the cards and slide the two portions of the pack together.

A shuffle of this sort should be made about three times to mix the cards thoroughly. The alternative Poker shuffle, made by holding a portion of the pack loosely in one hand and dropping the remaining cards into it from the other hand, is not proper in most games, while the riffle-shuffle is proper in any game including Poker.

In dealing, hold the pack in one hand and with the other hand slide the cards off one by one, moving both hands a few inches toward the player who is to receive the next card. It is not proper to remove each card with the thumb and forefinger and flip it, or set it down, on the table.

Do not look at the bottom card, either before or during the deal.

3. An inexperienced player, or anyone sitting in a game with better players, is likely to be nervous and uncertain. This feeling should be concealed as much as possible. The other players will prefer to have a bid or play made promptly even though it turns out to be wrong, than to have anyone sit in long periods of indecision through fear. Nothing makes other players more uncomfortable than to have a player moan, "Oh, dear, I just don't know *what* to do."

4. During the game, avoid conversation on matters not related to the game.

5. Don't delay the game by discussing what should have happened or what might have happened on a previous hand. Above all:

Don't express sympathy for a loser—including yourself when you are losing.

When a hand has just gone very well for you, don't talk to anyone about it.

Don't point out your opponents' mistakes to them. This is even worse than criticizing your partner for his mistakes.

6. When watching others play, make no comment and ask no questions. If possible, sit behind one player and look at his hand only. Having seen one player's hand, do not shift your position to look at another's; this might imply that the first hand you saw is not very good or very interesting, and thus your action would give information to some other player.

CONTRACT BRIDGE

and other games of "The Whist Family"

Contract Bridge is the "hobby" game of more millions of people than is any other card game played in the English-speaking countries and throughout the world. It is first in the affections of the ultra-fashionable circles that frequent Palm Beach, Newport and other famous resorts; and it is equally the property of all walks of life, all sections of the United States and all types of card players from those who play seriously in clubs and tournaments to those who play casually in their homes.

"THE WHIST FAMILY"—The principle of Contract Bridge goes back more than 400 years in England. Whist, the basic game, developed into Bridge (1896), then Auction Bridge (1904), and finally Contract Bridge (1925). Whist and Auction Bridge still have many followers, but since about 1930 Contract Bridge has been most popular.

WHY CONTRACT BRIDGE IS POPULAR—Contract Bridge is an ideal game for the entertainment of guests, especially when married couples get together, because it is a partnership game and husband-and-wife do not have to play against each other. It is as ideally adapted for play by clubs which meet weekly in groups of eight, twelve or more; for large card parties; and for tournament play, in clubs or homes, among serious players.

But the most fascinating feature of Contract Bridge is that it is equally enjoyable to the casual player, who does not want to take any game too seriously, and to the scientific player who wishes to study and master the intricacies of the game.

HOW TO LEARN CONTRACT BRIDGE—The following pages describe the fundamentals of the game, together with its rules, ethics, and proprieties. For those who wish to learn the game well, there are hundreds of books, and thousands of professional teachers who give lessons in Bridge; but the best and quickest way to learn is to play in actual Bridge games as often as possible.

How to Play Contract Bridge

Condensed from The Laws of Contract Bridge, © 1963 by the American Contract Bridge League.

Preliminaries

NUMBER OF PLAYERS—Four, two against two as partners. Five or six may take part in the same game, but only four play at a time.

THE PACK—52 cards. Two packs, of contrasting back designs, are invariably used. While one pack is being dealt, dealer's partner shuffles the other pack for the next deal.

RANK OF SUITS—Spades (high), hearts, diamonds, clubs.

RANK OF CARDS—A (high), K, Q, J, 10, 9, 8, 7, 6, 5, 4, 3, 2.

THE DRAW—A shuffled pack is spread face down on the table and each player draws one card, but not one of the four cards at either end. A player who exposes more than one card must draw again. No player should expose his card before all have drawn.

The player drawing the highest card deals first. He chooses his seat and the pack with which he will deal; next-highest is his partner and sits across the table from him; the two others take the other two seats. If two players draw cards of the same rank, as ♡ 6 and ♧ 6, the rank of the suits determines the higher card.

PRECEDENCE—When five wish to play, the draw establishes order of precedence. Example: North draws ♧ A, South ♤ K, East ♧ 5, West ♡ 2 and a fifth players draws ♢ 2. North and South play as partners against East and West. After the first rubber the fifth player plays and West sits out; after the next rubber West reenters the game and East sits out, and so on until North has sat out a rubber, after which the fifth player sits out again. The procedure is the same with six players, except that two sit out each rubber.

THE SHUFFLE—The player on dealer's left shuffles the cards and places them at the dealer's left. The dealer (after shuffling again, if he wishes) sets the cards down at his right to be cut.

THE CUT—The player at dealer's right must lift off a portion of the pack (not fewer than four cards nor more than forty-eight) and set it down toward dealer. Dealer completes the cut.

THE DEAL—Dealer deals thirteen cards to each player, one card at a time, face down, in clockwise rotation beginning with the player at his left.

ROTATION—The turn to deal, to bid and to play always passes from player to player to the left.

The Auction

CALLS—After looking at his cards, each player in turn beginning with dealer must make a *call* (pass, bid, double or redouble). If all four pass in the first round, the deal is passed out and there is a new deal by the next dealer in turn. If any player makes a bid in the first round, the bidding is opened.

PASSING—When a player does not wish to bid, to double or to redouble, he says "Pass."

BIDDING—Each bid must name a certain number of tricks in excess of six (called *odd-tricks*) which the bidder agrees to win, and a suit which will become the trump suit, if the bid becomes the contract; thus: "One spade" is a bid to win seven tricks (6+1) with spades as trumps. A bid may be made in no-trump, meaning that there will be no trump suit. The lowest possible bid is one, and the highest possible bid is seven.

Each bid must name a greater number of odd tricks than the last preceding bid, or an equal number of a higher denomination. No-trump is the highest denomination, outranking spades, Thus, a bid of two no-trump will overcall a bid of two hearts, a bid of four diamonds is required to overcall a bid of three hearts.

DOUBLING AND REDOUBLING—Any player in turn may double the last preceding bid if it was made by an opponent. The effect of a double is to increase the value of odd-tricks, overtricks and undertrick penalties (see Scoring Table, page 27) if the doubled bid becomes the contract.

Any player in turn may redouble the last preceding bid if it was made by his side and doubled by an opponent. A redouble again increases the scoring values.

A doubled or redoubled contract may be overcalled by any bid which would be sufficient to overcall the same contract undoubled; thus, if a bid of two diamonds is doubled and redoubled, it may still be overcalled by a bid of two in hearts, spades or no-trump and by a bid of three clubs, or by any higher bid.

INFORMATION AS TO PREVIOUS CALLS—Any player in turn may ask to have all previous calls made in the auction restated, in the order in which they were made.

FINAL BID AND THE DECLARER—When a bid, double or redouble is followed by three consecutive passes in rotation, the auction is closed. The final bid in the auction becomes the *contract*. The player who, for his side, first bid the denomination named in the contract becomes the *declarer*. If the contract names a trump suit, every card of that suit becomes a *trump*. Declarer's partner becomes *dummy*, and the other side become *defenders*.

The Play

LEADS AND PLAYS—A play consists of taking a card from one's hand and placing it, face up, in the center of the table. Four cards so played, one from each hand in rotation, constitute a trick. The first card played to a trick is a *lead*.

The leader to a trick may lead any card. The other three hands must follow suit if they can, but, if unable to follow suit, may play any card.

OPENING LEAD; FACING THE DUMMY HAND—The defender on declarer's left makes the first lead. Dummy then spreads his hand in front of him, face up, grouped in suits with the trumps at his right.

WINNING OF TRICKS—A trick containing a trump is won by the hand playing the highest trump. A trick not containing a trump is won by the hand playing the highest card of the suit led. The winner of each trick leads to the next.

DUMMY—Declarer plays both his and dummy's cards, but each in proper turn. Dummy may reply to a proper question but may not comment or take an active part in the play; except that he may call attention to an irregularity and may warn declarer (or any other player) against infringing a law of the game; as by saying, "It's not your lead," or asking, "No spades?" when a player fails to follow suit to a spade lead. See Dummy's Rights, page 32.

PLAYED CARD—Declarer plays a card from his own hand when he places it on the table or names it as an intended play; from dummy, when he touches it (except to arrange dummy's cards) or names it. A defender plays a card when he exposes it, with apparent intent to play, so that his partner can see its face. A card once played may not be withdrawn, except to correct a revoke or in the course of correcting an irregularity.

TAKING IN TRICKS WON—A completed trick is gathered and turned face down on the table. Declarer, and the partner of the defender winning the first trick for his side, should keep in front of him all tricks won by his side, so arranged that it is apparent how many tricks that side has won, and the sequence in which they were won.

CLAIM OR CONCESSION OF TRICKS BY DECLARER—If declarer claims or concedes one or more of the remaining tricks, or otherwise suggests that play be curtailed: Play should cease, and declarer, with his hand face up on the table, should forthwith make any statement necessary to indicate his intended line of play. A defender may face his hand and may suggest a play to his partner. If both defenders concede, play ceases and declarer is considered to have won the tricks claimed. If a defender disputes declarer's claim—see page 35.

CLAIM OR CONCESSION OF TRICKS BY A DEFENDER—To claim or concede any part of the remaining tricks, a defender should show his hand, or part of it, to declarer only. A defender's concession is not valid unless his partner also concedes.

TRICK CONCEDED IN ERROR—The concession of a trick which cannot be lost by any play of the cards is void.

INSPECTING TRICKS DURING PLAY—Declarer or either defender may, until his side has led or played to the next trick, inspect a trick and inquire which hand played any card to it.

The Scoring

When the last (thirteenth) trick has been played, the tricks taken by the respective sides are counted and their number agreed upon. The points earned by each side in that deal are then entered to the credit of that side on the score sheet. See the Scoring Table on page 27 for the point values.

Any player may keep a score. If only one player keeps score, both sides are equally responsible to see that the score for each side is correctly entered.

Each side has a *trick score* and a *premium score*.

TRICK SCORE—If declarer made his contract, the trick-point value of the odd-tricks he bid for is entered to the credit of his side in its trick score (called "below the line"; see page 25).

PREMIUM SCORE—Odd-tricks won by declarer in excess of

his contract are *overtricks* and are scored to the credit of his side in its premium score (called "above the line"; see page 25). Honors held in one hand, and premiums for slams bid and made, for winning the rubber, and for undertricks are scored to the credit of the side earning them, in its premium score.

UNDERTRICKS—When declarer wins fewer odd-tricks than he bids for, his opponents score, in their premium score, the undertrick premium for each trick by which he fell short of his contract.

SLAMS—If a side bids and makes a contract of six odd-tricks (all but one trick) it receives the premium for a *little slam;* seven odd-tricks (all the tricks), the premium for a *grand slam.*

VULNERABLE—A side which has won its first game toward the rubber becomes *vulnerable.* It is exposed to increased undertrick penalties if it fails to make a contract, but receives increased premiums for slams, and for overtricks made in doubled or redoubled contracts.

HONORS—When there is a trump suit, the A, K, Q, J and 10 of that suit are honors. If a player holds four trump honors in his hand, his side receives a 100-point premium whether he is declarer, dummy or a defender; five trump honors in one hand, or all four aces at a no-trump contract, 150-point premium.

GAME—When a side amasses 100 or more points *in trick points* (whether these points are scored in one or more hands), it wins a game. Both sides then start at zero trick score on the next.

RUBBER—When a side has won two games, it receives the premium for the rubber—500 points if the other side has won one game, 700 points if the other side has not won a game. The scores of the two sides are then totaled, including both trick points and premium points, and the side which has scored the most points has won the rubber. The players then draw again for partners and seats (page 20) and a new rubber is begun. (Or they may pivot—see pages 55-56.)

BACK SCORE—After each rubber, each player's standing, plus (+) or minus (—) in even hundreds of points, is entered on a separate score called the back score. An odd 50 points or more count 100, so if a player wins a rubber by 950 he is +10, if he wins it by 940 he is +9.

Four-deal Bridge, or Chicago, or Club Bridge

In a cut-in game, a player who is "cut out" often has a long wait till the rubber ends and he can get back in. Playing Four-deal Bridge, a player seldom has to wait more than 15 or 20 minutes. The game is often called "Chicago" because it originated in the Standard Club of Chicago, Ill.

A round consists of four deals, one by each player in turn. Vulnerability is automatic, as follows:

First deal: Neither side vulnerable.

Second and third deals: Dealer's side vulnerable, opponents not vulnerable (even if they previously made game).

Fourth deal: Both sides vulnerable.

A passed-out deal is redealt by the same dealer. There is a bonus of 300 for making game when not vulnerable and 500 when vulnerable. A part-score carries over as in rubber bridge and can help to make game in the next deal or deals, but is canceled by any game. There is a bonus of 100 for making a part-score on the fourth deal. After four deals have been played, the scores are totaled and entered on the back score, as in rubber bridge, and there is a new cut for partners, seats, and deal.

Some play that on the second and third deals the dealer's side is *not* vulnerable and the opposing side *is* vulnerable.

More points are usually scored in Four-deal Bridge than in the same number of deals at rubber bridge—estimates vary from 15% to 50% more. This is chiefly because at least one side is vulnerable in three deals out of four.

Illustration of Contract Bridge Scoring

(a) We bid two hearts and win nine tricks, scoring 60 points below the line (trick-score) for 2 tricks at hearts bid and made (30 each), and 30 points above the line (honor-score) for 1 overtrick at hearts. We now have a part-score of 60 toward game.

(b) We bid two clubs and make four-odd, scoring 40 points trick-score for 2 tricks bid and made (20 each), completing our game (100 points), so a line is drawn across both columns to show end of first game of rubber. We also score 40 points for 2 overtricks at clubs (20 each), and 100 points for four honors in one hand (one of us held ♣ A K J 10). *We are now vulnerable.*

(c) We bid four hearts and are doubled and set one trick.

They score 200 for defeating our contract because we are vulnerable.

(d) They bid four spades but take only 9 tricks, being set 1. We score 50 points, for they are not vulnerable and we did not double. One of them held ♠ A Q J 10, so they score 100 points for honors even though they did not make their contract.

(e) We bid and make one no-trump. This scores 40 points for us below the line. We need only 60 points more to make a game.

(f) They bid and make three no-trump, scoring 40 for the first, 30 for the second, and 30 for the third trick over six (100 points below the line), a game. Another horizontal line is drawn across both columns, marking end of second game. Our part-score no longer can count toward a game. *Now both sides are vulnerable.*

(g) We bid two spades and are doubled. We are set 3 tricks, and the opponents held 100 honors as well. They score 800 for the set and 100 for the honors.

(h) We bid and make six diamonds, a small slam, scoring 120 points trick-score, 750 for a little slam, and 500 for winning the rubber.

WE	THEY
500 (h)	
750 (h)	
50 (d)	100 (g)
100 (b)	800 (g)
40 (b)	100 (d)
30 (a)	200 (c)
60 (a)	
40 (b)	
40 (e)	100 (f)
120 (h)	
1730	1300
1300	
+430	

Adding the score for both sides we have 1730 points, they 1300; we win the rubber by 430. This gives us a 4-point rubber (see "Back Score," page 24).

Irregularities in Contract Bridge

THE SCOPE OF THE LAWS—The Laws are designed to define correct procedure and to provide an adequate remedy where a player, by irregularity, gains an unintentional but unfair advantage. The Laws are not designed to prevent dishonorable practices. Ostracism is the ultimate remedy for intentional offenses.

CONTRACT BRIDGE SCORING TABLE

	ODD TRICKS BID AND WON IN	UNDOUBLED	DOUBLED
TRICK POINTS FOR CONTRACTORS	Clubs or Diamonds, each	20	40
	Hearts or Spades, each	30	60
	No-Trump { first { each subsequent	40 30	80 60

Redoubling doubles the doubled points for Odd Tricks.
Vulnerability does not affect points for Odd Tricks.
100 Trick Points constitute a game.

	Overtricks	NOT VULNERABLE	VULNERABLE
PREMIUM POINTS FOR CONTRACTORS | DEFENDERS	Undoubled, each	TRICK VALUE	TRICK VALUE
	Doubled, each	100	200
	Making Doubled or Redoubled Contract }	50	50
	Undertricks Undoubled, each	50	100
	Doubled { first { each subsequent	100 200	200 300

Redoubling doubles the doubled points for Overtricks and
Undertricks, but does not affect the points for making
Doubled Contracts.

PREMIUM POINTS FOR CONTRACTORS | HOLDER	Honors in { All Honors One Hand { Four Trump Honors	150 100
	Slams Bid { Little, not vulnerable 500, vuln. and Won { Grand, not vuln. 1000, vuln.	750 1500
	Rubber { Two game Points { Three game	700 500

Unfinished Rubber—Winners of one game score 300 points.
If but one side has a part score in an unfinished game, it
scores 50 points. Doubling and Redoubling do not affect
Honor, Slam, or Rubber points. Vulnerability does not affect
points for Honors.

©—The National Laws Commission.

NEW SHUFFLE AND CUT—Before the first card is dealt, any player may demand a new shuffle and cut. There must be a new shuffle and cut if a card is faced in shuffling or cutting.

CHANGING THE PACK—A pack containing a distinguishable damaged card must be replaced. The pack originally belonging to a side must be restored if reclaimed.

REDEAL—There must be a redeal if, before the last card is dealt, a redeal is demanded because a player is dealing out of turn or with an uncut pack. There must be a redeal if the cards are not dealt correctly, if a card is faced in the pack or elsewhere, if a player picks up the wrong hand and looks at it, or if at any time (until the end of play) one hand is found to have too many cards and another too few (and the discrepancy is not caused by errors in play).

When there is a redeal, the same dealer deals (unless the deal was out of turn) with the same pack, after a new shuffle and cut.

MISSING CARD—If a missing card is found, it is deemed to belong to the deficient hand, which may then be answerable for exposing the card and for revoke through failure to play the card in a previous trick. But if a missing card is found in another hand, there must be a redeal; or in a trick, the law on defective trick (page 34) applies. If a missing card is not found, there must be a redeal.

SURPLUS CARD—If a player has a surplus card due to an incorrect pack or incorrect deal, there must be a redeal. If the surplusage is due to omission to play to a trick, the law on defective trick (page 34) applies.

DRAWING ATTENTION TO AN IRREGULARITY—Any player (except dummy if he has forfeited his rights) may draw attention to an irregularity. Any player may give or obtain information as to the law covering it. The fact that the offending side draws attention to its own irregularity does not affect the rights of the opponents.

ENFORCING A PENALTY—Either opponent (but not dummy) may select or enforce a penalty. If partners consult as to selection or enforcement, the right to penalize is canceled.

IMPROPER REMARKS AND GESTURES—If by remark or unmistakable gesture a player other than declarer: discloses his intentions or desires, the nature of an unfaced hand, the presence or absence of a card in an unfaced hand; or improperly suggests a lead, play or plan of play; the offender's side is subject to penalty as below. If the offense occurred:

(a) During the auction, either opponent may require the offending side to pass at every subsequent turn; and if that side becomes the defenders, declarer may require or forbid the opening lead of a specified suit by the offender's partner, for as long as he retains the lead.

(b) During the play, declarer or either defender (as the case may be) may require the offender's partner, on any one subsequent trick, to withdraw a lead or play suggested by the improper remark or gesture and substitute a card not so suggested.

CARD EXPOSED DURING THE AUCTION—If during the auction a player exposes a single card lower than a ten there is no penalty. If a player exposes an ace, king, queen, jack, or ten, or a lower card prematurely led, or more than one card, such cards must be left face up on the table and become penalty cards (see page 32) if the owner becomes a defender; and the partner of the offender must pass at his next turn.

IMPROPER CALL OVERCALLED—If the offender's left-hand opponent calls before the penalty for an illegal call has been enforced, the auction proceeds as though the illegal call had been a legal call, except that it becomes a pass if it was a bid of more than seven, a call after the auction is closed, a double or redouble when the only proper call was a pass or bid.

CHANGING A CALL—A player may change an inadvertent call without penalty if he does so without pause. Any other attempted change of call is void. If the first call was illegal, it is subject to the appropriate law. If it was a legal call, the offender may either:

(a) allow his first call to stand, whereupon his partner must pass at his next turn; or

(b) substitute any other legal call, whereupon his partner must pass at every subsequent turn.

INSUFFICIENT BID—If a player makes an insufficient bid, he must substitute either a sufficient bid or a pass. If he substitutes:

(a) The lowest sufficient bid in the same denomination, there is no penalty.

(b) Any other sufficient bid, his partner must pass at every subsequent turn.

(c) A pass (or a double or redouble, which is treated as a pass), his partner must pass at every subsequent turn, and if the offending side becomes the defenders, declarer may impose a lead penalty (see next paragraph) on the opening lead.

LEAD PENALTY—When declarer may impose a lead penalty he may specify a suit and either require the lead of that suit or forbid the lead of that suit for as long as the opponent retains the lead. When in the following pages only a "lead penalty" is cited, declarer has these rights. There are some other cases in which declarer has some control over a defender's lead, but not so much. In such cases, the exact penalty will be specified.

INFORMATION GIVEN IN CHANGING CALL—A denomination named, then canceled, in making or correcting an illegal call, is subject to penalty if an opponent becomes declarer: If a suit was named, declarer may impose a lead penalty (see above); if no trump was named, declarer may call a suit, if the offender's partner has the opening lead; if a double or redouble was canceled, the penalties are the same as when a pass is substituted for an insufficient bid.

BARRED PLAYER—A player who is barred once, or for one round, must pass the next time it is his turn to bid; a player who is barred throughout must pass in every turn until the auction of the current deal is completed.

WAIVER OF PENALTY—When a player calls or plays over an illegal call or play by his right-hand opponent, he accepts the illegal call or play and waives a penalty. The game continues as though no irregularity had occurred.

RETENTION OF THE RIGHT TO CALL—A player cannot lose his only chance to call by the fact that an illegal pass by his partner has been accepted by an opponent. The auction must continue until the player has had at least one chance to call.

CALL OUT OF ROTATION (OR "OUT OF TURN")—Any call out of rotation is canceled when attention is drawn to it. The auction reverts to the player whose turn it was. Rectification and penalty depend on whether it was a pass, a bid, or a double or redouble, as follows.

A call is not out of rotation if made without waiting for the right-hand opponent to pass if that opponent is legally obliged to pass; nor if it would have been in rotation had not the left-hand opponent called out of rotation. A call made simultaneously with another player's call in rotation is deemed to be subsequent to it.

PASS OUT OF TURN—If it occurs (a) before any player has bid, or when it was the turn of the offender's right-hand opponent, the offender must pass when his regular turn comes; (b) after there has been a bid and when it was the turn of the offender's partner, the offender is barred throughout; the offender's partner may not double or redouble at that turn; and if the offender's partner passes and the opponents play the hand, declarer may impose a lead penalty (page 30).

BID OUT OF TURN—If it occurs (a) before any player has called, the offender's partner is barred throughout; (b) after any player has called and when it was the turn of the offender's partner, the offender's partner is barred throughout and is subject to a lead penalty (page 30) if he has the opening lead; (c) after any player has called and when it was the turn of the offender's right-hand opponent, the offender must repeat his bid without penalty if that opponent passes, but if that opponent bids the offender may make any call and his partner is barred once.

DOUBLE OR REDOUBLE OUT OF TURN—If it occurs (a) when it was the turn of the offender's partner, the offender's partner is barred throughout and is subject to a lead penalty (page 30) if he has the opening lead, and the offender may not in turn double or redouble the same bid; (b) when it was the turn of the offender's right-hand opponent, the offender must repeat his double or redouble without penalty if that opponent passes but may make any legal call if that opponent bids, in which case the offender's partner is barred once.

IMPOSSIBLE DOUBLES AND REDOUBLES—If a player doubles or redoubles a bid that his side has already doubled or redoubled, his call is canceled; he must substitute (a) any legal bid, in which case his partner is barred throughout and if he becomes the opening leader declarer may prohibit the lead of the doubled suit; or (b) a pass, in which case either opponent may cancel all previous doubles and redoubles, the offender's partner is barred throughout, and if he becomes the opening leader he is subject to a lead penalty (page 23).

If a player doubles his partner's bid, redoubles an undoubled bid, or doubles or redoubles when there has been no bid, he must substitute any proper call, and his partner is barred once.

OTHER INADMISSIBLE CALLS—If a player bids more than seven, or makes another call when legally required to pass, he is deemed to have passed and the offending side must pass at every subsequent turn; if they become the defenders, declarer may impose a lead penalty (page 30) on the opening leader.

CALL AFTER THE AUCTION IS CLOSED—A call made after the aution is closed is canceled. If it is a pass by a defender, or any call by declarer or dummy, there is no penalty. If it is a bid, double or redouble by a defender, declarer may impose a lead penalty at the offender's partner's first turn to lead.

DUMMY'S RIGHTS—Dummy may give or obtain information regarding fact or law, ask if a play constitutes a revoke, draw attention to an irregularity, and warn any player against infringing a law. Dummy forfeits these rights if he looks at a card in another player's hand.

If dummy has forfeited his rights, and thereafter

(a) is the first to draw attention to a defender's irregularity, declarer may not enforce any penalty for the offense;

(b) warns declarer not to lead from the wrong hand, either defender may choose the hand from which declarer shall lead;

(c) is the first to ask declarer if a play from declarer's hand is a revoke, declarer must correct a revoke if able but the revoke penalty still applies.

EXPOSED CARDS—Declarer is never subject to penalty for exposure of a card, but intentional exposure of declarer's hand is treated as a claim or concession of tricks.

A defender's card is exposed if it is faced on the table or held so that the other defender may see its face before he is entitled to do so. Such a card must be left face up on the table until played and becomes a penalty card.

PENALTY CARDS—A penalty card must be played at the first legal opportunity, subject to the obligation to follow suit or to comply with another penalty.

If a defender has two or more penalty cards that he can legally play, declarer may designate which one is to be played.

Declarer may require or forbid a defender to lead a suit in which his partner has a penalty card, but if declarer does so the penalty card may be picked up and ceases to be a penalty card.

Failure to play a penalty card is not subject to penalty, but declarer may require the penalty card to be played and any defender's card exposed in the process becomes a penalty card.

LEAD OUT OF TURN—If declarer is required by a defender* to retract a lead from the wrong hand, he must lead from the correct hand (if he can) a card of the same suit; if it was a defender's turn to lead, or if there is no card of that suit in the correct hand, there is no penalty.

If a defender is required to retract a lead out of turn, declarer may either treat the card so led as a penalty card, or impose a lead penalty on the offender's partner when next he is to lead after the offense.

PREMATURE PLAY—If a defender leads to the next trick before his partner has played to the current trick, or plays out of rotation before his partner has played, declarer may require the offender's partner to play his highest card of the suit led, his lowest card of the suit led, or a card of another specified suit. Declarer must select one of these options and if the defender cannot comply, he may play any card. When declarer has played from both his hand and dummy, a defender is not subject to penalty for playing before his partner.

INABILITY TO PLAY AS REQUIRED—If a player is unable to lead or play as required to comply with a penalty (for lack of a card of a required suit, or because of the prior obligation to follow suit) he may play any card. The penalty is deemed satisfied, except in the case of a penalty card.

REVOKE—A revoke is the act of playing a card of another suit, when able to follow suit to a lead. Any player, including dummy, may ask whether a play constitutes a revoke and may demand that an opponent correct a revoke. A claim of revoke does not warrant inspection of turned tricks, prior to the end of play, except by consent of both sides.

CORRECTING A REVOKE—A player must correct his revoke if aware of it before it becomes established. A revoke card withdrawn by a defender becomes a penalty card. The non-offending side may withdraw any cards played after the revoke but before attention was drawn to it.

*A defender's drawing attention to declarer's lead from the wrong hand is equivalent to requiring its retraction.

ESTABLISHED REVOKE—A revoke becomes established when a member of the offending side leads or plays to a subsequent trick (or terminates play by a claim or concession). When a revoke becomes established, the revoke trick stands as played (unless it is the twelfth trick—see below).

REVOKE PENALTY—The penalty for an established revoke is two tricks (if available), transferred at the end of play from the revoking side to the opponents. This penalty can be paid only from tricks won by the revoking side after its first revoke, including the revoke trick. If only one trick is available, the penalty is satisfied by transferring one trick; if no trick is available, there is no penalty.

There is no penalty for a subsequent established revoke in the same suit by the same player.

A transferred trick ranks for all scoring purposes as a trick won in play by the side receiving it. It never affects the contract.*

REVOKES NOT SUBJECT TO PENALTY—A revoke made in the twelfth trick must be corrected, without penalty, if discovered before the cards have been mixed together. The non-offending side may require the offender's partner to play either of two cards he could legally have played. A revoke not discovered until the cards have been mixed is not subject to penalty, nor is a revoke by any faced hand (dummy, or a defender's hand when faced in consequence of a claim by declarer). A revoke by failure to play a penalty card is not subject to the penalty for an established revoke.

DEFECTIVE TRICK—A defective trick may not be corrected after a player of each side has played to the next trick. If a player has failed to play to a trick, he must correct his error when it is discovered by adding a card to the trick (if possible, one he could legally have played to it). If a player has played more than one card to a trick, he does not play to the last trick or tricks and if he wins a trick with his last card, the turn to lead passes to the player at his left.

DECLARER CLAIMING OR CONCEDING TRICKS — If declarer claims or concedes one or more of the remaining tricks (verbally or by spreading his hand), he must leave his hand face up on the table and immediately state his intended plan of play.

*For example, if the contract is 2 ♡ and declarer wins 8 tricks plus 2 tricks as a revoke penalty, total 10 tricks, he can score only 60 points below the line and the other 60 points go above the line.

If a defender disputes declarer's claim, declarer must play on, adhering to any statement he has made, and in the absence of a specific statement he may not "exercise freedom of choice in making any play the success of which depends on finding either opponent with or without a particular unplayed card."

Following curtailment of play by declarer, it is permissible for a defender to expose his hand and to suggest a play to his partner.

DEFENDER CLAIMING OR CONCEDING TRICKS—A defender may show any or all of his cards to declarer to establish a claim or concession. He may not expose his hand to his partner, and if he does, declarer may treat his partner's cards as penalty cards.

CORRECTING THE SCORE—A proved or admitted error in any score may be corrected at any time before the rubber score is agreed, except as follows. An error made in entering or failing to enter a part-score, or in omitting a game or in awarding one, may not be corrected after the last card of the second succeeding correct deal has been dealt (unless a majority of the players consent).

EFFECT OF INCORRECT PACK—Scores made as a result of hands played with an incorrect pack are not affected by the discovery of the imperfection after the cards have been mixed together.

CONCESSION OF A TRICK THAT CANNOT BE LOST—The concession of a trick that cannot be lost by any play of the cards is void if attention is drawn to the error before the cards have been mixed together. If a player concedes a trick he has in fact won (as by claiming nine tricks when his side has already won ten) the concession is void, and if the score has been entered it may be corrected as provided above.

Illustrations of Most Frequent Irregularities and Penalties

In all the following examples, the four players at the bridge table are designated as South, *declarer;* North, *dummy;* West and East, *defenders*. Their relative positions are:

NORTH *(Dummy)*

WEST   EAST

SOUTH *(Declarer)*

LEAD OUT OF TURN—West should make the opening lead, but East leads the ◇7. South may say to West, "Lead anything but a diamond." West may lead any spade, heart, or club; and East picks up the ◇ 7 and puts it in his hand. Or South may say to West, "Lead a diamond." West may lead any diamond in his hand, and East may pick up the ◇ 7 and play either it or any other diamond he may hold. Or South may permit West to make any lead he pleases, but in this case ◇ 7 becomes a penalty card: East must place it face up on the table in front of him and leave it there. The first time he can legally lead or play it he must do so, subject only to his duty to follow suit. Or, South may accept the ◇ 7 as a correct lead. In this case dummy exposes his hand and then South plays to the trick. West plays next and dummy last. If, after East's out-of-turn opening lead, South had inadvertently exposed his hand, the lead would have stood, South's hand would have become the dummy, and North would have become the declarer.

In another case, North makes an opening lead, thinking that West has won the contract. But South is the actual declarer. North's card is put back in his hand. There is no penalty against the declaring side for exposing cards, since the information so given can be utilized only by the opponents.

DECLARER LEADS FROM WRONG HAND—North (dummy) won the last trick, but South (declarer) leads the ♤ K. West says, "The lead is in dummy." South replaces the ♤ K in his own hand and must lead a spade from dummy. When South plays to that trick, he does not have to play the ♤ K if he has another spade he prefers to play. (If dummy had not held a spade, South could have led any card from dummy.)

West could accept the out-of-turn lead of the ♤ K, if he wished, by following to it at once, before either he or East made any remark about its irregularity.

REVOKE CORRECTED—South leads ◇ 6. West has some diamonds, but he plays ♧ 9. Dummy plays ◇ K and East plays ◇ 3. At this juncture West say, "Wait, I have a diamond."

There is time for West to correct his revoke, because it is not established—neither West nor East has led or played to the next trick. West must leave the ♧ 9 face up on the table as a penalty card. He may play any diamond he wishes, and he elects to play ◇ A. Now declarer may retract dummy's play of the ◇ K and substitute a small diamond. But East may not change his card.

In another case, South (the declarer) revokes and notices his error in time for correction. He replaces the revoke card in his hand, without penalty, and follows suit with any card he chooses.

REVOKE ESTABLISHED—South leads ♠ K. West has a spade, but plays ♡ 7. East wins the trick with the ♠ A and leads a heart.

It is now too late for West to correct his revoke. East, a "member of the offending side," has led to the next trick and the revoke is established. Play proceeds normally, and let us suppose that East-West win one more trick.

South's contract was two spades, and when play is ended he has won eight tricks. But, as the revoke penalty, he may take two of East-West's tricks and transfer them to his pile. That gives him ten tricks in all. He scores 60 below the line for making two spades, and 60 above the line for two over-tricks. Note that South does not get game for making ten tricks at spades. He bid only two spades, and that is all he can score toward game. Tricks transferred as the result of a revoke penalty are scored exactly as though won in play. If South, having bid two spades, had won ten tricks without the revoke, he could not have have made game; therefore he cannot make game as a result of the revoke penalty.

Finally, take a case in which West revokes, and East, who wins the trick, establishes the revoke by leading to the next trick; play continues, but East-West do not win another trick.

After the play is completed, South may take only one trick as the revoke penalty—the trick on which the revoke occurred. He is not entitled to any trick the defenders won before the revoke occurred, because obviously the revoke could have had nothing to do with how such tricks were won.

Proprieties in Bridge

The dealer should refrain from looking at the bottom card before completing the deal.

The other players should refrain from touching or looking at their cards until the deal is completed.

A player should refrain from—Calling with special emphasis, inflection or intonation; making a call with undue delay which may result in conveying improper information to partner; indicating in any way approval or disapproval of partner's call or play; making a remark or gesture or asking a question from which an inference may be drawn; attracting attention to the score, except for his own information; calling attention to the number of tricks needed to complete or defeat the contract; preparing to gather a trick before all four hands have played to it; detaching a card from his hand before it is his turn to lead or play; watching the place in a player's hand from which he draws a card.

Do not allow partner's hesitation or mannerism to influence a call, lead, or play. It is proper to draw inferences from an opponent's gratuitous acts, but at one's own risk.

It is proper to keep silent in regard to irregularities committed by one's own side, but it is improper to infringe any law of the game deliberately.

It is improper to employ any convention whose significance is known to partner but has not been announced to the opponents.

Outline of The Goren System of Bidding*

Proper play in Contract Bridge has two branches, bidding and play. To bid correctly, a player should first determine the value of his hand and then make the bid consistent with that value. There are various systems of hand-valuation. The system chiefly used in America is the "Point-Count System" advocated by Charles H. Goren. An authorized outline of the Goren System, approved by Mr. Goren, follows. It comprises the point-count method of hand-valuation and the requirements for bids.

See also *Leads* on page 47.

Goren Point-Count Table

High-Card Points	*Quick Tricks*
Ace = 4 pts.	A-K = 2
King = 3 pts.	A-Q = 1½
Queen = 2 pts.	A or K-Q = 1
Jack = 1 pt.	K-x = ½

High-card points (usually called simply *points*) are counted for nearly every bid. To them are often added dis-

*Authorized outline of the Goren System of Bidding as condensed from *Contract Bridge Complete*, *Contract Bridge in a Nutshell*, and *Point-Count Bidding Made Easy: A Self-Teacher*, all published by Doubleday & Co., New York, and from *Point Count Bidding* and *Contract Bridge for Beginners*, both published by Simon and Schuster, New York; all by Charles H. Goren.

tributional points, described below. Quick tricks are counted only for opening bids on borderline hands and, often, when considering a double of an opponent's bid.

GAME AND SLAM REQUIREMENTS—26 pts. will normally produce a game. 33 pts. will normally produce a small slam. 37 pts. will normally produce a grand slam.

Distributional Points
In Addition to High-Card Points

The Opening Bidder Counts For Original Bids

Void Suit = 3 pts.
Singleton = 2 pts.
Doubleton = 1 pt.
Add 1 pt. for all 4 aces
Deduct 1 pt. for an aceless hand.
Deduct 1 pt. for each unguarded honor (examples: Q-x, J-x, singleton K, Q, or J).

The Responder Counts When Raising Partner's Suit

Void Suit = 5 pts.
Singleton = 3 pts.
Doubleton = 1 pt.
Promote honors in partner's bid suit by 1 pt. (unless these honors already total 4 pts.).
Deduct 1 pt. from total distributional points if hand contains only three trumps or if hand has 4-3-3-3 distribution.

FOR REBIDS: After Partner has raised opening bidder's suit:
Add 1 additional pt. for the fifth card in the trump suit.
Add 2 additional pts. for the sixth and each subsequent trump.

Minimum Biddable Suits

For an Opening Bid

4-Card Suits—must contain 4 high-card points (example—K-J-x-x, A-x-x-x)
5-Card Suits
Any 5-Card Suit (x-x-x-x-x)

For a Response or Rebid

Q-10-x-x or better (example— Q-10-x-x, K-x-x-x, A-x-x-x)
Any 5-Card Suit (x-x-x-x-x)

Rebiddable Suits

4-Card Suits No 4-card suit is rebiddable
5-Card Suits Must be Q-J-9-x-x or better
6-Card Suits Any 6-card suit is rebiddable (x-x-x-x-x-x)

Opening Bid Requirements

One of a suit   (a) 14-pt. hands must be opened.
                  (b) 13-pt. hands may be opened if a

	good rebid is available (a rebiddable suit or a second rebiddable suit).
	(c) All openings must contain two quick tricks.
	(d) A third-position opening is permitted with 11 pts. if hand contains a good suit.
Two of a suit *(forcing to game)*	(a) 25 pts. with a good 5-card suit (1 pt. less with a second good 5-card suit).
	(b) 23 pts. with a good 6-card suit.
	(c) 21 pts. with a good 7-card suit.
Three, four, or five of a suit *(preëmptive bids)*	Preëmptive bids show less than 10 pts. in high cards and the ability to win within two tricks of the contract vulnerable and within three tricks not vulnerable. They should usually be based on a good 7-card or longer suit.
One No-Trump	16 to 18 pts. (in no-trump bidding only high-card points are counted) and 4-3-3-3, 4-4-3-2 or 5-3-3-2 distribution with Q-x or better in any doubleton.
Two No-Trump	22 to 24 pts. and all suits stopped (J-x-x-x; Q-x-x; K-x; or better).
Three No-Trump	25 to 27 pts. and all suits stopped.

CHOICE OF SUITS—Generally speaking, bid your longest suit first. With two 5-card suits bid the higher-ranking first. With two or more 4-card suits, bid the suit immediately lower in rank to your short suit (doubleton, singleton, or void).

Responses

GENERAL PRINCIPLES—Any bid of a new suit by the responding hand is forcing on the opening bidder for one round. Thus, each time the responder bids a new suit the opener must bid again. If responder should jump, his bid is forcing to game.

With less than 10 pts., responder should prefer to raise partner if partner has opened in a major suit, and to bid a new suit himself at the one level in preference to raising a minor-suit opening bid. With 11 or 12 pts., responder can make two bids but should not force to game. With 13 pts. or more he should see that the bidding is not dropped before a game contract is reached. With 19 pts. he should make a strong effort to reach a slam.

RESPONSES TO SUIT-BIDS OF ONE—*Raise*. To raise partner's suit responder must have adequate trump support. This consists of J-x-x, Q-x-x, x-x-x-x, or better for a non-rebid suit; and Q-x, K-x, A-x, or x-x-x for a rebid suit.

Raise partner's suit to two with 7 to 10 pts. and adequate trump support.

Raise to three with 13 to 16 pts. and at least four trumps.

Raise to four with no more than 9 high-card points plus at least five trumps and a short suit (singleton or void).

Bid of a new suit. At one level requires 6 pts. or more. This response may be made on anything ranging from a weak hand, where responder is just trying to keep the bidding open, to a very powerful one when he is not sure where the hand should be played.

At two level requires 10 pts. or more.

Jump in a new suit requires 19 pts. or more (the jump shift is reserved for hands where a slam is very likely. Responder should hold either a strong suit or strong support for opener's suit).

No-trump responses (made on balanced hands). One no-trump requires 6 to 9 pts. in high cards (this bid is often made on an unbalanced hand if responder's suit is lower in rank than the opening bidder's and responder lacks the 10 pts. required to take the bidding into the two level).

Two no-trump requires 13 to 15 pts. in high cards, all unbid suits stopped, and a balanced hand.

Three no-trump requires 16 to 18 pts. in high cards, all unbid suits stopped, and 4-3-3-3 distribution.

RESPONSES TO SUIT-BIDS OF TWO—An opening bid of two in a suit is unconditionally forcing to game and responder may not pass until game is reached. With 6 pts. or less he bids two no-trump regardless of his distribution. With 7 pts. and one quick trick, he may show a new suit or raise the opener's suit. With 8 or 9 high-card points and a balanced hand, responder bids three no-trump.

RESPONSES TO PREËMPTIVE BIDS—Since the opener has overbid his hand by two or three tricks, aces, kings and potential ruffing values are the key factors to be considered when responder is contemplating a raise. One or two trumps constitutes sufficient support.

RESPONSES TO A ONE NO-TRUMP BID—*Balanced hands*. Raise to 2 N T with 8 or 9 pts., or with 7 pts. and a good 5-card suit. Raise to 3 N T with 10 to 14 pts. Raise to 4 N T with 15 or 16 pts. Raise to 6 N T with 17 or 18 pts. Raise to 7 N T with 21 points.

Unbalanced hands. With less than 8 pts. plus a 5-card suit, bid two diamonds, two hearts, or two spades. (Do not bid two clubs on a 5-card club suit.) With 8 pts. or more and a 4-card major suit, bid two clubs. (This is an artificial bid asking opener to show a 4-card major if he has one. See section on rebids by opening one no-trump bidder.) With 10 pts. and a good suit, bid three of that suit. With a 6-card major suit and less than 10 pts. in high cards, jump to game in the suit.

RESPONSES TO A TWO NO-TRUMP OPENING—*Balanced hands.* Raise to 3 N T with 4 to 8 pts. Raise to 4 N T with 9 to 10 pts. Raise to 6 N T with 11 or 12 pts. Raise to 7 N T with 15 pts.

Unbalanced hands. With a 5-card major suit headed by an honor, plus 4 pts., bid the suit at the three level. Show any 6-card major suit.

RESPONSES TO A THREE NO-TRUMP OPENING—Show any 5-card suit if the hand contains 5 pts. in high cards. Raise to 4 N T with 7 pts. Raise to 6 N T with 8 or 9 pts. Raise to 7 N T with 12 pts.

Rebids

REBIDS BY OPENING BIDDER—The opener's rebid is frequently the most important call of the auction, as he now has the opportunity to reveal the exact strength of his opening bid and therefore whether game or slam is in contemplation. His opening is valued according to the following table:

13 to 16 pts.	Minimum hand
16 to 19 pts.	Good hand
19 to 21 pts.	Very good hand

13 to 16 pts. *Minimum hand.* If partner has made a limit response (one no-trump or a single raise) opener should pass, as game is impossible. If partner bids a new suit at the one-level, opener may make a single raise with good trump support, rebid one no-trump with a balanced hand, or, with an unbalanced hand, rebid his own suit or a new suit (if he does not go past the level of two in the suit of his original bid).

16 to 19 pts. *Good hand.* If partner has made a limit response (one no-trump or a single raise) opener should bid again, as game is possible if responder has maximum values. If responder has bid a new suit, opener may make a jump

raise with four trumps, or jump in his own suit if he has a 6-card suit, or bid a new suit.

19 to 21 pts. *Very good hand.* If partner has made a limit response (one no-trump or a single raise) opener may jump to game in either denomination, according to his distribution. If responder has bid a new suit, opener may make a jump raise to game with four trumps, or jump to game in his own suit if it is solid. With a balanced hand and 19 or 20 pts., opener should jump to two no-trump. With 21 pts. he should jump to three no-trump. With 22 pts. and up he should jump in a new suit (forcing to game and suggesting a slam).

REBIDS BY OPENING NO-TRUMP BIDDER—*Two-club convention* (usually called the Stayman Convention).* When the responder bids two clubs, the opening bidder must show a 4-card biddable major suit if he has one:

With four spades, he bids two spades;

With four hearts, he bids two hearts;

With four cards in each major, he bids two spades;

With no 4-card major suit, he bids two diamonds.

Opening no-trump bidder must pass: When responder raises to two no-trump and opener has a minimum (16 pts.); when responder bids two diamonds, two hearts, or two spades, and opener has only 16 or 17 points and no good fit for responder's suit; when responder bids three no-trump, four spades, or four hearts.

Defensive Bidding

OVERCALLS—An overcall is a defensive bid (made after the other side has opened the bidding). Prospects for game are not as good as they are for the opening bidder, in view of the announced adverse strength, and safety becomes a prime consideration. Overcalls are therefore based not on a specified number of points but rather on a good suit. Generally speaking the overcaller should employ the same standards as a preëmpter; he should be able to win in his own hand within two tricks of his bid if vulnerable and within three tricks not vulnerable.

ONE NO-TRUMP OVERCALL—An overcall of one no-trump is similar to a one no-trump opening bid and shows 16 to 18 pts. with a balanced hand and the opening bidder's suit well stopped.

---

* Introduced by Samuel M. Stayman of New York. The name "two-club convention" is also, more often, applied to the use of an opening two-club bid as an artificial game-forcing bid; see page 46.

JUMP OVERCALL—Any jump overcall, whether it is a single, double or triple jump, is preëmptive in nature and shows a hand weak in high cards but with a good suit that will produce within three tricks of the bid if not vulnerable and within two tricks vulnerable.

TAKEOUT DOUBLES (also called *negative* or *informatory* doubles)—When a defender doubles and all the following conditions are present: (a) his partner has made no bid; (b) the double was made at the doubler's first opportunity; (c) the double is of one, two or three of a suit—it is intended for a takeout and asks partner to bid his best (longest) suit. This defensive bid is employed on either of two types of hand: (1) a hand of opening-bid strength where the doubler has no good or long suit of his own but has good support for any of the unbid suits; and (2) where the doubler has a good suit and so much high-card strength that he fears a mere overcall might be passed out and a possible game missed.

OVERCALL IN OPPONENT'S SUIT (cue-bid)—The immediate cue-bid (example: opponent opens one heart; defender bids two hearts) is the strongest of all defensive bids. It is unconditionally forcing to game and shows approximately the equivalent of an opening forcing bid. It normally announces first-round control of the opening bid suit and is usually based on a void with very fine support in all unbid suits.

ACTION BY PARTNER OF OVERCALLER—The overcaller's bid is based on a good suit; therefore less than normal trump support is required to raise (Q-x or x-x-x). A raise should be preferred by the partner to bidding a suit of his own, particularly if the overcaller has bid a major. The partner of the overcaller should not bid for the sole purpose of keeping the bidding open. A single raise of a one-no-trump response should be made only in an effort to reach game. If appropriate values are held, a leap to game is in order, since a jump raise is not forcing.

ACTION BY PARTNER OF TAKEOUT DOUBLER—In this situation, the weaker the hand the more important it is to bid. The only holding that would justify a pass would be one that contained four defensive tricks, three in the trump suit. The response should be made in the longest suit, though preference is normally given to a major over a minor.

The doubler's partner should value his hand as follows: 6 pts., fair hand; 9 pts., good hand; 11 pts., probable game.

Doubler's partner should indicate a probable game by jumping in his best suit, even if it is only four cards in length.

Since the partner of a doubler may be responding on nothing, it is a good policy for the doubler to subsequently underbid, while doubler's partner should overbid.

ACTION BY PARTNER OF THE OPENING BIDDER (when the opening bid has been overcalled or doubled)—When the opener's bid has been overcalled, the responder is no longer under obligation to keep the bidding open; so a bid of one no-trump or a raise should be based on a hand of at least average strength. Over a takeout double, the responder has only one way to show a good hand—a redouble. This bid does not promise support for opener's suit but merely announces a better-than-average holding. Any other bid, while not indicative of weakness, shows only mediocre high-card strength.

Slam Bidding

When the two partners have been able to determine that they have the assets for a slam (33 pts. between the combined hands plus an adequate trump suit), the only thing that remains is to make certain that the opponents are unable to cash two quick tricks. Various control-asking and control-showing bids have been employed through the years, but only three have stood the test of time—Blackwood, Gerber, and cue-bids (individual ace-showing).

BLACKWOOD CONVENTION*—After a trump suit has been agreed upon, a bid of four no-trump asks partner to show his total number of aces. A response of five clubs shows either no aces or all four aces; five diamonds shows one ace; five hearts shows two aces; five spades shows three aces. After aces have been shown, the four-no-trump bidder may ask for kings by now bidding five no-trump. The responder to the five-no-trump bid now shows kings: by bidding six clubs if he has no king, six diamonds if he has one king, etc., but six no-trump if he has all four kings.

GERBER CONVENTION**—This convention is similar to Blackwood in that it asks for the number of aces. Its advantage lies in the fact that it initiates the response at a lower level. A sudden bid of four clubs where it could not possibly have a natural meaning (example: opener, one no-trump; re-

---

*Devised 1934 by Easley Blackwood of Indianapolis, Indiana
** Devised 1938 by John Gerber of Houston, Texas

sponder, four clubs) is Gerber and asks partner to show the number of his aces. If he bids four diamonds, he shows no aces; four hearts, one ace, etc. If the asking hand desires information about kings, he bids the next-higher suit over his partner's ace-showing response. Thus, if the responding hand has bid four hearts over four clubs to show one ace, a bid of four spades would now ask him for kings and he would now reply four no-trump to show no king, five clubs to show one king, etc.

CUE-BIDDING (individual ace-showing)—The Blackwood and Gerber conventions are designed to cover only a small number of potential slam hands. Many slams depend on possession of a specific ace, rather than a wholesale number of aces. Cue-bids are employed in such cases. *For example:* Opener bids two spades, responder bids three spades, opener now bids four clubs; the four-club bid shows the ace of clubs and invites responder to show an ace if he has one. The responder "signs off" by bidding the agreed trump suit.

Other Contract Bridge Conventions

CLUB CONVENTION—This method of bidding was devised by Harold S. Vanderbilt, who invented the modern game of Contract Bridge, and for that reason it is often called "the Vanderbilt Club." It is very popular in Europe. An opening bid of one club is artificial—it does not necessarily show a club suit but it shows a strong hand with 3½ or more quick tricks. The opener's partner must respond one diamond if he has less than 2 quick tricks. Any other response shows at least 2 quick tricks. After the opening bid and response the partners show their suits naturally.

TWO-CLUB CONVENTION—This convention, used by many expert players, is usually combined with "weak two-bids." An opening bid of two clubs is artificial, not necessarily showing a club suit but showing a very powerful hand. It is forcing to game. The opener's partner must respond two diamonds if he has a weak hand. Any other response shows strength, usually at least 1½ quick tricks. An opening bid of two diamonds, two hearts, or two spades is a preëmptive bid, made on a fairly weak hand that includes a good 5- or 6-card suit but does not have 13 or more points.

UNUSUAL NO-TRUMP—If a player bids two no-trump after the opposing side has opened the bidding, and when his partner has not bid, the two-no-trump bid is a convention showing a two-suited hand (usually with five or more cards in each of the two minor suits). The partner of the two-no-trump bidder is required to respond in his best minor suit, even if it is a three-card or shorter suit.

Conventional Leads
(Contract or Auction Bridge)

HOLDING IN SUIT	LEAD AT SUIT BIDS	LEAD AT NO-TRUMP
A-K-Q alone or with others	K, then Q	K, then Q
A-K-J-x-x-x-x	K, then A	A, then K*
A-K-J-x-x or A-K-x-x-x(-x)	K, then A	Fourth best
A-Q-J-x-x	A**	Q
A-Q-10-9	A**	10***
A-Q-x-x(-x)	A	Fourth best
A-J-10-x	A**	J
A-10-9-x	A	10
A-x-x-x(-x)	A	Fourth best
A-K-x	K	K
A-K alone	A	K**
K-Q-J alone or with others	K, then J	K, then Q
K-Q-10 alone or with others	K	K
K-Q-x-x(-x-x)	K	Fourth best
K-Q alone	K	K
K-J-10 alone or with others	J	J
K-10-9-x	10	10
Q-J-10 or Q-J-9 alone or with others	Q	Q
Q-J-x or Q-J	Q	Q
Q-J-8-x (four or more)	Q	Fourth best
Q-10-9 alone or with others	10	10
J-10-9 or J-10-8 alone or with others	J	J
J-10-x or J-10	J	J
J-10-x-x or more	J	Fourth best
10-9-8 or 10-9-7, alone or with others	10	10
10-9-x-x(-x)	10	Fourth best
K-J-x-x(-x-x)	Fourth best	Fourth best
Any other four-card or longer suit not listed above	Fourth best	Fourth best

LEADS IN PARTNER'S BID SUIT

HOLDING IN SUIT	LEAD AT SUIT-BIDS	LEAD AT NO-TRUMP
A-x, K-x, Q-x̄, J-x, 10-x, or any other doubleton	High card	High card
J-10-x or x-x-x	Highest	Highest
A-J-x or A-x-x	Ace	Lowest
K-J-x, K-x-x, Q-10-x, Q-x-x, J-x-x	Lowest	Lowest
Q-J-x(-x)	Q	Q
A-x-x-x or better	A	Fourth best
A-K-x(-x) or K-Q-x(-x)	K	K
Any other 4 or more cards	Fourth best	Fourth best

Party Bridge

Pointers for Hostesses

The host or hostess should make all decisions as to what form of Bridge is to be played. She should tell her guests at what table they are to play and what form of Bridge (regular Rubber Bridge, Pivot Bridge, Progressive Bridge, etc.) is to be played. She should consider the probable desires of her guests, but should not consult them. Leaving such decisions to the guests usually serves only to make them uncomfortable and may even cause arguments and disagreements among them.

THE CASUAL GAME—When a Bridge game or party is not planned in advance, there are seldom more guests than will make up a single table, or at most two tables (eight players).

Four, five or six players may play a "cut-in" game at one table. The host or hostess should play in the game; the guests will not mind sitting out in their proper turns, and it is embarrassing to them if the hostess insists on sitting out.

If the group includes a husband and wife who may not wish to play against each other, the hostess may suggest a "set match" in which the couple are always partners; in a five- or six-hand game, there may be a "semi-set match" in which the couples are partners whenever they are both in the game at the same time. The hostess should not make this

---

*The lead of the ace of an unbid suit at a no-trump contract requests partner to play his highest card of the suit led, even the king or queen, unless dummy reveals that such a play might risk losing a trick.

**Usually not a good lead at this contract.

***When dummy seems likely to have the king, the queen is a better lead.

suggestion, however, if the married couple are better players than the other guests, or if they are thought to be.

If one player is better than the others, Pivot Bridge (page 55) should be suggested, so that everyone will have equal opportunity to play with the better player.

With six players, it is advisable to set up a second card table and provide cards so that the two players who are sitting out may amuse themselves by playing a two-hand game such as Gin Rummy, Russian Bank, Canasta, or Samba, while waiting for the rubber to end.

Seven players are the most inconvenient number. They cannot very well all play in the same Bridge game. It may be best to try to arrange some game in which all seven can play at once, instead of Bridge. Otherwise the hostess must sit out and let six play.

Eight players make two tables of Bridge. The hostess should arrange the placing of the players at the respective tables. If all are married couples, it is usually wiser to split them up than to have any couple at the same table. If four of the players are quite good and the other four weaker, the four good players should be put together; but the reason for the grouping should not be mentioned.

THE PLANNED BRIDGE PARTY—When guests are invited to play Bridge, the hostess can decide in advance what form of the game is to be played. It may be best merely to play Rubber Bridge; serious players may wish to play Duplicate Bridge (page 57); but the most popular game is Progressive Bridge.

HINTS TO THE HOSTESS—Place the tables in as nearly circular arrangement as possible so that in moving from one table to another the guests will never have difficulty finding their next table.

Each table should have its number conspicuously placed on it, and should be provided with at least two score-pads and pencils, and with two unopened packs of cards; it is most proper if the cards at all tables are of the same quality.

Prepare the tally cards in advance. Some tally cards have the "table and couple numbers" printed on them; others must be properly marked with pen or pencil. Two separate piles of tally cards should be made (of different-colored tallies); each pile should contain one tally for each table and couple number; thus, a card marked "Table 1—Couple 1" in each pile. As the guests arrive, each lady draws a card from one pile, and each gentleman from the other pile, so that (if there are equal numbers of ladies and gentlemen) the game will begin with a mixed couple as partners at each table.

When all guests are seated, make a clear announcement of the rules of the game (a specimen announcement is given below).

Provide at least: A prize for the highest score and a "booby" prize for the lowest score; at mixed parties, there should be two prizes for each, one for the ladies and one for the gentlemen; at unmixed parties there should be a prize for the second-highest score, but no second booby prize. Special prizes may be offered for the first slam bid and made, the most slams, the highest score in any round, etc.

The Progressive Bridge Laws (next page) say that each player must subtract his opponents' score from his own after each round is completed. This is the only logical way to determine the winner, but it is usually unpopular. Since it is the duty of the hostess to please her guests, it is usually wiser for the hostess to let each player score all the points he makes.

But whatever the scoring system, insist that each player enter his opponents' score for each round on his tally card, as well as his own. At the end of the game, add up the "My Score" totals on all the cards and the "Opponents' Score" totals on all the cards; unless these totals are the same, there is an error in addition or in entering a score on one of the tallies. When the prizes are valuable, it is worth while checking to see where the error occurred, to make sure the prize is not given to the wrong person because of a scoring error.

When it appears that all tables but one have finished, walk to that table so that the progression may be called just as soon as the last deal is finished and while those players are adding and entering their scores.

Urge the guests to call you when there is any irregularity for which a penalty is demanded. When angry arguments arise, it is no crime for the hostess to make compromises so that each side gets the full score it would have had if the irregularity had never occurred.

There may be exactly as many rounds as there is time for. About twenty minutes before she wants the game to end, the hostess may say, when calling the progression, "This will be the last round. At the end of this round, add up your scores, write your names on the tallies, and bring them to me."

The following is a specimen announcement that the hostess may make before the game begins, with such changes as the circumstances require:

"For this first round, the two ladies draw for deal; high deals. After the first round, the visiting lady—the one who has just come to the table—will deal.

"You will play four deals in each round, one by each player. If a hand is passed out, it is not dealt over—each side simply scores zero for that deal.

"On the first deal, neither side is vulnerable; on the next two deals, the dealer's side is vulnerable and the other side is not; on the last deal, both sides are vulnerable.

"After the fourth deal, add up your scores, but wait till I call the progression. Then the couple with the high score at each table will move to the next table and change partners, except at Table 1, where the couple with the high score will remain and not change partners, and the losing couple will go to Table (the table with the highest number.)

"You get 500 points extra for game in one hand, vulnerable; 300 points extra for game in one hand, not vulnerable; and 50 points extra when you bid and make a contract which is not game.

"Doubling and redoubling are permitted, but no one may score more than 1,000 points in a single hand, except by bidding and making a slam.

"Please call me if there is anything you do not understand."

Before planning or starting the game, the hostess should carefully read the Laws of Progressive Bridge and be sure that she understands them.

The Laws of Progressive Bridge

(Copyright, 1935, by National Laws Commission. Reprinted by permission.)

1. ARRANGEMENT OF TABLES—The game is played by two or more tables of four players each. The tables are numbered consecutively from Table No. 1 to the highest number.

Comment: It is customary to provide each table with two decks of cards having different backs. The tables should be numbered conspicuously for the convenience of the players, and each one should be provided with one or more pencils, and a score pad showing contract scoring.

2. TALLY CARDS—Prior to the beginning of play, the game director or committee prepares individual tally cards, one for each player. Each tally card bears a table number and designates a position (North, South, East, or West) at the table. The tally cards may be drawn at random by the players or

assigned by the game director, as he prefers. When play is called, each player takes the position assigned by his tally card.

Comment: At mixed parties it is customary to arrange the tallies and seat assignments so that a gentleman will always have a lady as a partner and vice versa. This is accomplished by having tallies of two different kinds or colors, one for the ladies and the other for the gentlemen.

3. A ROUND—A round consists of four deals, one by each player. When all tables are through play, the game director gives a signal and the players move to their positions for the next round according to the type of progression used.

Comment: Each round should take about 20 minutes and the average session of play is from 6 to 7 rounds.

4. A DEAL PASSED OUT—Only four hands are dealt at each table, one by each player. If a deal is passed out (that is, if all four players pass at their first opportunity to declare), the deal passes to the left and both sides score zero for that deal.

5. METHOD OF PROGRESSION—At the conclusion of each round, the winning pair at Table No. 1 remain and the losing pair move to the last table. At all tables except Table No. 1, the losers remain and the winners move up one table toward Table No. 1.

Comment: The above is the standard method of progression, but this may be waived or altered to suit the wishes of the game director or the players. Special tallies may be arranged or obtained, assigning positions for each round in such a way as to give each player as wide a variety of partners as possible. Another method is to have the ladies progress one way and the gentlemen the other way.

6. SELECTION OF PARTNERS—At mixed parties, it is customary but not essential for a gentleman to play with a lady partner and vice versa. If the standard method of progression is used, the visiting lady at each table becomes partner of the gentleman who remains.

If the players are all of the same sex, the four players at each table draw cards to determine partners at the start of each round. The two new arrivals at each table draw first, and the one drawing higher has choice of seats and is the first dealer. The one drawing lower sits at the left of the first dealer. The two players who remain at the table from the preceding round then draw, the higher becomes the partner of the dealer. Thus all players change partners after each round.

Comment: Since the chief function of Progressive Bridge is social, it is preferable to change partners at each round. However, if for some reason a pair contest is desired, the same partnerships may be retained throughout by simply progressing as described in Law No. 5 without changing partners at the next table. Another method is to have the original N-S pairs remain in the same positions throughout the game, and to have the E-W pairs progress one table at a time until they reach Table No. 1, and then go to the last table. In this case, the progression is followed automatically, regardless of which pair wins at each table.

7. DRAW FOR DEAL—Unless the dealer is already determined under Law No. 6, the four players at a table draw for first deal. The player who draws highest is the first dealer and may select either deck.

PROGRESSIVE BRIDGE SCORING—*Comment:* With the exceptions specifically mentioned below, the scoring for Progressive Bridge is exactly the same as for Rubber Bridge:

Each deal is scored and recorded separately, and no trick points are carried over from one deal to the next.

Game is 100 points for tricks bid and made in one deal. The game premium is 300 points, if not vulnerable, and 500 points if vulnerable, and it is allowed only when game is bid and made in one deal.

A premium of 50 points is scored for making any contract less than game. This premium is in addition to the value of the tricks made. Premiums for a small and grand slam are allowed only if bid for.

8. SCORING LIMITS—A side may not score more than 1,000 points in a single deal, except in the case of a slam contract fulfilled.

Comment: It is not correct to prohibit doubles or redoubles. The limitation of penalties avoids the necessity of this restriction.

9. VULNERABILITY—The first deal of each round shall be played and scored as if neither side were vulnerable.

The second and third deals of each round shall be played and scored as if the dealer's side were vulnerable and the other side not vulnerable.

The fourth deal of each round shall be played and scored as if both sides were vulnerable.

Comment: This is the most desirable method of determining vulnerability in Progressive Bridge, but if preferred all deals may be played as though neither side were vulnerable, or all deals as though both sides were vulnerable. In any event, the method should be announced before play starts.

10. RECORDING THE SCORE—One of the four players at each table is appointed to record the score. He enters the result of each deal on the score pad separately and, at the end of the round, totals all the points made by each side.

He enters on the individual tally of each player the points made by that player's side and also the points made by the opponents.

Comment: Correctly designed tallies provide spaces to record both "My Score" and "Opponents' Score." It is important that both be entered on the tally, for otherwise the record would be meaningless.

11. COMPUTING TOTAL SCORES—At the conclusion of the game, each player totals his score. He also totals the scores of his opponents, as recorded on his tally, and subtracts his opponents' total from his own. The difference, plus or minus as the case may be, is recorded in the space provided at the bottom of his tally.

Comment: Let us suppose that a player scores 2,460 points, and the opponents score 1,520 points against him. This makes his net score +940 for the entire session. On the other hand, if a player scores only 1,650 points, and the opponents score 1,940 points against him, then his net score for the session is —290 points. Do not make the mistake of recording only plus scores, for that method gives false results, and is likely to lead to improper doubling and redoubling.

12. DETERMINING THE WINNER—The player with the largest plus score is the winner. Other players with plus scores rank in descending order followed by the players with minus scores, the one with the largest minus being last.

Comment: The method of awarding prizes is left to the discretion of the game director. At mixed parties it is usual to award one or more prizes to the highest-scoring ladies and one or more prizes to the highest-scoring gentlemen.

Progressive Rubber Bridge

Progressive Rubber Bridge is a variation of the usual progressive game. It has proved increasingly popular, and may in time supplant the usual form. It follows the methods of progression and change of partners described in the preceding laws, but the scoring is somewhat different.

Under this arrangement it is preferable to play 6 or 8 deals to a round, or to fix the length of a round by a definite time limit—say 30 minutes. If the length of a round is determined by a time limit, any deal which has been started before time is up may be completed, but no new hand may be dealt.

Rubber scoring is used. [See the scoring instructions on pages 26-27.] As many rubbers as possible are completed during the time allotted. A rubber completed in two games carries a bonus of 700 points. A three-game rubber carries a bonus of 500 points. If a side has won one game toward a rubber and the other side has not won a game, 300 points are allowed for the single game won. If a rubber is unfinished and one side has made one or more part-score contracts in an unfinished game, but the other side has made no part-score in that game, the side with the part-score(s) adds 50 points to its score.

Vulnerability is determined by the state of the score and not according to Law No. 9 in the Progressive Code. A side is vulnerable when it has won a game and remains vulnerable until the conclusion of that rubber. However, vulnerability lapses at the conclusion of a round and a new rubber is started at the beginning of each new round.

At the end of a round each player enters on his tally only his net gain or loss—not his total score. At the end of the session these net gains and losses are totaled and the player's final score, plus or minus as the case may be, is entered at the bottom of this tally.

[If each side is permitted to enter all the points it has scored, without subtracting its opponents' score; and if each side has scored a game toward an unfinished rubber, then each side adds 300 points to its score; and if each side has a part-score in an unfinished game of an unfinished rubber, then each side adds 50 points to its score.]

The Laws of Pivot Bridge

(Copyright, 1935, by National Laws Commission. Reprinted by permission.)

Pivot Bridge is played by four (or five) players at a table. This form may be used for a single table or for large gatherings in which it is desirable to have each table play as a separate unit without progression by the players.

The game is so arranged that each player plays with each other player at his table both as partner and opponent. There are two methods of play: first, four deals may be played to a round, one deal by each player, and the players change partners at the end of each four deals; second, rubbers may be played, and the players change partners at the end of each rubber.

If four deals to a round are played, the scoring is exactly the same as in Progressive Bridge; if rubbers are played, the scoring is exactly the same as in Rubber Bridge. The laws given below explain only the method of rotation in changing partners, not scoring, vulnerability, etc., which are covered elsewhere.

1. DRAW FOR PARTNERS—The players draw cards for partners and deal and for a choice of seats and deck. The player who draws highest is the first pivot, and he deals first and has the choice of seats and decks. The player who draws second highest is the pivot's first partner; the player who draws third highest sits at the pivot's left during the first round; the player who draws fourth sits at the pivot's right; and if a fifth player is present, he does not participate in the first round or rubber.

2. CHANGING PARTNERS (FOR FOUR PLAYERS)—During the first three rounds or rubbers, the players change positions as indicated in the following diagram:

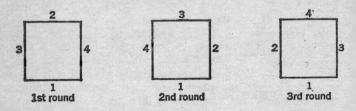

After the third round or rubber, the players again cut for position and partners.

3. CHANGING PARTNERS (FOR FIVE PLAYERS)—If five players desire to play at the same table, they may be accommodated in this manner:

For the first round or rubber, the players take the positions indicated by their draw for position under Law No. 1. For rounds of one to five, they take the positions indicated in the following diagram:

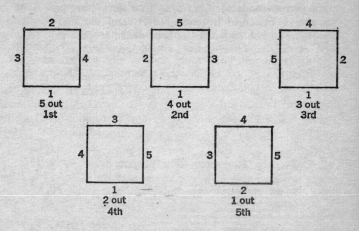

At the end of each five rounds, the players again draw for positions and partners.

Comment: This arrangement permits each player to play with each other player once as partner and twice as opponent, and each player sits out one round in turn.

4. DETERMINING THE WINNER—At the completion of each round or rubber, the player enters on his tally both his own score and that of his opponents. Each player totals his own and his opponents' scores separately and records the difference, plus or minus as the case may be, at the bottom of his tally. The player having the highest plus score is the winner and the others rank in descending order according to their scores.

Duplicate Bridge

Duplicate Bridge is the only form of the game played in tournaments, but is equally adapted to play in homes and clubs. It is considered the supreme test of skill among card games. The following description and the laws of the game are condensed, by permission, from The Laws of Duplicate Contract Bridge, ©1949 by the National Laws Commission of the American Contract Bridge League.

NUMBER OF PLAYERS—Four players in two partnerships may play Replay Duplicate. Eight or more players may play a pair game, an individual game, or a team-of-four match.

EQUIPMENT—A set of duplicate boards, or trays, and one pack of cards for each board. Each board has four pockets, corresponding to the compass points, for holding the hands of the respective players. The face of each board is marked with an arrow pointing toward the "North" pocket, and with an indication of the dealer and vulnerability. There should be at least 16 boards to a set, numbered consecutively, with dealer and vulnerability as follows:

DEALER	VULNERABILITY
N—1, 5, 9, 13	Neither—1, 8, 11, 14
E—2, 6, 10, 14	N-S only—2, 5, 12, 15
S—3, 7, 11, 15	E-W only—3, 6, 9, 16
W—4, 8, 12, 16	Both—4, 7, 10, 13

Boards numbered 17 to 32, if used, correspond to boards 1 to 16 respectively, except in their identifying numbers.

SHUFFLE AND DEAL—Any player, in the presence of an opponent or of the tournament director, prepares a board by shuffling the pack of cards and dealing it, one card at a time face down, into four packets, each of which he inserts in a pocket of the duplicate board.

THE AUCTION—The arrow on the board is pointed in the direction of the room designated as North. Each player takes the hand from the pocket nearest him, and counts his cards to make sure he has thirteen. The player designated as dealer calls first, and the auction proceeds as described on page 21 until the contract is determined. There is no redeal when a hand is passed out.

THE PLAY—The opening lead, exposure of dummy, and subsequent play are as described on page 22, except: After a trick is completed, each player retains possession of his card and places it face down on the table directly in front of him, pointed lengthwise toward the partners who won the trick. Declarer plays dummy's cards by naming or touching them, and dummy turns them and keeps them in front of him.

SCORING—The score of each board is independent of the scores of the other boards, and trick points scored on one board cannot count toward game on a subsequent board. No rubber premium is scored. Instead the following premiums are scored:

	DECLARER'S SIDE	
	VULNERABLE	NOT VULNERABLE
For bidding and making a game contract	500	300
For making a contract of less than game	50	50

If match-point scoring is used to determine the winner of the game, there is no premium for holding honors in one hand.

In other respects the scoring of each board follows the schedule shown on page 27.

DETERMINING THE WINNER—Match-point scoring is always used in individual games, is most often used in pair games, and may be used in team-of-four games or replay games. Cumulative (or "total-point") scoring may be used in pair and team-of-four games. These methods are explained on pages 64-67.

Irregularities in Duplicate Bridge

Rubber Bridge and Duplicate Bridge are governed by the same laws so far as the nature of the two games makes it possible. The procedure described on pages 19-23, and the penalties and rectifications of irregularities described on pages 28-37 govern in Duplicate Bridge except as provided below.

TOURNAMENT DIRECTOR—One person, who may be a player, must be appointed to conduct and supervise the game or tournament. His duties include: listing the entries; selecting suitable movements and conditions of play; maintaining discipline; administering the laws; assessing penalties and assigning adjusted scores; collecting and tabulating results.

DRAWING ATTENTION TO AN IRREGULARITY—The Director must be summoned as soon as attention is drawn to an irregularity. Players do not have the right to assess or waive penalties on their own initiative.

ADJUSTED SCORE—The Director may assign an adjusted score when the laws provide no penalty which will fully indemnify a non-offending contestant for an opponent's irregularity, or when no rectification can be made that will permit normal play of the board; but may not assign an adjusted score on the ground that the penalty provided by the laws is unduly severe or unduly advantageous to the non-offending side. An adjusted score may be assigned by altering the total-point score on the board, or by the assignment of zero or more match-points. Penalty points may be assessed against the offending side, indemnity points given to the non-offending side; these need not balance.

BIDDING AND PLAYING CONVENTIONS—A player may make any call or play (including an intentionally misleading call such as a "psychic" bid) except that he may not make a call or play based on a partnership understanding unless the opposing pair may reasonably be expected to understand its meaning, or unless his side has announced its use before either member has looked at his hand. If the Director decides that a pair has been damaged through its opponents' failure to make such announcement, he may assign an adjusted score.

The Director, on a player's request, may require the player who made a call or play to leave the table and his partner to explain its meaning.

The Director (or other authority) may forbid the use of such conventions as might place other contestants at a disadvantage or take too long to explain.

DUMMY'S RIGHTS—In addition to the rights stated on page 32, dummy may: notify the Director of any matter that may affect the legal rights of his side; keep count of the tricks won and lost; draw attention to another player's card played to the preceding trick and pointed in the wrong direction. He may play the cards of the dummy hand as directed by declarer; if he places in the played position a card that declarer did not name, the error may be corrected before a card has been led to the next trick and a defender may withdraw a card played after the error but before attention was drawn to it. If dummy (in the Director's opinion) suggests a play, the Director may require or forbid declarer to play that card or its equivalent.

ERROR IN PLAY FROM DUMMY—Declarer may change his designation of a card to be played from dummy if he does so practically in the same breath, or if he designated a card that is not there.

IMPROPER INFORMATION—If a player receives improper information about a board, he should notify the Director, who shall require that the board be played and scored normally if that seems feasible, and otherwise shall assign an adjusted score. Examples of improper information: looking at the wrong hand; seeing another player's card before the auction begins; overhearing calls or remarks; partner's improper remark or gesture.

REVOKE TIME LIMIT—A revoke made in the twelfth trick must be corrected if discovered before all four hands have been returned to the board. An established revoke is not subject to penalty if attention is first drawn to it after the round has ended and the board has been moved. In all other respects the provisions stated on page 34 apply.

CLAIMS AND CONCESSIONS—The concession of a trick which cannot be lost by any play of the cards is void, provided the error is brought to an opponent's attention before the round has ended and the board has been moved. The concession of a trick the player has in fact won is void, provided the error is brought to the Director's attention within 30 minutes after the end of the session.

If a claim or concession is disputed, the Director must be summoned and no action should be taken without him. The Director determines the result on the board, awarding any doubtful trick to the claimant's opponents.

CORRECTION OF SCORING ERRORS—A time limit should be established for the correction of errors in recording scores; it should be no less than 30 minutes nor more than 24 hours after the posting of the Official Score. To change a score because an opponent has received improper information, a contestant must notify the Director within 30 minutes after the end of the session.

WRONG NUMBER OF CARDS—If the Director decides that one or more pockets of the board contained an incorrect number of cards, he should correct it if possible, and should then require that the board be played normally unless a player gained information of sufficient importance to warrant assigning an adjusted score.

INTERCHANGED CARDS—If the cards or hands in a board become interchanged during a session, the Director rates separately each group that played identical boards, as follows: Each pair receives 1 match point for each lower score in the same group, ½ match point for each identical score in the same group, and ½ match point for each pair in the other group(s).

DISCIPLINARY PENALTIES—For an error in procedure (failure to count cards, playing the wrong board, etc.) which requires an adjusted score for any contestant, the Director may assess a penalty against the offender (10% of the maximum match-point score on one board is recommended). A similar indemnity may be awarded to a contestant who is required to take an adjusted score through no fault of his own. The Director may increase the penalties for flagrant or repeated violations. In total-point play, 100 total points are equivalent to 1 match point.

APPEALS—If there is a tournament or club committee in charge, appeal may be made to it from any ruling of the Director on a question of disputed fact or an exercise of discretionary power. Appeals from the Director's rulings on points of law may be made only to the National Laws Commission, 33 West 60th St., New York 23, N. Y.

Duplicate Bridge for Homes and Clubs
Replay Duplicate—for Four Players

Replay Duplicate is a contest between two pairs. It is played in two sessions, called the *original play* and the *replay*.

The players take places, one being designated North. The boards are shuffled, and are played with the arrows pointing North. Any number of boards is feasible.

A separate score slip is kept for each board. At the close of the session the boards and score slips are laid aside where they will be undisturbed.

At some later time, the same four players take the same relative positions about the table. The boards are replayed with the arrows pointing East. Again a separate score slip is kept for each board.

The scoring may be by match points or total points. If the former method is used, each deal is treated as a separate match. The pair having the better net score on a deal is credited with 1 point. The final scores are the totals of these match points.

If total-point scoring is employed, the two slips for each deal are compared, and the pair having the net plus score is credited with that amount. The net scores for all deals, so determined, are totaled, and the pair having the larger total wins the difference.

Replay Duplicate is popular as a home game among foursomes that meet weekly for social Bridge. It can easily be played in a continuous series of sessions. Half of the time in each session is devoted to the original play of new boards, and half to the replay of old boards.

The game tends to become a test of memory rather than of bridge skill. To check this tendency the following measures are recommended:

1. Do not play the boards in consecutive order. Choose the board to be played next at random from the stack.

2. Avoid comment of any sort about the deal after its original play.

3. Allow at least a week to elapse between the original play and the replay.

It is sometimes desired to make the game a test of skill in the play alone. The bidding during the original play is then recorded, and for the replay this bidding is read to fix the contract and declarer.

Individual Contests—for Eight or Twelve Players

In an individual game, each player plays once with every other as partner, and twice against every other as opponent.

The initial seating of the players in games for two or three tables is shown below:

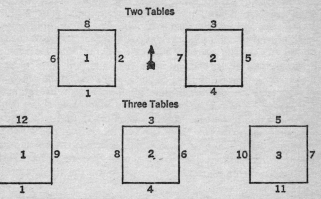

Two Tables

Three Tables

The game may be conducted without guide cards, thus:

1. Allow the players to take places at random. Reserve the North position at Table 1 for the supervisor; this player is "anchor," retaining his seat throughout the game.

2. From this schedule inform each player of his number, and tell him who is the player of the next-lower number.

3. Announce that after each round, all players but the anchor will progress, each player taking the seat vacated by the player of next-lower number. (Player 1 follows Player 7 or 11 respectively.)

A new set of boards is played in each round. The set is played at all tables, the boards being circulated at convenience. The eight-player game requires seven rounds, with a total of 14, 21, or 28 boards. The twelve-player game requires eleven rounds, and the only feasible number of boards is 33.

The scoring of individual contests is by match points, as explained on page 67.

Team-of-four Contest—for Eight Players

The team-of-four match between two teams has long been recognized as the most accurate test of Bridge skill known. Two tables are provided, in different rooms if possible. One pair of Team 1 sits N-S at Table 1, and the other pair sits E-W at Table 2. The members of Team 2 take the remaining positions, its E-W pair playing at Table 1 and its N-S pair at Table 2.

The number of boards to be played should be a multiple of 4. From one to one and one-half hours are usually required for the play of twelve boards. The first fourth of the boards are placed on Table 1 and the second fourth on Table 2. These boards are shuffled, dealt, played and scored.

The two tables then exchange boards, each replaying the ones played at the other table. Care must be taken to see that in every case the arrow points toward the North player.

When the boards have been replayed, the two pairs of Team 2 exchange places, retaining the same partners but playing against the other pair of opponents. The remaining boards are divided equally between the two tables, to be shuffled, dealt, played, scored, exchanged and replayed as explained above.

When all the boards have been replayed, the team whose members, considering all boards and all scores, have a net plus score, is the winner.

Mitchell Pair Games—for Three or More Tables

The Mitchell game is the simplest and most popular of the Duplicate pair movements.

One way of the room is arbitrarily designated the North-South direction, regardless of the actual compass direction. The tables are numbered and arranged in numerical order with Table No. 1 at the North end of the room. With players of average speed about 24 boards can be played in three hours.

The entire number of boards to be played is equally divided into as many sets as there are tables. The method of distribution depends upon whether the number of tables is odd or even. With an odd number of tables, one set is placed on each table, beginning with Table 1, which receives the lowest numbered set of boards, the next set on Table 2, and so on.

Each pair of players takes as its pair number the number of the table at which it starts play. At Table 4, for example, would be North-South pair 4 and East-West pair 4. These numbers are retained throughout the contest.

When the signal to commence play is given, the boards at each table are bid, played, and scored. (See page 58 for scoring laws, and page 67 for an illustration of match-point scoring.)

When the play of the original set of boards at each table has been completed the tournament director gives the signal to progress. The North-South pairs remain stationary. The East-West pairs move to the next-higher-numbered table. The boards are moved to the next-lower-numbered table. This progression is continued until each East-West pair has played against each North-South pair, and each pair has played each set of boards.

DISTRIBUTION OF BOARDS AND PROGRESSION FOR AN EVEN NUMBER OF TABLES—The sets of boards are distributed regularly until half of them have been placed on the tables. *The next set is placed on a stand or chair,* known as the relay stand. Following this, each of the remaining tables receives its regular quota of boards, except the last table, *which receives none.* The pairs at this table play, simultaneously with Table 1, the boards which have been allotted to Table 1, passing the boards back and forth between the two tables. The first and last tables share the same boards throughout the contest.

The relay stand is always placed *exactly halfway between the first and last tables.* The players at the lower-numbered table next to the relay table shuffle the relay boards. These boards, however, are not played in the first round.

The North-South pairs do not progress. The East-West pairs progress to the next-higher-numbered table in the same manner as for an odd number of tables. The boards are passed to the next-lower-numbered table, except that from the higher-numbered table above the relay stand the boards are passed to the relay stand. The lower-numbered table next to the relay stand secures its boards from the relay stand, taking the set of boards that was not in play during the preceding round. The boards that were played simultaneously by the first and last tables are passed to the next-to-last table. INCOMPLETE TABLE—If an odd number of pairs enter the game so that one table is incomplete, the odd pair is seated E-W at the highest-numbered table, assuming that table number for its pair number. This pair does not play the first round, but at the completion of the round moves to Table 1 and enters the regular progression. Each E-W pair in its proper turn sits out one round when it comes to the last, or incomplete, table. In distributing the boards and arranging the progression, the odd pair (or half table) is considered a regularly constituted table; for example, 5½ tables would require the arrangement for 6 tables and 8½ tables would require the arrangement for 9 tables.

COMPARING SCORES—In the Mtichell game all N-S pairs play the same hands, and all E-W pairs play the same hands. Therefore each pair can compare scores only with others in its own direction, and there are really two separate contests —one for N-S pairs, and one for E-W pairs. There will be one pair of winners in each group, and they should receive equal prizes or honors.

MATCH-POINT SCORING FOR THE MITCHELL GAME—Match-point scoring is the most popular and the most equitable method for duplicate play. In this method all scores made by N-S pairs on a given deal are tabulated in a vertical column for purposes of comparison. Each score receives one match point for each other N-S score it beats and ½ match point for each N-S score it ties. For example, in a section of 9 tables, there would be 9 scores; the highest score would have beaten 8 others and would therefore receive 8 match points; the second-highest score would have beaten 7 others and would receive 7 points, etc. The E-W scores are similarly tabulated and compared among themselves.

Each deal is rated separately, and when all have been rated the total number of match points awarded to each pair is computed. The match-point figure on each deal represents the number of pairs beaten on that deal, and the match-point total represents the total number of pairs beaten on all deals. The pair having the greatest number of match points in each group is the winner in that group.

The simplest method of recording scores is to provide a traveling score slip for each board, which remains with the board throughout the game, and on which all results for the board are recorded. Pads of traveling score slips are available from many suppliers.

A traveling score slip is folded, in such a way that its face cannot be seen, and tucked in one of the pockets of each board. After the play of that board is completed at each table, the North player unfolds the traveling score slip, enters the score (plus or minus) of his pair on the line corresponding to his pair number, and returns the slip to the board.

Howell Movement

The Howell movement is one in which each pair plays one set of boards against each other pair. The movement is somewhat complicated, and in order to direct the movement of the players and the boards Howell movement guide cards are necessary. These may be obtained in sets for any number of tables.

International Match Points

Team-of-four contests for world and national championships are scored by "international match points" (IMP). On each deal a team's net score is determined and this score is translated into international match points by the following schedule.

AGGREGATE	MATCH POINTS	AGGREGATE	MATCH POINTS
0 - 10	0	750 - 890	13
20 - 40	1	900 - 1090	14
50 - 80	2	1100 - 1290	15
90 - 120	3	1300 - 1490	16
130 - 160	4	1500 - 1740	17
170 - 210	5	1750 - 1990	18
220 - 260	6	2000 - 2240	19
270 - 310	7	2250 - 2490	20
320 - 360	8	2500 - 2990	21
370 - 420	9	3000 - 3490	22
430 - 490	10	3500 - 3990	23
500 - 590	11	4000 - and up	24
600 - 740	12		

AUCTION BRIDGE

There is no difference whatsoever between Auction Bridge and Contract Bridge except in the scoring. Pages 23-26 cover the procedure in Auction Bridge, and pages 27-37 cover the irregularities. But whereas in Contract Bridge declarer's tricks count toward game or slam only if he bid for them, in Auction Bridge declarer's overtricks count toward game or slam just as do the tricks he bid for. Auction Bridge scoring is as follows:

SCORING—Provided declarer has won at least the number of odd-tricks named in his contract, declarer's side scores for each odd-trick won:

	Undoubled	Doubled	Redoubled
With no trump	10	20	40
With spades trump	9	18	36
With hearts trump	8	16	32
With diamonds trump	7	14	28
With clubs trump	6	12	24

Game and Rubber. When a side scores, in one or more hands, 30 points or more for odd-tricks, it has won a game and both sides start fresh on the next game. When a side has won two games it wins the rubber and adds to its score 250 points.

Doubles and Redoubles. If a doubled contract is fulfilled, declarer's side scores 50 points bonus plus 50 points for each odd-trick in excess of his contract. If a redoubled contract is fulfilled, declarer's side scores 100 points bonus plus 100 points for each odd-trick in excess of his contract. These bonuses are additional to the score for odd-tricks, but do not count toward game.

Undertricks. For every trick by which declarer falls short of his contract, his opponents score 50 points; if the contract is doubled, 100 points; if it is redoubled, 200 points.

Honors. The side which holds the majority of the trump

honors (A, K, Q, J, 10), or of the aces at no-trump, scores:

For 3 honors (or aces) 30
For 4 honors (or aces), divided 40
For 5 honors, divided 50
For 4 trump honors in one hand 80
For 4 trump honors in one hand, 5th in partner's hand. 90
For 4 aces in one hand at no-trump 100
For 5 honors in one hand 100

Slams. A side which wins twelve of the thirteen tricks, regardless of the contract, scores 50 points for a small slam. A side which wins all thirteen tricks, regardless of the contract, scores 100 points for grand slam.

Points for overtricks, undertricks, honors and slams do not count toward game. Only odd-tricks count toward game, and only when declarer fulfils his contract.

Games Based on Bridge

Honeymoon Bridge (Two-Hand Bridge)

NUMBER OF PLAYERS—TWO.

THE PACK—52 cards.

RANK OF CARDS AND SUITS—As in Contract Bridge (page 20).

THE SHUFFLE, CUT AND DEAL—Each draws; the player drawing the higher card deals first. Each player may shuffle, dealer last, and dealer's opponent must cut. Dealer gives each player 13 cards, one at a time, and places the remaining cards face down in the center as the *stock*.

THE PLAY—Non-dealer leads first. It is necessary to follow suit to the lead if able. Play is at no-trump, as in Contract Bridge. After each trick, each player draws a card from the stock, the winner of the previous trick drawing first and then leading to the next trick. Tricks won during this period have no scoring value.

BIDDING AND FINAL PLAY—When the last card of the stock has been drawn, dealer may bid or pass. Bidding then proceeds as in Contract Bridge until a bid, double or redouble is followed by a pass. The player who does not make the final bid leads first and thirteen tricks are played with or without a trump suit as determined by the final contract.

SCORING—Auction or Contract Bridge scoring may be used.

IRREGULARITIES—If a player revokes during the first thirteen tricks; or draws out of turn from the stock, or in drawing sees the face of more than one card; his opponent, when next he draws, may look at the two top cards of the stock and select either.

Three-Hand (Cutthroat) Bridge

NUMBER OF PLAYERS—Three.

THE PACK—52 cards. Two packs are used as in Contract Bridge.

THE DRAW—Draw for deal and seats only. High deals.

THE SHUFFLE AND CUT—Player at dealer's left shuffles (dealer may shuffle last) and player at dealer's right cuts.

THE DEAL—Four hands are dealt as in Contract Bridge, an extra or "dummy" hand being dealt between the players at dealer's left and right.

THE BIDDING—Dealer bids first and bidding proceeds until any call is followed by two passes.

THE PLAY—The highest bidder becomes declarer; the other two players become defenders, and the defender at declarer's left makes the opening lead. The dummy is then spread out between the two defenders and play proceeds as in Contract Bridge.

SCORING—Either the Auction Bridge or Contract Bridge scoring table may be used. A separate score is kept for each player. If declarer makes his contract, the points are scored to his credit; if he is defeated, each of his opponents scores the undertrick penalties. If the defenders or either of them hold honors, both defenders score for them. In three-hand Auction Bridge, the first player to win two games receives 250 points bonus; in three-hand Contract Bridge, he receives 700 points if neither opponent has a game, 500 points if either opponent has a game.

SETTLEMENT—Each player settles separately with each other player, paying or collecting the difference in their scores to the nearest 100 points, 50 or more counting as 100.

IRREGULARITIES—*During the auction,* any improper double may be canceled by the player who is doubled and thereafter neither opponent may double him at any contract. There is no penalty for any other improper call, which may be canceled by either opponent or condoned by agreement of both opponents. If a player improperly looks at any card in the.

dummy, he is barred from the auction thereafter. *During the play*, the laws of Contract Bridge (page 26) apply.

Trio (Contract Bridge for Three)
Introduced by George S. Coffin of Waltham, Massachusetts

PLAYERS—The three players are designated as South, North, and East, seated in those compass positions. South and North are partners against East and the dummy, which is in the West position.

PRELIMINARIES—As in Three-hand Bridge. After the deal the entire dummy hand is faced and is seen by all players during the bidding.

BIDDING—South always bids first, then North, then East, and so on in rotation. Any player may become declarer, though East always plays the dummy.

PLAY—The player (which may be dummy) at declarer's left makes the opening lead and play proceeds as in Bridge.

SCORING—Score is kept as in Contract Bridge, with East and dummy constituting one side and North-South the other. Hence, East wins or loses doubly, North and South each singly. After each rubber the North player moves into the seat at his right and becomes South, and the previous South player becomes East.

Towie (For Three or More)
Introduced by Leonard Replogle of New York City

PLAYERS—Only three play at a time, but there may be as many as seven in the game and all participate in the scoring of every hand.

PRELIMINARIES—Four hands are dealt, then the dealer turns up six cards of the dummy (hand opposite him).

BIDDING AND PLAY—The three players bid. High bidder becomes declarer and after the opening lead (by the player at his left) he turns up the rest of the dummy and places it opposite him. Play proceeds as in Bridge.

SCORING—Contract Bridge scoring may be used, but most players use special scoring in which down three, vulnerable and doubled, counts 1,000 (called *towie*). A separate scoring column is used for each player. If declarer makes his contract he scores the trick-score plus 500 for his first game and 1,000 for his second (rubber) game. If declarer is defeated, every player (active or inactive) scores the undertrick penalties.

GOULASH—If a contract worth at least 100 trick-points is not reached, each player sorts his hand into suits, these hands are stacked and the pack is cut, and the same dealer redeals them in three rounds—5, 5 and 3 cards at a time. Six of dummy's cards are turned up and bidding begins again.

RETIREMENT—When there are more than three in the game, each player becomes inactive after being declarer. Players re-enter in the order in which they went out, except that a vulnerable player may not re-enter as long as any player is not vulnerable.

Cutthroat Contract (For Four Players)
Introduced by S. B. Fishburne of Tulsa, Oklahoma

PLAYERS—Four, but with no fixed partnerships.

BIDDING—As in Contract Bridge, except: (a) the opening bidder must have at least 13 high-card points or 3 quick tricks (see page 38) and if he does not he pays a penalty of 300 points to each other player; (b) after an opening bid of one club to four spades, the next player must bid at least four no-trump; (c) if no one opens the bidding, a goulash (see above) is dealt by the same dealer.

PARTNERSHIPS—The high bidder selects any player to be his partner. That player may accept and score with declarer, or reject and score with the opponents, but in any case his hand is dummy and the players change seats if necessary to put it opposite declarer. After this, declarer's left-hand opponent may double; if he does not, declarer's right-hand opponent may double; and if either doubles, declarer (or then dummy, if he has accepted) may redouble. Play proceeds as in Contract Bridge.

SCORING—A separate score is kept for each player. The first player to win two games scores 700 for rubber if neither defender is vulnerable and 500 if either defender is vulnerable. A dummy who has accepted gets only 300 for game if he is not vulnerable. Both defenders, plus dummy if he has rejected, score undertrick penalties. The value of undertrick penalties depends solely on whether declarer is vulnerable or not vulnerable.

Blackout (Oh Pshaw)

PLAYERS—Three to seven. Best for four or five. Each plays for himself.

THE DEAL—Each game comprises a series of deals; in the

first deal, each hand receives one card; in the second deal, 2 cards; and so on to the limit. With four players, there are 13 deals; with five players, 10 deals; with three players it is advisable to limit the game to 15 deals.

THE TURN-UP—Having completed the deal, the dealer turns up the next card of the pack. The turn-up fixes the trump suit for that deal. When the last deal leaves no odd card to turn up, the deal is played at no-trump.

THE BIDDING—Beginning with eldest hand, each player in turn bids *exactly* the number of tricks that he thinks he can win. Thus, on the first deal the possible bids are "One" and "Zero." The total of all bids need not be equal to the number of tricks in play. It is a duty of the scorekeeper to announce, after the dealer has bid, "Over," or "Under," or "Even," according to how the total of bids compares with the number of tricks.

THE PLAY—Eldest hand makes the opening lead. Each hand must follow suit to a lead if able; if unable, the hand may trump or discard at will. A trick is won by the highest card of the suit led, or, if it contains trumps, by the highest trump. The winner of a trick leads to the next.

OBJECT OF PLAY—To win exactly the number of tricks bid, neither more nor less.

SCORING—A scorekeeper must be appointed to record the bids as well as to enter the results. A running account is kept of each individual's cumulative score.

A player who takes more or less tricks than his bid scores nothing for the hand and loses nothing. For making his bid exactly, a player scores 10 points plus the amount of his bid. (Practice is not standardized as to the scoring of "Zero" bids. In different localities the score is 10, 5, or 5 plus the number of tricks in the deal.)

The player with the highest cumulative score at the end of the game wins. Each player settles with every other player on the difference in their final scores. (*Variant.* The winner gets a bonus of 10 points.)

IRREGULARITIES—There is no penalty for a bid out of turn, but such a bid must stand. The turn to bid reverts to the rightful player. A player may change his bid without penalty before the player at his left bids.

A lead or play out of turn must be retracted on demand of any player, and the card played in error must be left face up on the table and played at the first legal opportunity. A card exposed in any way but by legal play in turn becomes exposed and is treated in the same way.

A player is entitled to be informed at any time how much any other player has bid, and how many tricks each player has won. Each player should keep his tricks arranged in an orderly fashion so that they may be counted by inspection.

WHIST

NUMBER OF PLAYERS—Four, two against two as partners. For the procedure when more than four want to play, see the Laws of Whist on the next page.

THE PACK—52 cards. Two packs of contrasting back designs should be used, one being shuffled while the other is dealt.

RANK OF CARDS—In play, A (high), K, Q, J, 10, 9, 8, 7, 6, 5, 4, 3, 2. In drawing for partners and deal, ace is low.

THE DRAW—Cut, or draw from a spread pack, for partners; the two highest play against the two lowest. Low card has choice of cards and seats.

THE SHUFFLE AND CUT—Any player may shuffle, the dealer last; the player at the dealer's right cuts (see Laws).

THE DEAL—The dealer gives one card at a time, face down, to each player, in clockwise rotation beginning with the player on his left, until he comes to the last card, which is the trump card.

THE TRUMP CARD—The dealer must place the last card of the pack face up on the table before him, and every card of its suit becomes a trump. When it is the dealer's turn to play to the first trick, he picks up the trump card and it becomes part of his hand.

OBJECT OF PLAY—To win tricks.

THE PLAY—The turn to play is from player to player in clockwise rotation. The player at dealer's left makes the first lead, and may lead any card. Each player in turn thereafter must play a card, following suit if able. If not able to follow suit a player may play any card. Four cards so played (including the card led) constitute a trick.

A trick containing any trump is won by the player of the highest trump; a trick not containing a trump is won by the player of the highest card of the suit led. The winner of each trick leads to the next.

SCORING—Each odd-trick (trick in excess of six) counts one point for the side winning it.

The Laws of Whist

Condensed from the Laws of the American Whist Congress.

THE GAME—A game consists of 7 points, each trick above six counting 1. The value of the game is determined by deducting the losers' score from seven.

SHUFFLING—Before every deal, the cards must be shuffled. In all cases the dealer may shuffle last.

CUTTING—The dealer must present the pack to his right-hand adversary to be cut; the adversary must take a portion from the top of the pack and place it toward the dealer. At least four cards must be left in each packet. The dealer must reunite the packets by placing the one not removed in cutting upon the other. If in cutting or reuniting the separate packets a card is exposed, the pack must be reshuffled by the dealer and cut again.

If the dealer reshuffles the pack after it has been properly cut, he loses his deal.

DEALING—When the pack has been properly cut and reunited, the dealer must distribute the cards, one at a time, to each player in regular rotation at his left. The last, which is the trump card, must be turned up before the dealer. At the end of the hand, or when the deal is lost, the deal passes to the player next to the dealer on his left, and so on to each in turn.

There must be a new deal by the same dealer:

a. If any card except the last is faced in the pack.
b. If, during the deal or during the play of the hand, the pack is proven incorrect or imperfect, but any prior score made with that pack shall stand.

If, during the deal, a card is exposed, the side not in fault may demand a new deal, provided neither of that side has touched a card. If a new deal does not take place, the exposed card is not liable to be called.

Anyone dealing out of turn, or with his adversaries' pack, may be stopped before the trump card is turned; after which the deal is valid, and the packs, if changed, so remain.

MISDEALING—It is a misdeal:

a. If the dealer omits to have the pack cut, and his adversaries discover the error before the trump card is turned and before looking at any of their cards.

b. If he deals a card incorrectly and fails to correct the error before dealing another.

c. If he counts the cards on the table or in the remainder of the pack.

d. If, having a perfect pack, he does not deal to each player the proper number of cards and the error is discovered before all have played to the first trick.

e. If he looks at the trump card before the deal is completed.

f. If he places the trump card face downward upon his own or any other player's cards.

A misdeal loses the deal unless during the deal either of the adversaries touches a card, or in any other manner interrupts the dealer.

THE TRUMP CARD—The dealer must leave the trump card face upward on the table until it is his turn to play to the first trick; if it is left on the table until after the second trick has been turned and quitted, it is liable to be called. After it has been lawfully taken up it must not be named, and any player naming it is liable to have his highest or his lowest trump called by either adversary. A player may, however, ask what the trump suit is.

IRREGULARITIES IN THE HANDS—If, at any time, after all have played to the first trick (the pack being perfect), a player is found to have either more or less than his correct number of cards, and his adversaries have their right number, the latter, upon the discovery of such surplus or deficiency, may consult and shall have the choice:

a. To have a new deal; or,

b. To have the hand played out; in which case the surplus or missing cards are not taken into account.

If either of the adversaries also has more or less than his correct number, there must be a new deal.

If any player has a surplus card by reason of an omission to play to a trick, his adversaries can exercise the foregoing privilege only after he has played to the trick following the one in which the omission occurred.

CARDS LIABLE TO BE CALLED—The following cards are liable to be called by either adversary:

a. Every card faced upon the table otherwise than in the regular course of play, but not including a card led out of turn.

b. Every card thrown with the one led or played to the current trick. The player must indicate the one led or played.

c. Every card so held by a player that his partner sees any portion of its face.

d. All the cards in a hand lowered or shown by a player so that his partner sees more than one card of it.

e. Every card named by the player holding it.

All cards liable to be called must be placed and left face upward on the table. A player must lead or play them when they are called, providing he can do so without revoking. The call may be repeated at each trick until the card is played. A player cannot be prevented from leading or playing a card liable to be called; if he can get rid of it in the course of play, no penalty remains.

If a player leads a card better than any of his adversaries hold of the suit, and then leads one or more other cards without waiting for his partner to play, the latter may be called upon by either adversary to take the first trick, and the other cards thus improperly played are liable to be called; it makes no difference whether he plays them one after the other or throws them all on the table together.

A player having a card liable to be called must not play another until the adversaries have stated whether or not they wish to call the card liable to the penalty. If he plays another card without awaiting the decision of the adversaries, such other card also is liable to be called.

LEADING OUT OF TURN—If any player leads out of turn, a suit may be called from him or his partner the first time it is the turn of either of them to lead. The penalty can be enforced only by the adversary on the right of the player from whom a suit can rightfully be called.

If a player so called on to lead a suit has none of it, or if all have played to the false lead, no penalty can be enforced. If all have not played to the trick, the cards erroneously played to such false lead are not liable to be called, and must be taken back.

PLAYING OUT OF TURN—If the third hand plays before the second, the fourth hand may also play before the second. If the third hand has not played, and the fourth hand plays before the second, the latter may be called upon by the third hand to play his highest or lowest card of the suit led; or, if he has none, to trump or not to trump the trick.

ABANDONED HANDS—If all four players throw their cards on the table, face upward, no further play of that hand is permitted. The result of the hand, as then claimed or admitted, is established; provided, that if a revoke is discovered, the revoke penalty attaches.

REVOKING—A revoke may be corrected by the player making it, before the trick in which it occurs has been turned and quitted, unless either he or his partner, whether in his right turn or otherwise, has led or played to the following trick, or unless his partner has asked whether or not he has any of the suit renounced. If a player corrects his mistake in time to save a revoke, the card improperly played by him is liable to be called.

The penalty for revoking is the transfer of two tricks from the revoking side to their adversaries. It can be enforced for as many revokes as occur during the hand. The revoking side cannot win the game in that hand. If both sides revoke, neither side can win the game in that hand.

The revoking player and his partner may require the hand in which the revoke has been made to be played out, and score all points made by them up to score of six.

The revoke can be claimed at any time before the cards have been presented and cut for the following deal, but not thereafter.

MISCELLANEOUS—Any one, during the play of a trick, and before the cards have been touched for the purpose of gathering them together, may demand that the players draw their cards.

If any player says, "I can win the rest," "The rest are ours," "We have the game," or words to that effect, his partner's cards must be laid upon the table, and are liable to be called.

If a player is lawfully called upon to play the highest or lowest of a suit, or to trump or not to trump a trick, or to lead a suit, and unnecessarily fails to comply, he is liable to the same penalty as if he had revoked.

In all cases where a penalty has been incurred, the offender must await the decision of the adversaries. If either demands a penalty to which they are entitled, such decision is final.

Bouré or Booray

This game, combining features of Ecarté and Poker, is most popular with Creoles of the Louisiana region and French-Canadians of that and other regions (according to Bennett W. Richards, on whose description the following rules are based).

NUMBER OF PLAYERS—Two to seven. Each plays for himself.

THE PACK—52 cards, ranking A (high), K, Q, J, 10, 9, 8, 7, 6, 5, 4, 3, 2, in each suit.

THE ANTE—For each deal there is a pot to which each player antes. The current dealer decides the amount of the ante to be contributed by each player (the same for all, including the dealer), but usually a maximum is placed on the ante by agreement.

THE DEAL—Players draw or cut for first deal; after that, the turn to deal passes to the left. Only the dealer shuffles and the player at his right cuts. Five cards are dealt to each player, one at a time, face down, in rotation to the left. The dealer turns up the next card, which fixes the trump suit, and announces the suit.

THE DRAW—After looking at his cards, each player may discard his hand and forfeit his ante, or may stay in and have a chance to win the pot but also be subject to additional losses. Each active player in turn to dealer's left may then discard one or more cards and receive replacements from the deck, as in Draw Poker. A player may stand pat. A limit may be placed on the number of cards drawn, three or four cards, depending on the number of players who stay in.

THE PLAY—When the draw is completed, the player at dealer's left leads and the cards are played out in tricks (one card from each player in turn). The leader must lead his highest trump if he has the ace, king and/or queen. To each trick a player in turn must follow suit if able, "play over" (play a higher card than any previously played) if able, and play a trump if unable to follow suit; but a player unable to follow suit need not over-trump, and if unable to follow suit or trump, a player may play any card. A trick is won by the highest card of the suit led unless a trump is played, in which case the highest trump wins. The winner of a trick leads to the next trick and may lead any card in his hand, except that if he holds the ace, king and/or queen of trumps he must lead his highest trump.

OBJECT OF PLAY—To win the most tricks; and to win at least one trick.

THE SCORING—The player who wins the most tricks wins the pot. If two players win two tricks each, or if five players win one trick each, they divide the pot equally. A player who stays in but fails to win a trick must contribute an amount equal to the current pot, which however is added to the next pot and not to the winnings of the winner of the current pot.

POKER

Poker is called the national card game of the United States, and has been so called for a hundred years, yet its growth in popularity has never been so rapid as in recent years, when new millions have discovered its appeal to ladies as well as to men, and its suitability to casual play in homes as well as to serious play in clubs. Nearly every American either understands Poker, or wants to; and part of the charm of the game is that it is so easy to learn and to play enjoyably.

Poker Fundamentals for Beginners

How to Learn Poker—While Poker is played in innumerable forms, it is really necessary to understand only two basic things:

1. The values of the Poker hands.
2. The principles of betting in Poker.

A player who understands these can play without difficulty in any type of Poker game.

Number of Players—Any number of players from two to fourteen may play in one of the various forms of Poker. Most experienced players consider seven or eight players ideal, but five or six make an excellent game.

Everyone plays for himself. There are no partnerships, even when a husband and wife play in the same game.

Object of the Game—To win the pot. The pot is composed of all bets made by all players in any one deal. Each bet means that the player thinks or hopes he has the best hand. When every player has bet as much as he want to, the players show their hands and the best hand wins the pot.

The Poker Hands—A Poker hand consists of five cards. The value of a hand depends on whether it contains one of the following combinations:

Straight flush, the highest possible hand: all five cards of the same suit and in sequence, as the 6, 7, 8, 9 and 10 of diamonds. The highest-ranking straight flush is the A, K, Q, J, and 10 of one suit, called a *royal flush.*

Four of a kind ranks next under a straight flush, as, four aces, or four sixes. It does not matter what the fifth, unmatched card is.

A full house is three cards of one rank and two cards of another rank, as 8-8-8-4-4, and ranks next under four of a kind.

A *flush* is five cards of the same suit, but not all in sequence, and ranks next below a full house.

A *straight* is five cards in sequence, but not all of the same suit. It loses to a flush or higher hand, but beats anything else.

Three of a kind rank next under a straight.

Two pairs, as Q-Q-7-7-4, rank next under three of a kind.

One pair beats any hand containing no pair but none of the higher-ranking combinations named above.

And below the rank of hands containing one pair are all the no-pair hands, which are rated by the highest card they contain, so that an ace-high hand will beat a king-high hand, and so on.

The first thing a beginning player should do is to learn and remember these combinations and their relative values. They are stated in greater detail on page 109.

How the Betting Works—In the course of each Poker deal, there will be one or more *betting intervals* in which the players have an opportunity to bet on their hands.

Before the cards are even dealt, the rules of the Poker game being played may require that each player put an initial contribution (called an *ante)* of one or more chips into the pot, to start it off.

Each betting interval begins when any player in turn makes a bet of one or more chips. Each player in turn after him must either *call* that bet (by putting into the pot the same number of chips); or may *raise,* which means that he puts in more than enough chips to call; or may *drop,* which means that he puts no chips in the pot, discards his hand, and is out of the betting until there is another deal and he receives a new hand.

When a player drops, he loses all chips he has previously put into that pot. Unless a player is willing to put into the pot at least as many chips as any player before him has put in, he must drop.

A betting interval ends when the bets have been equalized —that is, when each player has put into the pot exactly as many chips as each other player, or has dropped. There are usually two or more betting intervals for each Poker deal. After the final betting interval, each player who has met all the bets shows his hand face up on the table, and the best Poker hand takes the pot. This is called the *showdown*.

If at any time a player makes a bet or raise that no other player calls, that player wins the pot without showing his hand.

Check is a Poker term that means the player wishes to remain in the pot without betting. In effect, it is "a bet of nothing." A player may check provided no one before him in that betting interval has made any bet. If any other player has bet, he must at least call the bet or drop. If all the players check, the betting interval is over.

In each betting interval, one player is designated as the first bettor, according to the rules of the game. The turn to bet moves from player to player to the left, and no one may check, bet, or even drop, except when his turn comes.

How to know When to Bet—The ranking of Poker hands, given above, is based on mathematics. The less likely you are to be dealt a certain hand, the higher it ranks and the more likely you are to win the pot if you hold such a hand. For example, you should not expect to be dealt a straight flush more than once in 65,000 hands; but you should be dealt two pair about once in every 21 hands, and about one in two hands that you hold should have at least one pair.

You should not bet unless you think your hand may be the best, and you cannot bet intelligently unless you know what constitutes a good hand, a fair hand, and a bad hand. On page 123 there is a guide to the average winning hand in each of the most popular forms of Poker. The beginner is advised to glance at this before playing, until he has become familiar with the various forms of the game.

The Two Main Forms of Poker—Though there are many different forms of Poker nearly all of them fall into either of two main types. One of these is Draw Poker, or Closed Poker; the other is Stud Poker, or Open Poker. Both of these, and other forms of Poker, are described later (pages 90-95).

General Principles in Poker

The following section applies to all Poker games, regardless of the form of Poker played.

FORM OF POKER TO BE PLAYED—Unless the host, or the rule of a club, has already established the game, the players should first decide what form of Poker they will play. There are two factors that should influence their decision: the number of players, and whether or not they are all experienced players or include some very inexperienced players. The following selections are recommended.

2, 3 or 4 Players: Stud Poker in any form. Perhaps one of the "Dealer's Choice" games (page 99). Usually only very experienced players play Draw Poker with so few players, and they often used a stripped deck (page 14).

5 to 8 Players: Any form of Poker.

9 to 10 Players: Five-card Stud Poker.

More than 10 Players: One of the "Dealer's Choice" games in which fewer than five cards are dealt, such as Hurricane or Three-card Monte; or Spit-in-the-Ocean without a draw (all on pages 102-103); or form two tables.

Dealer's Choice: In social Poker games including both men and women it is often advisable to play Dealer's Choice [of games], especially since men and women often have different tastes in choice of games. See page 99.

WILD CARDS—Especially when Dealer's Choice is played, there are likely to be cards of various kinds designated as wild. The most usual choices are:

The joker. Recently, when most packs of cards include two jokers for use in such games as Canasta, Poker players are increasingly adding to the pack two jokers, both wild.

The bug. This is the joker, but its wildness is limited: It counts as an ace; or as a card of any suit for purposes of making a flush; or as a card of any rank and suit for purposes of making a straight or straight flush.

Deuces. "Deuces wild" is a very popular form of Draw Poker. Every deuce is wild. Sometimes the joker is included as a fifth wild card.

One-eyes. The king of diamonds and the jacks of spades and hearts show only one eye, the other face cards all two eyes. These three one-eyed cards are often designated as wild cards.

Low hole card, in Seven-card Stud; each player's hole card, in Five-card Stud Poker; lowest card in the hand, in Draw Poker; etc. When such a card is designated, it means every card of that rank *in that player's hand is wild,* but the fact that a certain rank of card is wild in one player's hand does not make that same rank of card wild in other players' hands.

There are special laws governing wild cards; see page 107.

LAWS AND ETHICS—In every game, a *written* code of Poker laws should be adopted and should be final for settling all questions. No Poker laws are universally followed, there being many local customs and preferences; but the Poker laws in this book (pages 107-121) embrace the latest customs of the most expert games and are recommended for adoption. It is an immemorial tradition of Poker that any club or group of players may make special rules, called "house rules," to suit their personal preferences, but house rules also should be written down.

TIME LIMIT—Before play begins, the players should set a time limit and stick to it. Violation of this principle may eventually turn pleasant sessions into unpleasant ones.

CARDS—Poker was once a one-pack game, but today virtually all games in clubs and among the best players use two packs, one red and one blue (or of other contrasting colors). This speeds up the game, for one pack is being shuffled and prepared for the next deal while the other pack is being dealt. The procedure is as follows: While the deal is in process, the *previous* dealer assembles all the cards from the pack he dealt with, shuffles them, and places them at his left. When the time comes for the next deal, they are passed to the next dealer. *For example:* There are seven players, designated as A, B, C, D, E, F, G. The dealer is D. He deals with the red pack. During his deal, as the players drop or discard they toss the cards in his direction. At the end of his deal, he gathers up these cards. While E is dealing with the blue pack, D is shuffling the red pack, which he then places at his left, between himself and E. When E's deal ends, it becomes F's turn to deal. E passes the red pack to F at his left, then assembles and shuffles the blue pack. F proceeds to deal with the red pack. In many games in which two packs are used, the dealer's left-hand opponent instead of his right-hand opponent cuts the pack.

Poker-sized cards (wider than the bridge size) are preferred in most clubs, but there is no rule to this effect and the narrower cards are increasingly used in home games in which ladies play.

In clubs, it is customary to change cards frequently and to permit any player to call for new cards whenever he wishes. When new cards are introduced, both the blue and the red packs are replaced. In some clubs, the player who calls for new cards must pay for them; but in most club games there is a "kitty" (see next paragraph) from which new cards are paid for.

THE KITTY—By unanimous or majority agreement the players may establish a special fund called a "kitty." Usually the kitty is built up by "cutting" (taking) one white chip from each pot in which there is more than one raise. The kitty belongs to all the players equally. It is used to pay for new cards (see above), or for refreshments. Any chips left in the kitty when the game ends are divided equally among the players who are still in the game. Unlike the rule in some other games, such as Pinochle, when a player leaves a Poker game before it ends he is not entitled to take his share of chips in the kitty.

CHIPS—Poker is almost always played with poker chips. For a game of seven or more players there should be a supply of at least 200 chips. Usually, the white chip is the unit, or lowest-valued chip, worth whatever the minimum ante or bet is; a red chip is worth 5 whites, and a blue chip is worth 10 whites or 2 reds. If the limit in the game is 5, there should be 100 whites and 100 reds. If the limit is 10, there should be 100 whites, 50 reds, and 50 blues. At the start of the game, each player takes a number of chips—the same for each player—known as a *takeout*. A practical takeout might be 10 whites, 4 reds, and 2 blues, making 50 units in all.

BANKER—One player must be designated as banker, to keep the stock of chips and the record of how many have been issued to each player. Players should have no private transactions or exchanges among themselves; a player with surplus chips may return them to the banker and receive credit for them, while a player requiring more chips should obtain them only from the banker.

BETTING LIMITS—There are different ways of fixing a betting limit. Some limit is conceded to be necessary. Once fixed, the limit should be unalterable throughout the game. The limit may be any one of the following popular ones:

1. *Fixed limit.* No one may bet or raise by more than a stipulated number of chips; for example, 2, or 5, or 10. Usually, this limit varies with the stage of the game: In Draw Poker, if the limit is 2 before the draw, it is 4 after the draw. In Stud Poker, if the limit is 1 in the first three betting intervals, it is 2 in the final betting interval (and, often, 2 whenever a player has a pair showing).

2. *Pot limit.* The limit for any bet or raise is the number of chips in the pot at the time the bet or raise is made. (This means that a player who raises may count as part of the pot the number of chips required for him to call. If there are 6 chips in the pot, then a bet of 4 is made, the total is 10 chips; it requires 4 chips for the next player to call, making 14; and he may then raise by 14 chips). When pot limit is played, there should still be some maximum limit, such as 50 chips.

3. *Table stakes.* This, and especially table stakes with pot limit, has become one of the most popular forms of fixing a limit. The limit for each player is the number of chips he has in front of him: If he has only 10 chips, he may bet no more than 10 and he may call any other player's bet to that extent. No player may withdraw any chips from the table, or return them to the banker, until he leaves the game. A player may add to his stack, but only between the showdown (or the time that he drops) in one pot and the beginning of the next deal.

The custom of table stakes, in which a player may "call a sight" (that is, stay in for the showdown) for all the chips he has, produces occasional side pots. For example: A has 40 chips, B 80, C 150, D 200. A bets 20; B calls; C raises 50. This bet *taps* A (requires him to put up all his chips to call). C puts only 40 chips in the pot, 20 to call, 20 to raise; the 30 chips that represent the remainder of his raise go into a side pot. D calls, putting 40 chips in the main pot and 30 in the side pot. A calls, putting his remaining 20 chips in the main pot. Now A can stay through to the showdown, regardless of the additional bets of other players, and if he has the highest hand he will win the main pot. B calls, putting 20 chips in the main pot and 30 in the side pot. In the next betting interval, A is not concerned. B checks and C bets 50, tapping B. Of C's 50 chips, 10 go into the first side pot and 40 begin a second side pot. D calls, putting 10 in the first side pot and 40 in the second. B calls for 10, closing the first side pot. At the showdown, the highest of the four hands will win the main pot; the highest hand as among B, C and D will win the first side pot; the higher hand as between C and D will win the second side pot.

But when a player drops he loses interest in all side pots. Suppose, in the example just given, there is still another betting interval, in which C bets 30 chips and D drops. By dropping, D loses his interest in the main pot and the first side pot, as well as in the second side pot; for he has conceded that C has a better hand, and therefore C succeeds to D's rights in all pots.

4. *Whangdoodles, or Roodles.* In a fixed limit game, it is often agreed that following any very good hand—say, a full house or better—there will be a round of Jackpots in which everyone antes (even if that is not the custom in the game) or in which everyone antes double, and the limit is doubled for that round. A round means one deal by each player. When it comes around to the deal of the first player, the usual limit and customs of the game are resumed.

5. *Poverty Poker.* A maximum limit is put on the number of chips any player may lose. Each takes out one stack at the start; if he loses that stack, the banker issues him another, not charging him for it; and, in many cases, the player can get still a third stack free before he drops out of the game. (Some limit should be placed on the number of free stacks so that a player will have the incentive to play carefully.)

No Limit, Sky's the Limit, Freezeout, and other methods have been common; they are still played by a few; but from a practical standpoint they are obsolete.

LIMITS ON RAISES—It is not unusual to limit the number of raises any one player may make to three (in some circles, two) in each betting interval; or to have no more than three raises—no matter by whom—in any betting interval.

POKER—PRINCIPAL FORMS

Draw Poker

There are several methods of playing Draw Poker, but they differ chiefly in the rules governing betting. The essential features of the game, common to all varieties, are:

Each player receives five cards, all dealt face down, one at a time, in rotation beginning at the dealer's left.

Upon completion of the deal there is a betting interval. The player at the dealer's left has the first right or obligation to bet.

When the first betting interval is ended, each active player in turn, beginning with the active player at the dealer's left, may discard one or more cards and the dealer then gives him, from the top of the undealt portion of the pack, face down, as many cards as he discarded. This is the *draw*. A player may, if he wishes, *stand pat* (draw no cards).

After the draw, there is another betting interval, followed by a showdown.

NOTE: The rules of the draw and the treatment of irregularities or disputed procedure are covered by the Laws of Poker beginning on page 106, and especially by paragraphs 26 to 30 of those laws.

BASIC FORMS OF DRAW POKER—All games of Draw Poker fall into one of two classes, depending on the betting rules:

1. *Pass and Out,* also called *Pass Out* or *Bet or Drop.* In each turn a player must make a bet—the minimum allowed, if there has been no bet before him—or must drop. In most games, this applies only before the draw. After the draw, a player may check. In some games, however, each player must bet or drop before and after the draw.

2. *Pass and Back In.* At his first turn, a player may pass rather than bet, provided no player before him has made a bet. The first player to make a bet is said to *open.* Once the pot is opened, each player in turn has another chance to stay in or to drop. After the draw, a player may check.

The game most often played "pass and out" is Blind Opening; the game most often played "pass and back in" is Jack-pots (both described below).

THE ANTE—The players must decide in advance which of two methods they will adopt for the ante: Either (a) each player antes one white chip before the deal, or (b) the dealer antes, for example, one white or red chip, before the deal.

SPECIAL HANDS—To create more playable hands, and so en-liven the game, many players give special value to one or more hands that are not among the traditional Poker hands. The special hands most often played are:

Big cat, or *big tiger:* King high, eight low, no pair, as K-J-10-9-8. Ranks next under a flush; beats a little cat, any dog, or a straight.

Little cat, or *little tiger:* Eight high, three low, no pair, as 8-7-5-4-3. Loses to a big cat or flush, beats a dog or a straight.

Big dog: Ace high, nine low, no pair, as A-Q-J-10-9. Loses to a cat or flush, beats a little dog or a straight.

Little dog: Seven high, deuce low, no pair, as 7-6-4-3-2. Beats a straight, loses to a big dog, a cat, or a flush.

When dogs and cats are played, they usually are the only special hands played. The following are other special hands that are usually played only in games in which the cat and dog are not recognized:

Skeet, or *pelter.* A hand containing 9, 5, 2, two other low cards, no pair; as 9-7-5-3-2. Beats a straight, loses to a flush. Some play that one of the two odd cards must be between the nine and five in rank and the other must be between the five and deuce in rank, so that 9-5-4-3-2 would not be a skeet.

Skip straight, Dutch straight, or *kilter.* Five cards in alter-nate sequence, as Q-10-8-6-4 or K-J-9-7-5. Beats three of a kind, loses to a straight.

Round-the-corner straight. A sequence such as 3-2-A-K-Q. This is simply the lowest-ranking straight; 5-4-3-2-A beats 4-3-2-A-K, which beats 3-2-A-K-Q, etc. When both skip straights and round-the-corner straights are played, the skip straight ranks higher.

Blaze. Any five face cards; beats any other two-pair hand, loses to three of a kind.

Fourflush. Seldom played except in Stud Poker. Beats a pair, loses to two pair.

Special flushes. Some play that since a cat, dog or skeet

beats a straight, a cat flush, dog flush or skeet flush beats a
straight flush and becomes the highest-ranking hand in the
game, unless a wild card makes possible five of a kind, which
is always the highest hand.

Breaking ties. Ties between two special hands of the same
rank are broken the same as with any other no-pair hands,
so that of two little dogs, 7-6-4-3-2 would beat 7-5-4-3-2.

Jackpots

Usually each player antes one white chip before the deal.

When the deal is completed, each player in turn, beginning
at the left of the dealer, has the right to *open* (make the first
bet), or to pass. In Jackpots, the word pass is equivalent to
check; pass is an ambiguous term in Poker, because sometimes it means check, sometimes it means drop. A player may
not open unless he has jacks or better—a pair of jacks, or a
hand that would beat a pair of jacks in a showdown.

If no one opens, through the dealer, everyone (or the next
dealer) antes again and there is a new deal by the next
dealer in turn.

If any player opens, the first betting interval has begun.
Each other player in turn after him (including players who
passed on the first round) must drop, call, or raise, until this
betting interval ends. There is then the draw, as in all forms
of Draw Poker, another betting interval in which each player
may check until a bet is made, and the showdown.

The player who opens must "show openers" before he can
discard his hand. He need show only as many cards as will
prove to the other players that he had the requirements. Of
course, if he is in the showdown he must show his entire
hand. (See page 117 for the rules on showing openers, and
false openers.)

PROGRESSIVE JACKPOTS—This is the same as Jackpots except
that if no one opens, on the next deal queens or better are
required to open; on the next, if two in a row are passed out,
kings or better are required; on the next, aces or better; and
some run the series all the way up to two pair or better.

JACKS OR BOBTAIL TO OPEN—Many play that one may open
either on a pair of jacks or better; or on any bobtail, that is,
four cards of the same suit, called a fourflush, or a bobtail
straight, which is four cards in sequence that can become a
straight if the card at either end of the sequence is drawn.
(8-7-6-5 is a bobtail, because either the nine or the four will

make it a straight; A-K-Q-J is not, because only a single card, the ten, will fill it; 9-8-6-5 is not, because only a seven will fill it, this being called an "inside straight.")

OPEN ON ANYTHING—The rules are the same as in Jackpots except that there is no minimum requirement for opening, and so the player who makes the first bet need not show openers at any stage. It is usually played "pass and out" before the draw, with checking permitted after the draw.

Blind Opening
(Blind Tiger, or Blind and Straddle)

Dealer antes one chip, which does not count as a bet. The player at dealer's left (formerly called the *age*, or *edge*) must open blind for one chip and the player at his left must raise blind by putting in two chips, so each pot begins with four chips. The compulsory raise was formerly called the *straddle*.

The cards are then dealt. The player at the left of the blind raiser is the first to take voluntary action. He may either call by putting in two chips, raise by putting in three chips, or drop. The limit before the draw is one chip, so no player may raise by more than that amount.

The betting then proceeds normally. The dealer's ante does not count toward what he must put in to call or raise, but the blind opener's one-chip bet and the blind raiser's two-chip bet do count; therefore, if no one has raised, the blind opener can stay for one chip and the blind raiser is in automatically.

After the draw, the limit is two chips. The betting begins with the blind opener if he is still in, and otherwise with the active player nearest his left. Players may check until a bet is made.

BLIND AND STRADDLE—In this earlier form of blind opening, the first blind bet and the first straddle (blind raise) are compulsory. The player at the left of the compulsory straddler may then straddle again (raise blind) by betting four chips; if he does, the player at his left may straddle by betting eight; and so on. In most games, there is a limit of one or two voluntary straddles. The limit before the draw is determined by the last straddle: If there was only one straddle, the limit is one chip; if there was a second straddle (four chips), the limit is two; if there was a third straddle (eight chips), the limit is four. After the draw, voluntary betting begins with the player at the left of the last straddler. The limit after the draw is twice the limit before the draw.

ENGLISH OR AUSTRALIAN POKER—This is blind opening in which a player who raises can double the preceding bet. Raising is called doubling.

BLOCK SYSTEM—In this game, twenty-five chips are put into the pot before play starts: these chips consist of a 19-chip ante of the dealer, a 2-chip blind opening by the player at the left of the dealer, and a compulsory raise to 4 chips by the second player on the left of the dealer. The third player then has the first privilege of betting, after he has looked at his cards. The limit of any player's raise before the draw consists of 2 chips. After the draw the limit for any raise is the total number of chips bet by each player before the draw (the 19-chip ante not counting as a bet).

Stud Poker

In Stud Poker, each player receives one or more hole cards, face down, and the remainder of his cards face up. After each player is dealt at least one upcard, and after each round of dealing (one card per player) thereafter, there is a betting interval before the dealing is resumed. NOTE: Procedure and the treatment of irregularities in Stud Poker are covered by the Laws of Poker beginning on page 106 and especially by paragraphs 31 to 38 of those laws.

Five-card Stud

Two to ten may play. (As a practical matter, as many as fourteen may play in the same game, on the assumption that a certain number of players will drop and there will be enough cards to go around. However, more than ten usually make an unwieldy game.)

There is no ante.

The dealer gives each player a face-down card and then each player a face-up card. The first betting interval then begins.

In the first betting interval, the player with the high card *must* start the pot with a bet of at least the minimum agreed upon by the players (such as one white chip). In any later betting interval the first bettor and players after him may check, unless and until a bet is made.

The first bettor in each betting interval is the player with the highest card or the highest Poker combination showing.

If two or more players are tied for highest, the one nearest the dealer's left (that is, the one dealt first) is the first bettor.

Following the first betting interval, the dealer gives another face-up card to each active player in rotation; there is another betting interval, another round of face-up cards to the remaining active players, another betting interval, then a final round of face-up cards and a final betting interval. If two or more players remain after the final betting interval, there is a showdown in which each player turns up his hole card. If a bet or raise goes uncalled in any betting interval, the pot is taken and the deal passes in rotation.

A player who drops must immediately turn down all his face-up cards.

It is the dealer's duty, after each round of cards is dealt, to designate the first bettor (as by saying, "First king bets," "Pair of sixes bets," etc.); and, after the third and fourth face-up cards are dealt, also to indicate holdings that may become straights or flushes ("Possible straight," "Possible flush"). A possible straight or flush has no effect on determination of the first bettor, except that in some games players agree that a fourflush will beat a pair in the showdown, and in these games a fourflush showing in the final betting interval bets against a pair showing.

In a very large game, if there are not enough cards left in the pack to complete the dealing of the final round, the dealer may *flash* a card from the top of the pack (turn it face up on the table) and this card serves as the common fifth of all hands.

Seven-card Stud
(Down the River, Peek Poker, or Seven-toed Pete)

Two to eight may play. In the initial deal, each player receives two cards face down and then one card face up, all dealt one at a time in rotation. There is then a betting interval. Each active player then receives three more face-up cards and one more face-down card, in that order, with the deal interrupted for a betting interval after each round of cards is dealt. In the showdown, each player turns up all his hole cards and selects five of his seven cards as his hand; he must separate these five cards from the other two, which he discards. The cards then speak for themselves, as in any other form of Poker, and the player may not reclaim his two discards if he finds he could have made a better five-card combination.

In other respects the procedure is the same as in Five-card Stud (see above).

High-Low Poker

The basic idea of High-Low Poker is that the best Poker hand and the worst Poker hand split the pot. The original purpose of High-Low was to give holders of poor cards a chance to play. The game was found to be so excellent that it rivals regular Poker in popularity, and a derivative of it—Low Poker, or Lowball (page 97), in which every pot goes to the lowest hand—is one of the principal card games played in the western part of the United States.

FORMS OF HIGH-LOW POKER—Any form of Poker may be played high-low; most games in which there are many wild cards, and most Seven-card Stud games, are now played high-low. In a high-low game there are usually two winners of the pot, the player with the highest hand taking one-half the pot and the player with the lowest hand taking the other half, the high hand taking the odd chip if the pot will not divide evenly. But in some cases there may be a single winner, thus:

DECLARATIONS—Some play that after the final betting interval, but before the showdown, each player must declare whether he is trying for high, or for low, or for both. There are three methods of declaring, and the players should agree in advance which will be used. The methods are:

(a) Each player in turn, beginning with the player on the dealer's left, states whether he is playing for high or low, before any hands are shown to the table.

(b) Before any hands are shown, each player decides mentally whether he is playing for high or low. If he decides upon low, he takes a white chip in his hand without letting other players see it; a red chip if he decides upon high. When all have decided, the players expose the colors of their chips. If all players in the call decide the same way, the best hand that way takes the whole pot.

(c) Playing for both high and low. In addition to taking a white or red chip, as explained in the preceding paragraph, the player may take a blue chip to signify that he is contending for both high and low. The player selects mentally two hands of five cards each from among the cards that he holds: this is possible when playing with wild cards or in Seven-card Stud. If a player claims both high and low, and is tied or beaten on either, he loses any title to the pot. If no one wins in full accordance with his declaration, all declarations are disregarded and the active players divide the pot equally.

SEVEN-CARD HIGH-LOW STUD—Each player in the showdown may select any five of his cards as his high hand and any five as his low hand; he may win both ways and take the entire pot.

RANK OF LOW HANDS—In most high-low games, the usual rank of Poker hands is observed; therefore, the lowest possible hand is 7-5-4-3-2, not all of one suit. Between 8-7-4-3-2 and 8-6-5-4-3, the 8-6 hand is the lower, because in Poker it would lose to the 8-7 hand.

It is common practice to observe one of the following variations in ranking the hands:

Ace low. In trying for low, one may call an ace the lowest card in his hand, whereupon the lowest possible hand becomes 6-4-3-2-A in two or more suits, and even among pairs, playing for low, a pair of aces is a lower hand than a pair of deuces.

Wild cards low. Any wild card ranks as a "zero" and the relative low rank is determined by the other cards; therefore, with deuces wild, 7-5-4-3-2 is not so low as 7-5-4-2-2. Some play that wild cards may duplicate other cards in the hand without pairing them, so that, with ace counting low and the joker wild, 6-4-3-2-A is not so low as 6-4-3-A-joker, the latter being "double-ace low."

JACKS BACK—Regular Jackpots Draw Poker is played, but if no one opens the pot, every player has another chance to open for a Lowball pot. If this pot is not opened (but it almost always is), the deal passes.

Low Poker or Lowball

In Lowball only low hands count; every pot is won by the lowest hand. The ace is always low; two aces are the lowest pair. Straights and flushes do not count, so the lowest possible hand is A-2-3-4-5 regardless of suits; this hand is called a "bicycle" or "wheel" (named after Bicycle brand playing cards). Usually the joker is added to the pack as the "bug," representing the lowest card not actually held in the hand.

Lowball is always played "pass and out." There are no minimum requirements for opening the pot and each player in every turn before the draw must bet or drop. After the draw a player may check. The betting after the draw always begins with the active player nearest the dealer's left.

CALIFORNIA LOWBALL—The following rules are typical of those followed for Lowball games in the Poker clubs of California, where this game is most popular.

Only the dealer and one or two players to his left ante; the total of their antes is the limit before the draw. [For example, if the limit before the draw is 2 chips, dealer antes 1 and the player at his left antes 1. If the limit is 3, dealer and the two players at his left ante 1 each. However, no more than three players ante; if the limit were 5, dealer would ante 1 and the other two players 2 each.] The limit after the draw is twice the limit before the draw.

The first turn to open is the player at the left of the last ante. The game is "pass and out" before the draw. The antes all count toward meeting the bets of other players.

After the draw it is permissible to check but a player who checks may not thereafter raise, but may only call. [In some clubs, a player who checks a seven-high or better loses all interest in additions to the pot; that is, if he calls a bet and loses, he loses everything; if he calls a bet and wins, the bettor withdraws his bet and the winner gets only the pot as it was when he checked.]

Five cards constitute a hand. More or less, hand is dead.

Card off table is dead. Card faced in deck is dead.

If a card seven or under is faced by dealer before draw, player must accept it; eight or over, he may accept or reject it and receive another card (off the top of the pack, before the dealing to other players is resumed).

Card faced by dealer after draw is dead and player receives additional card after other players receive theirs. If dealer faces his own card he must take it.

Player must take number of cards he calls for. If he says "Give me two—no, I mean three," he still gets two. If he fouls his hand, hand is dead. Draw up to five cards.

All players must keep cards at table level in sight. Hand held below table level is dead.

When players call for cards dealer "burns" (discards) top card face down and then fills players' requirements.

All called hands must be shown. Full five cards spread.

A hand thrown away cannot be retrieved if any card touches any other card or cards.

Player is responsible for his own hand. If fouled by another player hand is dead.

If player makes insufficient bet he must add additional chips or forfeit that already bet. Money once in pot may not be removed.

No string bets. Player cannot go back to his stack in order to raise unless he has announced "Raise" clearly.

All hands must be played out. No splitting pots unless an actual tie.

Poker Variations—Dealer's Choice

In Dealer's Choice, each dealer in turn has the privilege of naming the form of Poker to be played and to designate the ante, wild cards, betting rounds, rank of hands, etc.

Sometimes the dealer will select a standard form of Poker, but more often the game selected has some unusual rules, especially one of those described below. In addition to the wild cards listed on page 85, the dealer may make almost any rank of card wild, or each player's first card, or third card, or lowest card, etc. In some cases certain cards are made penalty cards, nullifying the value of wild cards or even making the entire hand foul.

The dealer may not require any player to ante more than any other player. If a game such as Jackpots is selected and no one opens, the same dealer deals again and everyone antes again.

Variations of Five-Card Stud Poker

FIVE-CARD STUD, LAST CARD DOWN—This is regular Stud Poker, with the fifth card dealt face down instead of up.

MEXICAN STUD, OR FLIP, OR PEEP-AND-TURN—The first two cards are dealt to each player face down. Players look at their cards and select one to be placed face up. The concealed card is then wild for each player. After a round of betting, another card is dealt around face down. Each player decides which of the two concealed cards to turn face up, and which to keep in his hand for a wild card. Another round of betting follows. The process continues until each player has four cards exposed before him, and one wild card concealed in his hand. This card is wild only for the player who holds it, and likewise wild are all other cards of the same denomination as the concealed card, held by the same player. After the final round of betting, all those players still in the game show their concealed cards and announce the value of their hands. The game is often played high-low.

FIVE-CARD STUD, LAST CARD OPTIONALLY DOWN—This game is similar to standard Stud Poker, except that the player may turn up his hole card before the last round is dealt and ask for his fifth card face down.

PISTOL, OR HOLE-CARD STUD—This is played according to the standard laws of Stud Poker, except that there is a betting interval after the first (hole) card is dealt, making five betting intervals in all. Usually the dealer must bet on the first (hole) card and the high up-card must bet on the next round.

ACEY-DEUCEY—A form of two-card Poker popular in the U. S. Army. Each player is dealt two cards, one up and one down. He may stand on the cards he is dealt, or at any later time, or he may draw by discarding one of his cards and being dealt a replacement (when his turn comes). If he discards a face-down card, the replacement is dealt face down; if he discards a face-up card, the replacement is dealt face up. If he draws one card he pays the pot one chip; for a second card he pays two chips, and for a third card five chips. Betting begins when all hands have stood. High card bets, as in Stud Poker. The game is usually played high-low. Only pairs and high cards count. Highest hand is A-A; lowest hand is A-2, since the ace is treated as low when the player tries for low (but A-A is never a low pair). Winners split the total pot, including bets and chips paid to draw cards.

Variations of Seven-card Stud Poker

SEVEN-CARD FLIP—Four face-down cards are dealt to each player. After examining them he may turn up any two of them. There is a betting interval, then play proceeds as in regular Seven-card Stud, with three more cards dealt, two up and one down, a betting interval following each.

In another variation, each player first receives two cards, one up and one down, followed by a betting interval; then another two cards, one up and one down, and another betting interval; then two cards a third time and a betting interval; then a seventh card face down. Each player then discards one of his face-down cards and one of his face-up cards, leaving himself with three concealed cards and two exposed cards. The final betting interval and showdown follow.

DOUBLE-BARRELED SHOTGUN, OR TEXAS TECH—Each player is dealt three cards face down, then there is a betting interval; another face-down card, another betting interval; a fifth face-down card, a third betting interval. There is then a draw as in Draw Poker. After the draw, each player turns up one card, followed by a betting interval; another card, followed by a betting interval; and so on, until each has four cards face up and one face down, after which there is a final betting interval and a showdown. Cards are turned up simultaneously, the dealer giving a signal.

BASEBALL—Seven-card Stud is played, with all nines and threes wild; but when a three is dealt face up, the player to whom it is dealt must either match the pot (put into the pot as many chips as are already in it)—or drop. Any four dealt face up entitles the recipient to an additional hole card, which the dealer immediately gives him, face down, from the top of the pack. Baseball may also be played as a five-card Stud game.

FOOTBALL—The same as Baseball, except that sixes and fours are wild, a four requires a player to match the pot or drop, and a deuce entitles a player to an extra hole card.

HEINZ—Fives and sevens are wild, but a player dealt one of these cards face up must match the pot or drop.

WOOLWORTH—Fives and tens are wild. A player dealt a five face up must pay 5 chips to the pot or drop, and a player dealt a ten face up must pay 10 chips to the pot or drop.

OMAHA—Each player receives two cards down. Five cards are dealt to the center, face down. There is a betting interval. Then the center cards are turned up one by one, with a betting interval after each. Each player makes his hand from his own two cards plus the five in the center.

HOLD 'EM—The same as Omaha, but after the first betting interval three cards are turned up in the center. The last two cards are turned up one at a time.

BULL—Each player receives three cards face down. He arranges them in any order he wishes, but may not thereafter change the order. There is a betting interval. Then each player receives four face-up cards, with a betting interval after each. Then each player turns up his first face-down card, followed by a betting interval, and his second face-down card, following by the final betting interval. The last cards are then turned up for the showdown. The game is usually played high-low and a player may win both high and low.

SIX-CARD STUD—The first five cards are dealt as in regular Five-card Stud, but after the fourth betting interval each player receives a second hole card. After a final betting interval each player selects five of his six cards as his hand.

EIGHT-CARD STUD—The same as Seven-card Stud except that each player receives an eighth card, dealt either up or down, as the dealer may decide in advance.

Variations of Draw Poker

DEUCES WILD—This is a regular game of Jackpots with all four deuces wild.

COLD HANDS—Each player puts up an agreed ante, then five cards are dealt to each player one at a time, face up, and the highest hand takes the pot. There is no draw and no betting.

STRAIGHT POKER—This was the original form of Poker. Each player is dealt five cards, face down; they bet, then there is a showdown. There is no draw.

SPIT IN THE OCEAN—Only four cards are dealt to each player. The next card in the pack is turned face up in the center of the table and is considered as the fifth card in each player's hand. This card is wild, and the others of the same denomination are also wild throughout the game. After a betting interval, there is a draw as in any Draw Poker game, except that each player draws to a four-card hand, then a final betting interval and a showdown.

THE WILD WIDOW—Five cards are dealt face down to each player. Before the last round of cards is dealt, a card is turned up in the center; the other three cards of that rank are wild. There is a betting interval, then the draw and final betting interval.

VARIATIONS OF SPIT IN THE OCEAN—The many variations of this game are usually played high-low.

In one of them, three cards are dealt face down in the center, and four to each player. The center cards take the place of the draw. Each of these cards is turned up, one at a time, followed by a round of betting. The players have the option of using center cards to complete their hands. On the showdown, each player selects a Poker hand of five cards, combining any of the center cards with the cards in his own hand.

One game is called Cincinnati, Lame Brains, and by other names. Five cards are dealt to each player and another hand of five cards face down on the table. The center cards are turned up one at a time, with a round of betting after each is exposed. Each player selects a hand of five cards from among the cards in his own hand and the five on the table. Sometimes this game is played with the center card on the table wild, and sometimes with the lowest card on the table wild.

In the variation called Round the World, each player is dealt four cards and there are four cards in the center of the table, face down. The game is played for a high hand only. The center cards are turned up one at a time, with a round of betting after each card is exposed.

SHOTGUN—Three cards are dealt to each player face down and there is a round of betting. Other rounds of betting follow the dealing of the fourth and fifth cards. Players still in the game draw to improve their hands, and there is a final round of betting.

HURRICANE—Only two cards are dealt to each player, and the highest hand that can be held consists of two aces. The game is played as Straight Poker, or it can be played with the draw. Sometimes wild cards are added, and sometimes it is played high-low with deuces wild, so that 2-A is the perfect hand—a pair of aces for high, 2-A (or double-ace, ace and wild card) low.

THREE-CARD MONTE—One card is dealt to each player face down and two cards face up, with a round of betting following the dealing of each card. The usual rank of Poker value is used, except that there cannot be two pairs, full house, or four of a kind. Straights and flushes are composed of three cards only. With wild cards, this becomes a high-low game as does Hurricane.

SHOW FIVE CARDS—Seven cards are dealt face down to each player, and each player looks at his cards. At a signal from the dealer, each player turns up one of his cards on the table. Before giving the signal, the dealer should inquire whether everyone is ready. After the cards are exposed, there is a round of betting. After the betting is completed, the dealer gives the signal for the exposure of the second cards. All these second cards must be exposed at the same time.

The process continues until all players in the game have five cards exposed before them for the showdown. The game is usually played high-low. It is not unusual for player to change his mind during the game and try for a low hand rather than a high one, according to the cards exposed by other players.

Whiskey Poker

The dealer gives five cards, face down, to each player and an extra hand ("widow") of five cards in the middle of the table. He must deal to each player in turn around to the left, one card at a time, then the widow, then himself last. Each player, beginning at the dealer's left, has the option of exchanging his hand for the widow, or keeping it as it is. If he takes up the widow, he places his five cards face up on the table and they become the new widow. Each player in turn has the option of taking up one card or all of the new widow and replacing it with cards from his hand. If a player wishes to play his original hand, he signals by knocking on the table, but he cannot draw and knock at the same time.

The process of exchanging cards continues around the table until some player knocks. A knock means that this player will show his present hand when it is his turn next around the table, and that thus each player has only one more chance to exchange cards. No player may draw after he has once knocked. A player may knock before the widow is exposed, if he wishes to.

If no one takes the widow until it comes around to the dealer, the dealer must either take up the widow for himself, or turn it face up on the table. Even if the dealer knocks, and does not take up the widow, he must spread it on the table for each player to see and draw once more. A player may pass in any turn—that is, decline either to exchange or to knock; but he may not pass in two consecutive turns. Having passed on the previous round, he must either exchange or knock.

After the knock and the final round of draws, all hands are shown to the table. The highest takes the pot, if a pot has been made by an ante from all. The lowest pays the forfeit agreed upon beforehand. Some players prefer to have a round of betting before the showdown.

Knock Poker

This is an excellent game for three to five players. Each

antes one chip, and the dealer gives each player five cards as in Draw Poker. The undealt cards are placed in the center to form the *stock*. The player at dealer's left draws the top card and then discards one card, and thereafter each player in turn may draw the top card of the stock or the last previous discard, as in Rummy.

Any player, after drawing and before discarding, may *knock*. He then discards and each other player has one turn to draw and discard, until it comes back to the knocker, who does not have another turn. Each player, after drawing, must drop out, immediately paying the knocker one chip; or may stay in.

When the last player before the knocker has drawn and discarded, there is a showdown among all who have stayed in. If the knocker has the high hand, every player who stayed in pays him two chips. If any other player ties the knocker, they divide the winnings except for chips paid to the knocker by the players who dropped out. If the knocker does not have the high hand he pays two chips to every player who stayed in, and the player with the high hand gets the antes.

Bonuses (not always played). Everyone pays these bonuses, even a player who has dropped: 2 chips for knocking and winning without drawing a card; 4 chips for winning with a royal flush; 2 chips for winning with any other straight flush; 1 chip for winning with four of a kind.

Irregularities. On the first round, a hand with six cards discards without drawing; a hand with four cards draws without discarding. Any other irregular hand is dead.

If a player draws more than one card from the stock, his hand is dead; the cards he drew on that turn are placed on the discard pile and the next player has his choice of them.

VARIANTS—Many people play that any player may knock whenever it is his turn; there is then a showdown without any further drawing, and the high hand wins the pot, which consists only of the antes. Others play that each player must put another chip in the pot every time he draws a card.

Other Dealer's Choice Games

The following games are not forms of Poker but are often played in Dealer's Choice games.

RED AND BLACK—Each player in turn, beginning at dealer's left, places any bet up to the limit, and names "red" or "black." Dealer gives the player five cards face up. If three or more are of the color named, dealer pays the bet; if three or more are of the opposite color, dealer collects the bet. If all five cards are of the same color, the bet is paid or collected double.

There are several other games also called Red and Black. One may be described as follows: Deal, bet and draw as in Draw Poker; but the object is to make up hands of high or low point values. The point values are: King, queen, jack and ten, 10 each; ace, 1; other cards their pip value. All red cards are plus values, all black cards minus values; thus the hand ♤ K, ♢ J, ♤ 8, ♧ 7, ♡ 3 would count minus 12. The high count and the low count divide the pot.

"BINGO"—Each player's hand (five cards) remains spread out in front of him. The dealer turns up cards from the top of the pack, one at a time. Each player having a card of the same rank as the one turned up (regardless of suit) must put on that card in his hand a number of chips corresponding to the rank of the card, 13 for a king, 12 for a queen, 11 for a jack, etc., 1 for an ace. If a player holds more than one card of the rank, he must put the total number of chips on each. The first player who has chips on all five of his cards takes all chips on all players' cards; if two or more go out on the same card, they divide these chips equally.

UP AND DOWN THE RIVER, OR PUT AND TAKE—Dealer then turns up five cards, one at a time, as "put" cards; each player having a card of the same rank as the card turned must put into the pot as many chips as the pip value of the card (13 for a king, 1 for an ace, etc.). After the fifth card, dealer then turns up five "take" cards and this time each player takes from the pot the pip value of any corresponding card in his hand. (*Variant.* Some play that the first card turned by dealer calls for 1 chip, the second card 2 chips, the third card 4 chips, the fourth card 8 chips and the fifth card 16 chips.) The dealer takes anything left in the pot, or supplies any deficiency.

GARBAGE—A series of the above games is sometimes played and the combination is called "Garbage" and by various other names in different localities.

Laws of Poker

The following laws, newly prepared for this edition, define

correct procedure and the rectification of irregularities.

No penalties are assessed or proposed for breaches of law. A penalty can punish the offender but cannot restore the rights of a player who may have been damaged. In some cases the players in a game decide on certain penalties to discourage persistent offenders. See also *Ethics* on page 121.

The laws have three main sections: General laws, applying to all forms of Poker; Draw (or closed) Poker laws; and Stud (or open) Poker laws.

General Laws

(This section covers the pack of cards; the rank of hands; the shuffle, cut, and deal; the betting; and the showdown.)

1. PLAYERS. Poker may be played by two to ten players. In every form of Poker each plays for himself.

2. OBJECT OF THE GAME. The object of Poker is to win the pot, either by having the best Poker hand (as explained below) or by making a bet that no other player meets.

3. (A) THE PACK. The Poker pack consists of 52 cards, divided in four suits: spades (♠), hearts (♡), diamonds (♢), clubs (♣). In each suit there are thirteen cards: A, K, Q, J, 10, 9, 8, 7, 6, 5, 4, 3, 2.

(B) JOKER. One or more jokers may be added to the pack. Each joker is a wild card.

(C) WILD CARDS. A joker or any other card or class of cards may be designated as wild by any of the following methods. The method must be selected in advance by the players in the game.

(1) The wild card may be designated by its holder to represent any other card that its holder does not have.

(2) The joker (in this case called the bug) may be designated by its holder to represent a fifth ace or any card needed to complete a straight, a flush, or any special hand such as a dog, cat, etc.

(3) Any wild card may represent any other card, whether or not the holder of the wild card also has the card designated. [This permits double- or even triple-ace-high flushes, etc.] A wild card, properly designated, ranks exactly the same as a natural card.

4. RANK OF CARDS. (A) A (high) K, Q, J, 10, 9, 8, 7, 6, 5, 4, 3, 2; A (low) only in the sequence 5-4-3-2-A.

(B) *Optional.* The ace may rank low in Low Poker (Lowball) or in High-Low Poker. When the ace is by agreement designated as low:

(1) In Low Poker, the ace is always low, so that A-A is a lower pair than 2-2.

(2) In High-Low Poker, the holder must designate the relative rank of the ace at the time that he shows his hand in the showdown, e.g., by saying "aces high" (in which case A-A beats K-K for high) or "aces low" (in which case A-A beats 2-2 for low but loses to 2-2 for high).

(c) In any pot to be won by the high hand, the ranking follows subsection (a) of this law, so that for example between two little dogs, 7-6-4-3-2 beats 7-5-4-3-2.

5. SEATING. (A) Players take seats at random unless any player demands, before the game begins, that the seats of the respective players be determined as provided in the next paragraph.

(B) When any player demand a reseating, the banker has first choice of seats. The first dealer (see paragraph 7) either may take the seat to left of the banker or may participate with the other players in having his position determined by chance. The dealer then shuffles the pack, has the cards cut by the player to his right, and deals one card face up to each player in rotation beginning with the player at his left. The player thus dealt the highest-ranking card sits at the right of the banker, the player with the next-highest card at the right of that player, and so on. If two players are dealt cards of the same rank, the card dealt first ranks higher than the other.

(c) After the start of the game no player may demand a reseating unless at least one hour has elapsed since the last reseating. A player entering the game after it begins must take any vacant seat. A player replacing another player must take the seat vacated by that player. Two players may exchange seats, after any showdown and before the next deal begins, provided no other player objects.

(D) When there is no banker, the dealer has first choice of seats.

6. THE SHUFFLE AND CUT. (A) Any player on demand may shuffle the pack before the deal. The pack should be shuffled three times in all, by one or more players. The dealer has the right to shuffle last and should shuffle the pack at least once.

(B) The dealer offers the shuffled pack to his right-hand opponent, who may cut it or not as he pleases. [When two packs are used, he offers the pack for a cut to his left-hand opponent.] If this player does not cut, any other player may cut. If more than one player demands the right to cut, the one nearest the dealer's right hand shall cut. Except in case of an irregularity necessitating a new cut, the pack is cut only once.

(c) The player who cuts divides the pack into two or three portions, none of which shall contain fewer than five cards, and completes the cut by placing the packet that was originally bottom-most on top. [If a card is exposed in cutting, the pack must be shuffled by the dealer and cut again. Irregularities requiring a new shuffle and cut are covered on page 112.]

7. THE DEAL. (A) At the start of the game any player shuffles a pack and deals the cards face up, one at a time to each player in rotation beginning with the player at his left, until a jack is turned up. The player to whom the jack falls is the first dealer. Thereafter, the turn to deal passes from each player to the player at his left. A player may not voluntarily pass his turn to deal.

(B) The dealer distributes the cards from the top of the pack, one card at a time to each player in clockwise rotation, beginning with the player at his left and ending with himself.

8. RANK OF HANDS. Poker hands rank, from highest to lowest:

(A) Straight flush—five cards of the same suit in sequence. The highest straight flush is A, K, Q, J, 10 of the same suit, called a royal flush. The lowest straight flush is 5, 4, 3, 2, A of the same suit. As between two straight flushes, the one headed by the highest card wins. [When any card of the pack is designated as wild—see 3 (c)—a straight flush loses to five of a kind, which is the highest possible hand.]

(B) Four of a kind—four cards of the same rank. This hand loses to a straight flush but beats any other hand. As between two hands each containing four of a kind, the four higher-ranking cards win. [When there are several wild cards, it is possible for two players to hold four of a kind of the same rank. In this case, the winning hand is the one with the higher-ranking fifth card.]

(c) Full house—three cards of one rank and two cards of another rank. As between two full houses, the one with the higher-ranking three of a kind is the winner. [When there are several wild cards, two players may have full houses in which the three-of-a-kind holdings are of the same rank; the higher of the pairs then determines the winning hand.]

(D) Flush—five cards of the same suit. As between two flushes, the one containing the highest card wins. If the highest cards are of the same rank, the higher of the next-highest cards determines the winning hand, and so on; so that ♦ A-K-4-3-2 beats ♥ A-Q-J-10-8, and ♠ J-9-8-6-4 beats ♥ J-9-8-6-3.

(E) Straight—five cards, in two or more suits, ranking consecutively; as 8, 7, 6, 5, 4. The ace is high in the straight A, K, Q, J, 10 and low in the straight 5, 4, 3, 2, A. As between two straights, the one containing the highest card wins, so that 6, 5, 4, 3, 2 beats 5, 4, 3, 2, A.

(F) Three of a kind—three cards of the same rank. As between two hands each containing three of a kind, the one with the higher-ranking three of a kind wins. [When there are several wild cards, there may be two hands containing identical threes of a kind. In such cases, the highest-ranking unmatched card determines the winner. If these cards are of the same rank, the higher-ranking fifth card in each hand determines the winner.]

(G) Two pairs—two cards of one rank and two cards of another rank, with an unmatched fifth card. As between two hands each containing two pairs, the one with the highest pair wins. If the higher pairs are of the same rank, the one with the higher-ranking second pair wins. If these pairs too are of the same rank, the hand containing the higher of the unmatched cards is the winner.

(H) One pair—two cards of the same rank, with three unmatched cards. Of two one-pair hands, the one containing the higher pair wins. As between two hands containing pairs of the same rank, the highest unmatched card determines the winner; if these are the same, the higher of the second-highest unmatched cards, and if these are the same, the higher of the lowest unmatched cards. For example 8, 8, 9, 5, 3 beats 8, 8, 9, 5, 2.

(I) No pair. This loses to any hand having a pair or any higher-ranking combination. As between two no-pair hands, the one containing the highest card wins; if these two cards are tied, the next-highest card decides, and so on, so that A, 8, 7, 4, 3 loses to A, 9, 7, 4, 3 but wins from A, 8, 7, 4 2.

Two hands that are identical, card for card, are tied, since the suits have no relative rank in Poker.

9. BETTING. (A) All the chips bet go into the center of the table, forming the pot. Before putting any chips in the pot, a player in turn announces whether he is betting, calling, or raising; and, if he is betting or raising, how much. A player may not raise by any amount less than the bet he called, or the previous raise if any, unless there is only one player besides himself in the pot.

(B) If every player in turn, including the dealer, passes, there is a new deal by the next player in rotation and the ante (if any) is repeated. If any player bets, each player in turn after him must either call, or raise, or drop.

(C) In each betting interval, the turn to bet begins with the player designated by the rules of the variant being played, and moves to each active player to the left. A player may neither pass nor bet until the active player nearest his right has put the correct number of chips into the pot or has discarded his hand.

(1) In Draw Poker, the first in turn before the draw is the player nearest the dealer's left. The first in turn after the draw is the player who made the first bet before the draw, or, if he has dropped, the active player nearest his left.

(2) In Stud Poker, the first in turn in each betting interval is the player whose exposed cards are higher than those of any other player. If two or more players have identical high holdings, the one nearest dealer's left is first in turn. In the first betting interval, the high player must make a minimum bet. In any later betting interval, he may check without betting.

(D) Unless a bet has been made in that betting interval, an active player in turn may check, which means that he elects to remain an active player without betting. [In some variants of Poker, checking is specifically prohibited.]

(E) If any player bets, each active player in turn after him (including players who checked originally) must either drop, or call, or raise.

(F) No player may check, bet, call, raise, or drop, except in his proper turn. A player in turn may drop even when he has the privilege of checking. At any time that a player discards his hand, or permits it to be mixed with any discard, he is deemed to drop and his hand may not be reclaimed.

(G) Whenever only one active player remains, through every other player's having dropped, the active player wins the pot without showing his hand and there is a new deal by the next dealer in turn.

(H) No two players may play in partnership, and there may be no agreement between two or more players to divide a pot.

10. THE SHOWDOWN. When each player has either called the highest previous bet, without raising, or has dropped; or when every active player has checked; the full hand of every active player is placed face up on the table and the highest-ranking hand wins the pot. If two or more hands tie for the highest rank, they divide the pot evenly, an odd chip going to the player who last bet or raised. [It is customary for a player to announce the value of his hand. When there are wild cards he must announce the value of his hand and may then claim no higher hand.]

Irregularities

11. REDEAL. Any player, unless he has intentionally seen the face of any card required to be dealt to him face down, may call for a new shuffle, cut, and deal by the same dealer if it is ascertained, before the dealer begins dealing the second round of cards, that:

(1) a card was exposed in cutting;

(2) the cut left fewer than five cards in either packet;

(3) two or more cards are faced in the pack;

(4) the pack is incorrect or imperfect in any way [see paragraphs 3(A), 14, and 15].

(5) a player is dealing out of turn (see next paragraph).

If a player is dealing out of turn, and a redeal is called, the deal reverts to the proper player in turn. In a game in which every player antes, no one need ante again. Any other bet that has been put in the pot is forfeited to the pot. If no redeal or misdeal is called within the time limit provided, the deal stands as regular and the player at the left of the out-of-turn dealer will be the next dealer in turn.

12. MISDEAL. A misdeal—one due to the dealer's error—loses the deal, if attention is drawn to it by a player who has not intentionally seen any face-down card dealt to him. The deal passes to the next player in turn. Any ante made solely by the dealer is forfeited to the pot. If all players have anted equally, their antes remain in the pot and no one need ante again. A blind bet or raise may be withdrawn.

A misdeal may be called:

(A) by any player who has not intentionally seen any face-down card dealt to him, if before the dealer begins the second round of cards it is ascertained that the pack was not shuffled or was not offered for a cut;

(B) by any player to whom the dealer gives two face-up cards in Draw Poker or any other form of closed Poker, provided that player has not intentionally seen any face-down card dealt to him and has not contributed to the error; and provided he calls for the misdeal immediately;

(C) if the dealer gives too many cards to more than one player.

If the dealer stops dealing before giving every player enough cards, due solely to his omission to deal one or more rounds, it is not a misdeal and the dealer is required to complete the deal whenever the irregularity is discovered. [For example, if the dealer stops dealing after giving each player only four cards; or if the dealer gives the first five of seven players five cards each and the sixth and seventh players only four cards each, having stopped dealing after the fifth player on the last round.]

If the dealer deals too many hands, he shall determine which hand is dead, and that hand is discarded; but if any player has looked at any face-down card in any hand, he must keep that hand.

If the dealer deals too few hands, he must give his own hand to the first omitted player to his left. Any other player who has been omitted and who has anted may withdraw his ante.

13. EXPOSED CARD. (A) If the dealer exposes one or more cards from the undealt portion of the pack, after the deal is completed, those cards are dead and are placed among the discards. (See also Stud Poker, paragraph 35 on page 121.)

(B) There is no penalty against any player for exposing any part of his hand, and he has no redress. A player who interferes with the deal and causes the dealer to expose a card may not call a misdeal.

(C) Each player is responsible for his own hand and has no redress if another player causes a card in it to be exposed.

14. INCORRECT PACK. If it is ascertained at any time before the pot has been taken in that the pack has too many cards, too few cards, or a duplication of cards, the deal is void and each player withdraws from the pot any chips he contributed to it, any other laws of the game to the contrary notwithstanding; but the results of pots previously taken in are not affected.

15. IMPERFECT PACK. If the pack contains any card that is torn, discolored or otherwise marked so as to be identifiable from its back, the pack must be replaced before the deal in progress or any other deal can be completed; but the play of the pot in progress is not affected if the deal has been completed.

16. INCORRECT HAND. A hand having more or less than five cards (or any other number of cards designated as a player's hand in the Poker variant being played) is foul and cannot win the pot. If every other player has dropped, the pot remains and goes to the winner of the next pot.

[Players may agree that a hand with fewer than five cards is not foul, in which case its holder may compete for the pot with the best poker combination he can make with the cards he has.]

17. IRREGULARITIES IN BETTING. Chips once put in the pot may not be withdrawn except:

(A) By a player who, after he has anted, is dealt out—see paragraph 12 on page 112;

(B) In jackpots, when another player has opened without proper openers—see paragraph 30(c) on page 118;

(C) In Draw Poker, by the players who opened or raised blind, in case of a misdeal—see paragraph 12 on page 112;

(D) In Stud Poker, when the dealer has failed to deal a player any card face down—see paragraph 34 on page 121.

18. INSTALLMENT OR STRING BETS. A player's entire bet must be put in the pot at one time. Having put in any number of chips, he may not add to that number unless the original number was insufficient to call, in which case he may add exactly enough chips to call. If, however, he announced before putting in any chips that he was raising by a certain amount, and he puts in an amount insufficient for such a raise, he must on demand supply enough additional chips to equal the announced amount of his bet.

19. INSUFFICIENT BET. When a player in turn puts into the pot a number of chips insufficient to call, he must either add enough chips to call and may not raise; or he must drop and forfeit chips already put in the pot. When a player raises by less than the minimum permitted, he is deemed to have called and any additional chips he put into the pot are forfeited to it.

20. BET ABOVE LIMIT. If a player puts in the pot more chips than are permitted by the limit, it stands as a bet of

the limit and additional chips are forfeited to the pot. An exception is made in table stakes, when a player's bet exceeds the number of chips an opponent has; in that event, the player may withdraw the excess and either bet it in a side pot, or, if there are not other players willing or able to meet that bet in the side pot, restore those chips to his stack.

21. ANNOUNCEMENT IN TURN OF INTENTION TO PASS OR BET. If a player in turn announces that he passes or drops, his announcement is binding on him whether or not he discards his hand. If a player in turn announces a bet but does not put any chips in the pot, he is bound by his announcement and must if able supply such additional chips as are necessary to bring his bet up to the announced amount. In any event, other players who rely upon an announcement of intention do so at their own risk and have no redress in case under these rules the announcement need not be made good. [In many circles it is considered unethical to announce any intention and then not make good on it.]

22. ANNOUNCEMENT OUT OF TURN OF INTENTION TO PASS OR BET. If a player out of turn announces his intention to pass or drop when his turn comes, but does not actually discard his hand; or to make a certain bet, but does not actually put any chips in the pot; his announcement is void and he may take any action he chooses when his turn comes. Any other player who acts in reliance upon the announcement does so at his own risk and has no redress. [As in the case of paragraph 21, above, failure to make good on such an announcement, and especially if the announcement was intentionally misleading, is in many circles considered unethical.]

23. BET OUT OF TURN. If a player puts any chips in the pot out of turn, they remain there and the play reverts to the player whose turn it was. If any player to the offender's left puts chips in the pot, he has bet out of turn and is equally an offender. When the offender's turn comes, if the chips he put in were insufficient to call, he may add enough chips to call; if the amount was exactly sufficient to call, he is deemed to have called; if the amount was more than enough to call, he is deemed to have raised by the amount of the excess but cannot add chips to increase the amount of his raise; if no player before him has bet, he is deemed to have bet the number of chips he put in and any amount above the agreed limit is forfeited to the pot. If the chips he put in were in-

sufficient to call he may forfeit these chips and drop. He may never add chips to raise or to increase his raise.

24. PASS OUT OF TURN. The pass (act of dropping) out of turn is among the most damaging of Poker improprieties, but there is no penalty therefor except by agreement of the players. In any case the offender's hand is dead and he cannot win the pot.

25. IRREGULARITIES IN THE SHOWDOWN. (A) *Hand misstated.* If a player in the showdown announces a hand he does not actually hold, his announcement is void if attention is called to the error at any time before the pot has been taken in by any player (including the player who miscalled his hand). ["The cards speak for themselves."]

(B) *Designation of wild cards.* If in the showdown a player orally designates the suit or rank of a wild card in his hand, or implies such designation by announcing a certain hand, he may not change that designation (e.g., an announcement of Joker-J-10-9-8 as "jack-high straight" fixes the joker as a seven). A player may always show his hand without announcement and need not designate the value of a wild card unless another active player demands that he do so.

(c) *Concession of a pot.* A player who has discarded his hand after another player's announcement of a higher hand may not later claim the pot even if the announcement is determined to have been incorrect.

Draw Poker

26. THE DRAW. (A) When each player has exactly called the highest previous bet, without raising, or has dropped, the first betting interval ends. The dealer picks up the undealt portion of the pack, and each active player in turn to his left may discard one or more cards, whereupon the dealer gives him that number of cards, face down, from the top of the pack. A player need not draw unless he so chooses.

(B) If the dealer is an active player, he must announce how many cards, if any, he is drawing. At any time following the draw and before the first player in turn bets or checks in the final betting interval, any active player may ask any other active player how many cards he drew. The latter player must answer, but the questioner has no redress if the answer is incorrect. [It is considered unethical, however, to give an incorrect answer intentionally.]

(c) The dealer may not serve the bottom card of the pack. If the pack exclusive of this card does not suffice for the draw, the dealer must assemble all cards previously discarded, plus the bottom card of the original pack; shuffle these cards; offer them for a cut; and continue dealing. The cut shall be as provided in paragraph 6 (B) except that only an active player may cut. The opener's discards and the discards of any player yet to draw are excluded from the new pack if they have been kept separate and can be identified.

27. IRREGULARITIES IN THE DRAW. (A) *Wrong number of cards.* If the dealer gives a player more or less cards than he asks for in the draw, the error must be corrected if the player calls attention to it before he has looked at any of the cards. Unless a card has been served to the next active player in turn, the dealer must correct the error by supplying another card or restoring the excess to the top of the pack, as the case may be. If the next player has been served, the player may discard from his hand additional cards to accept an excess draw without going over a five-card hand; if he has already discarded and the draw is insufficient to restore his hand to five cards, his hand is foul. If the player has looked at any card of the draw and the entire draw would give him an incorrect number of cards, his hand is foul.

(B) *Card exposed.* If any card is exposed in the draw, whether or not it was faced in the pack, the player must accept the first such card but any additional exposed card to be dealt to him is dead and is placed among the discards. After the dealer has served all other active players, he serves additional cards due the player from the top of the pack.

(C) *Draw out of turn.* If a player allows a player at his left to draw out of turn, he must play without drawing, or drop. If he has already discarded any card, his hand is foul.

(D) A player may correct a slip of the tongue in stating the number of cards he wishes to draw, but only provided the dealer has not yet given him the number of cards he first requested.

(E) If a player discards a number of cards that would make his hand incorrect after the dealer gives him as many cards as he asked for, his hand is foul.

28. SHOWING OPENERS. The player who opens must prove that he held a legal hand of five cards including the strength (if any) required to open. If he is in the showdown he must show his entire hand face up. In any other case, before discarding his entire hand he must show his openers face up and his remaining cards, if any, face down.

29. SPLITTING OPENERS. The player who opened may split his openers (discard one or more cards essential to them) and he need not announce that he does so. He may put his discard in the pot, face down, for reference later. [For example, having opened with ♠ Q, ♡ Q, J, 10, 9, he may discard the ♠ Q and draw one card. It is not customary for the opener to put his discard in the pot, since he can usually demonstrate to the other players' satisfaction that he held openers.]

30. FALSE OPENERS. (A) If it is ascertained at any time that a player opened without proper openers, or that his hand contains too many cards, his hand is foul and all chips he has bet are forfeited to the pot.

(B) If false openers are discovered before the draw, any other player in turn to the offender's left (excluding those who passed in their first turns) may open and play continues; but any player except the offender may withdraw from the pot any chips he put in after the pot was falsely opened. If no one can open, the remainder of the pot remains for the next deal.

(C) If false openers are discovered after every player but the offender has dropped, each other player may withdraw from the pot any chips he put in after the pot was falsely opened.

(D) If false openers are discovered after the draw, and when any active player remains, play continues and the pot goes to the highest hand at the showdown, whether or not any player had openers. [If there is no hand at the showdown that is not foul, the pot remains and goes to the winner of the next pot. Regardless of other circumstances, a hand that has dropped can never win a pot.]

Stud Poker

31. BETTING IN STUD POKER. (A) In each betting interval the player with the highest exposed combination (as defined by paragraph 32) has the privilege of betting first. In the first betting interval, this player must bet at least the minimum established for the game. In any subsequent betting interval, this player may check.

(B) If in any betting interval every active player checks, the betting interval ends. Another round of cards is dealt, or there is a showdown, as the case may be. If in any betting interval any player bets, each active player in turn after him must at least call the highest previous bet or drop.

(c) At the start of each betting interval the dealer must announce which player bets first, naming the combination that gives such player the high exposed holding at that point (for example, "Pair of eights bets" or "First ace bets"). The dealer should also announce, after the third and fourth face-up cards are dealt, any player's combination that, when combined with his hole card, may make a one-card draw to a flush or straight (announced by saying "Possible flush" or "Possible straight").

[*Optional law.* In the final betting interval, a player may not check or call unless his full hand, including his hole card, will beat the exposed cards of the highest combination showing. Such player may, however, bet or raise. This rule, which is not recommended, is designed to protect players against making pointless calls; at the same time, it eliminates some bluffing opportunities. Like other optional rules, it should not apply unless there has been prior agreement among the players in the game that it will.]

32. INCOMPLETE HANDS. (A) Four or fewer exposed cards, for the purpose of establishing the first bettor in any betting interval, rank from highest to lowest as follows:

(1) Four of a kind; as between two such hands, the four higher-ranking cards are high.

(2) Three of a kind; as between two such hands, the higher-ranking three of a kind are high.

(3) Two pair; as between two such hands, the highest pair determines the high hand, and if the highest pairs are the same, the higher of the two lower pairs.

(4) One pair; as between two such hands, the higher pair is high; if two hands have the identical pair, the highest unmatched card determines the high hand, and if they are identical the higher of the two other cards.

(5) The highest card; if two players tie for highest card, the next-highest card in their respective hands determines the high hand, and so on.

(B) As between two holdings that are identical card for card, the one nearest the dealer's left is high for purposes of betting (but has no superiority over the other in the show-down).

[Flush and straight combinations of four or fewer cards have no higher rank, for determining the first bettor, than any other holdings including no pair; except when a fourflush is played to beat a pair, in which case a fourflush showing bets ahead of a pair.]

(c) If through the dealer's or his own error a player has all his cards exposed, all are taken into consideration for establishing the first bettor; and if at the start of the final betting interval such player has a straight, flush, full house or straight flush showing, his hand outranks any combination of exposed cards that his hand would beat in a showdown.

33. IRREGULARITIES IN DEALING STUD POKER. (A) At any time before the dealer begins dealing the second round of cards, a player who has not looked at a card dealt face down to him may call for a new shuffle, cut, and deal if it is ascertained that:

(1) the pack was not shuffled or cut;

(2) a card was exposed in cutting, or the cut left fewer than five cards in either packet;

(3) two or more cards are faced in the pack;

(4) the pack is incorrect or imperfect in any way;

(5) a player is dealing out of turn.

When there is a redeal, the same dealer deals again unless he was dealing out of turn, in which case the deal reverts to the proper player in turn.

(B) If the dealer deals too many hands, he shall determine which hand is dead, and that hand is discarded; but a player who has looked at the hole card of any hand must keep that hand.

(c) If the dealer deals too few hands, he must give his own hand to the first omitted player to his left.

(D) If the dealer gives a player two face-down cards instead of one on the first round of dealing, he omits that player on the second round of dealing and (unless the rules of the game require two hole cards, as in seven-card stud) he turns up one of the cards. The player who received the two cards may not look at them and then turn up one of them.

(E) If the dealer gives a player more than two cards on the first round of dealings, that player may require a redeal if he does so before the second round of dealing has begun. If the error is not noted until later, his hand is dead.

(F) If in dealing any round of face-up cards the dealer omits a player, he moves back the cards dealt later, so as to give each player the face-up card he would had if no irregularity had occurred; except that if attention is not called to the irregularity before the first bet is made in the ensuing betting interval, the hand of the player who was omitted is dead.

34. EXPOSED CARD. If the dealer gives any player a hole card face up, the player must keep that card and instead receive his next card face down. The player has no redress, except to receive his next card face down, unless the dealer repeatedly fails to correct the error until the player has four cards; at which point, if the dealer has never given him a face-down card, the player may if he wishes drop out, withdrawing from the pot all chips he has put in. If the player instead stays for his fifth card, and receives it also face up, he may withdraw his chips from the pot; but the player may instead remain in the pot.

35. DEAD CARDS. A card found faced in the pack during any round of dealing must be dealt to the player to whom it falls. A card at the top of the pack exposed during a betting interval, either because it is faced in the pack or because it is prematurely dealt, is discarded. In dealing the next round of face-up cards, the dealer skips the player to whom such card would have fallen, and deals in rotation, ending with the last player who would have received the exposed card if it had not been exposed. In each subsequent round of cards, on demand of any player the dealer must begin the rotation with the player who would otherwise have received the top card.

36. IMPOSSIBLE CALL. If the player last to speak in the final betting interval calls a bet when his five cards, regardless of his hole card, cannot possibly beat the four showing cards of the player whose bet he calls, his call is void and the chips may be retracted provided any player calls attention to his error before the hole card of any other active player is shown.

37. If the dealer errs in calling the value of a hand or in designating the high hand, no player has any redress; but if the first bet is made by the player incorrectly designated by the dealer, it is not a bet out of turn.

38. The dealer does not have the option of dealing a player's first card up and his second card down intentionally. A player may not turn up his hole card and receive his next card face down; if he turns up his hole card, he must play throughout with all his cards exposed.

Poker Ethics

The only safe guiding principle in Poker ethics is, "When

in Rome, do as the Romans do." In some games, a player may do anything to fool his opponents so long as he does not cheat; it is considered part of the skill of the game to do so, and by no means unsportsmanlike. In some games, it is considered unethical—at least sharp—to check on a good hand in the hope that someone else will bet and you can raise him. Since card-playing is a social pastime, a player is best advised to follow the standards of the other players and remain popular.

BLUFFING—To bluff, in Poker, is to make a bet on a hand you know, or believe, is not the best, in the hope that other players will believe you are strong and will drop. Bluffing is so much a part of Poker that the game would be no good without it. But some players believe you should not support your bluff by making remarks you know are untrue, as by announcing you have improved your hand in the draw when you have not.

INTENTIONALLY BREAKING THE RULES—In most circles it is not considered ethical to announce, out of turn, that you intend to bet, to raise, to drop, when actually you have no intention of so doing when your turn comes. It is safe to make such false announcements, because no penalty is provided for them; but regard for the other players should rule them out when they are not in accord with the code of ethics followed in the game you are playing. In no circle is it considered ethical to break the rules, as by passing out of turn, unless it is advantageous to you to do so; for in any other case you can hurt someone else without possibility of helping yourself.

PARTNERSHIPS, SPLITTING POTS—In all Poker circles it is considered unethical, and almost cheating, to play in partnership with another player or to split a pot rather than have a showdown.

BETTING BLIND—When a player announces that he is betting (or checking) "blind"—that is, without looking at his hand —he does so to avoid the stigma that in some games attaches to trap passes and sandbagging. Nevertheless, in nearly all circles it is considered unethical for a player to announce that he is betting or checking blind when in fact he has seen his hand.

Skillful Play at Poker

VALUES OF HANDS—A player must know what constitutes a good hand in the form of Poker he is playing. Following are the average winning hands in various forms of Poker, with seven players in the game:

Draw Poker, nothing wild	Jacks up
Five-card Stud	Aces or Kings
Seven-card Stud	Three eights
Draw Poker, joker wild	Three eights
Draw Poker, with the bug	Aces up
Draw Poker, deuces wild	Three aces
Draw Poker, high-low	Jacks up, high; 10 or 9, low
Lowball	9-6-x-x-x

WHEN TO STAY IN—Conservatism pays in Poker, and in a game with expert players it is necessary. The general rule is: You should stay in only in either of two cases, (a) you believe you have the best hand, or (b) the odds against your drawing the best hand are less than the odds offered by the pot.

The following table shows the hands on which you have an even chance of holding the highest hand originally dealt:

HAND REQUIRED	TO BEAT
Any pair	1 opponent
Eights	2 opponents
Jacks	3 opponents
Kings	4 opponents
Aces	5, 6, 7 opponents

POKER MATHEMATICS—The following tables are based on the theory of probabilities. Tables showing the relative numbers of "possible hands" are a guide to the value of your hand. For example, if you are dealt a flush there are only a few thousand hands that will beat you and some 2½ million that you can beat, so the odds are overwhelmingly in favor of your having the best hand. But in Draw Poker players have a chance to draw and improve their hands, so the ultimate odds must be reduced accordingly. The table on page 125 gives a player's chances in the draw.

Possible Poker Hands in a 52-Card Pack

Straight Flush	40
Four of a Kind	624
Full House	3,744
Flush	5,108
Straight	10,200
Three of a Kind	54,912
Two Pairs	123,552
One Pair	1,098,240
No Pair, less than above	1,302,540
Total	2,598,960

Chances of Improving a Hand on the Draw (Jackpots or Draw Poker)

Cards Held in Hand	Cards Drawn	Possible Improvement	Odds Against Making
One Pair	3	Two Pair	5 to 1
		Threes	8 to 1
		Full House	97 to 1
		Fours	359 to 1
		Anything	2½ to 1
One Pair and an Ace Kicker	2	Aces Up	7½ to 1*
		Another Pair	17 to 1*
		Threes	12 to 1
		Full House	119 to 1
		Fours	1080 to 1
		Anything	3 to 1*
Two Pairs	1	Full House	11 to 1*
		Anything	11 to 1*
Threes	2	Full House	15½ to 1
		Fours	22½ to 1*
		Anything	8½ to 1*
Threes and One Odd Card	1	Full House	14⅔ to 1
		Fours	46 to 1*
		Anything	11 to 1
Four Straight (Open-end)	1	Straight	5 to 1
Four Straight (One end or interior)	1	Straight	11 to 1
Four Flush	1	Flush	4¼ to 1
Four Straight Flush (Both ends open)	1	Straight Flush	22½ to 1
		Anything	2 to 1*
Four Straight Flush (Interior or end)	1	Straight Flush	46 to 1*
		Anything	3 to 1*
One Ace	4	Pair of Aces	3 to 1*
		Aces Up	14 to 1*

*From the book "Oswald Jacoby on Poker" published by Doubleday & Co., Inc., New York.

RUMMY (RUM)

Rummy is the best-known of all card games played in the United States. Its popularity is due partly to the fact that it is so simple. Any person with a knowledge of the basic game can easily learn any form of it. All the principal forms are described in the following pages. The basic game is described first.

NUMBER OF PLAYERS—Two to six. Each plays for himself. More than six players should play Double Rum, 500 Rum or Contract Rummy.

THE PACK—52 cards.

RANK OF CARDS—K (high), Q, J, 10, 9, 8, 7, 6, 5, 4, 3, 2, A. (*Variant.* In many forms of Rummy, the ace may rank either high or low).

THE SHUFFLE AND CUT—Draw or cut for deal; low deals. Each player may shuffle, the dealer last; it is customary for the dealer only to shuffle. The player at dealer's right cuts.

THE DEAL—Dealer gives one card at a time, face down, to each player in rotation to the left, until each player has: ten cards, when two play; seven cards, when three or four play; six cards, when five or six play. The remaining cards are placed face down in the center of the table, forming the *stock*. The top card of the stock is turned face up and placed beside the stock to found the *discard pile*.

When two play, the winner of each hand deals the next. When more than two play, the turn to deal passes from player to player to the left.

OBJECT OF PLAY—To form in one's hand *matched sets* consisting of: groups of three or four of a kind, as ♠ 9, ♢ 9, ♣ 9, or ♠ Q, ♡ Q, ♢ Q, ♣ Q; or *sequences* of three or more cards of the same suit, as ♢ J, ♢ 10, ♢ 9. In a sequence an ace may count only as low card.

THE PLAY—Each player in turn, beginning with eldest hand,

must draw one card—either the top card of the stock or the top card of the discard pile—and add it to his hand; he may then *meld*, or *lay down* on the table, face up, any matched set. He must then discard one card, face up, on top of the discard pile. If he drew the top card of the discard pile, he may not discard it in the same turn.

Laying off. A player in turn may add one or more matching cards from his hand to any matched set already shown on the table; thus, if threes are showing, he may add the fourth three; if ♡ 10 9 8 are showing, he may add ♡ J, or ♡ Q J, or ♡ 7, or ♡ 7 6.

Going out. When in this fashion a player gets rid of all his cards, he wins the game. If all his remaining cards are matched, he may lay them down without discarding on his last turn.

(*Variant*. In some circles each player's turn must end with a discard, so the game ends only when a player, having drawn, can lay down or lay off all cards but one remaining in his hand, then discards that card.)

If the last card of the stock has been drawn and no player has gone out, the next player in turn may either take the top of the discard pile, or may turn the discard pile to form a new stock (without shuffling it) and draw the top card, after which play proceeds.

(*Variant*. In a game sometimes called Block Rummy, play ends when the stock is exhausted and when any player refuses to take the last previous discard. All hands are shown and the player with the lowest count wins from each other player the difference in their counts; if two or more players tie for low count, they divide the winnings equally.)

(*Variant*. Some play that if any player discards a card which could be laid off, any other player may call "Rummy," lay off the card, and replace it with a discard from his hand. The first player to call rummy has this right; if two or more call simultaneously, the one nearest the player's left has the right.)

SCORING—Each player in the game pays to the winner the pip value of the cards remaining in his hand, whether they form matched sets or not; face cards count 10 each, aces 1 each, every other card its pip value.

A player *goes rummy* when he gets rid of all cards in his hand in one turn, without previously having laid down or laid off any cards; in this event every other player pays him double.

(*Variant.* Some play that no cards may be laid down until one player can go out all at once, and that the winner collects the pip value of his own hand from each other player. This variant is often played with ten cards dealt to each player, and only two or three players. Play always continues until some player goes out, and if the stock is exhausted before that time, it is shuffled and turned to make a new stock.)

Irregularities in Rummy

The following rules cover irregularities that may occur in any game of the Rummy family—including Canasta, Oklahoma, Continental and Contract Rummy, Gin Rummy, etc. In every case, the reader should also consult the specific rules of the game.

PLAY OUT OF TURN—If a player is not stopped before he has completed his turn by discarding, it stands as a play in turn and intervening players lose their turns. If the player out of turn has taken the top card of the stock, it is too late for rectification after he has added that card to his hand. If correction is required in time, the offender restores the card drawn and retracts any meld he may have made, and play reverts to the player in turn. The next paragraph (*Illegal Draw*) may apply.

ILLEGAL DRAW—If, by playing out of turn or by drawing more than one card from the top of the stock, a player sees a card to which he is not entitled, that card is placed face up on top of the stock. The next player in turn may either take the card or may have it put in the center of the stock, face down, and proceed to play as if no irregularity had occurred. If more than one card is so exposed at the top of the stock, the option of each player in turn is only to take the top such card remaining there, or the top face-down card of the stock, or (as always) the previous discard.

A player's illegal draw may not be corrected after he has discarded, but the section on *Incorrect Hand* may apply.

PREMATURE DISCARD—If a player discards without drawing, he may then draw from the stock (but may not meld after discarding) to restore his hand to the proper number of cards; except that if the next player in turn has drawn, the section on *Incorrect Hand* applies.

A player who discards more than one card may retract

either one, unless the next player has drawn it or unless the next player has already ended his turn.

INCORRECT HAND—A player with too many cards discards without drawing; a player with too few cards draws without discarding; one card in each turn until his hand is restored to the correct number. (This applies to a player who draws too many cards and adds them to his hand before correction is required.) A player may not meld in any turn in which his hand was incorrect. If, after a player goes out, another player has too many cards he simply pays the value of all cards in his hand; if he has too few cards, he is charged 10 points for each missing card. If the player who goes out is found to have too few cards, he retracts his meld and play continues.

REDEAL—There must be a redeal (by the same dealer) if more than one card is exposed in dealing or if more than one card is found faced in the pack. A player who is dealt an incorrect number of cards may demand a redeal before drawing in his first turn, but not thereafter.

There must be a redeal at any time it is discovered that the pack is incorrect, but the results of previous deals are not affected.

EXPOSED CARD—When each plays for himself, there is no penalty for exposure by a player of his own cards. In partnership play, a card exposed (unless it can legally be melded at that time) must be left on the table and discarded at the player's next opportunity. If a player has more than one exposed card, he may discard them in any order.

CARDS LAID DOWN ILLEGALLY—If a player lays down cards which are not in fact a matched set, they must be restored to his hand if discovered at any time before the cards have been mixed together; any card laid off on such a set remains on the table, but no card may be added to it unless three or more cards, which themselves form a matched set, have been laid off on it. If a player announces that he is out when he is not able to get rid of all his cards, he must lay down and lay off all he can. In either case play proceeds as if no irregularity had occurred.

SCORING ERRORS—An error in counting a hand may not be corrected after that hand has been mixed with other cards. An error in recording an agreed score may be corrected at any time.

Boat House Rum

The rules are as in regular Rummy (page 126) except:

Each player in turn may draw the top card of the stock; or, before drawing that card, he may take the top card of the discard pile and then either the next card of the discard pile or the top card of the stock. A player in turn may discard only one card. Play does not end until a player can lay down his entire hand at one time.

An ace counts either high or low in a sequence, and sequences may go around the corner as in ◇ 3, 2, A, K, Q.

In the settlement, a player pays only for cards in his hand which do not form matched sets; he may pay either one point for every unmatched card in his hand, or pip value of all unmatched cards (ace counting 11), as agreed.

Kaluki
(Also called Caloochi, Kaloochi, Kalougi)

The rules of Rummy (page 126) are followed, except:

Two 52-card packs plus four jokers are shuffled together, making a 108-card pack.

The game is best for two, three, or four, each for himself. Each is dealt fifteen cards (with five players, thirteen cards; with six, eleven cards).

Aces count 15 each, face cards 10 each, other cards their pip value. A player's first meld must count 51 or more. Ace is high or low, so A-2-3 or A-K-Q is a valid meld but not 2-A-K.

A player may not take the top discard, or lay off, until he has made his initial meld. He may take the discard to use it immediately in an initial meld.

Jokers are wild. A joker used in a meld counts the same number of points as the card it represent. A player in his turn, before melding or discarding, may trade the appropriate natural card for a melded joker in any player's meld.

The player who goes out scores all the points remaining in the other hands. A joker left in the hand counts 25. (*Variant.* The winner collects from each loser 1 point per card, 2 points for a joker.)

Double Rum
(Also called Coon-Can; see page 165)

A 106-card double pack is used, two full packs plus two jokers shuffled together. Ace may count either high or low in sequences. In the deal, each player receives ten cards.

A group may be any three or more cards of the same rank; thus, ♡ K, ♤ K, ◇ K. A joker is wild in any group or sequence. In laying off on a sequence which contains a joker, the joker may be moved if it was used at the end of the sequence, but not if it was used in the interior of the sequence. Thus, if ♡ 7, ♡ 6, joker are on the table, either ♡ 8 or ♡ 5 may be added; but if ♡ 7, joker, ♡ 5 were on the table, only ♡ 8 or ♡ 4 may be added. (A joker can thus be moved only once.)

In scoring, a player is charged 15 for each joker in his hand and 11 for each ace in his hand, other cards as in regular Rummy.

CANASTA

Canasta, a game of the Rummy family, was the most popular American game from 1951 through 1953 and is still played by millions. The game originated in Uruguay in the early 1940's, spread rapidly to Argentina and the rest of Latin America, and reached the United States about 1948. The word canasta means "basket" in Spanish. The first rules given below are the official rules, which very serious players use, but most players have adopted one or more of the variations described on page 141 and later pages.

NUMBER OF PLAYERS—Four, in two partnerships. (Canasta may also be played by two, three, five or six players. The special rules for these forms begin on page 141.)

THE PACK—108 cards—two regular packs of 52 cards, plus four jokers, all shuffled together.

WILD CARDS—The jokers and twos are wild. A wild card is melded only with natural cards and then becomes a card of the same rank.

THE DRAW—Partnerships may be determined by drawing cards from the deck. The player drawing highest card has choice of seats, plays first in the first deal, and has the player drawing the second-highest card as his partner.

In drawing the cards rank: A (high), K, Q, J, 10, 9, 8, 7, 6, 5, 4, 3, 2. Jokers are void. Suits rank: Spades (high), hearts, diamonds, clubs. Players drawing equal cards must draw again. A player drawing a joker, or more than one card, or one of the four cards at either end of the deck, must draw again.

Partners take places opposite each other.

THE SHUFFLE AND CUT—The first deal is made by the player who sits at right of the player who drew the highest card. Thereafter the turn to deal rotates clockwise (to the left).

Any player who wishes may shuffle the deck. The dealer

132

has the right to shuffle last. After it has been shuffled, the deck must be cut by the player at dealer's left.

THE DEAL—The dealer gives eleven cards to each player, one at a time clockwise, beginning with the opponent at his left and ending with himself.

The undealt remainder of the deck is placed face down in the center of the table, becoming the *stock*. The top card of the stock is turned face up beside it, forming the *upcard*. If the upcard is a joker, two, black or red three, one or more additional cards must be turned upon it until a natural card of rank ace to four appears.

RED THREES—A player finding a red three in his hand must, at his first turn, put it face up on the table and draw a replacement from the stock. A player who draws a red three from the stock must immediately place it face up on the table and draw a replacement. A player who takes the discard pile and finds a red three in it must place the three face up on the table, but does not draw a replacement.

Each red three has a bonus value of 100 points, but if one side has all four red threes they count 200 each, or 800 in all. The value of its red threes is credited (plus) to a side that has made any meld, or debited (minus) against a side that has made no meld, by the time the play ends.

THE PLAY—The opponent at the left of the dealer plays first. Thereafter the turn to play rotates clockwise (to the left). Each turn comprises: a draw, a meld (optional) after drawing, and a discard, which ends the player's turn.

The player in turn is always entitled to draw the top card of the stock. He may instead (subject to restrictions under *Taking the Discard Pile*) take the top card of the discard pile to use it in a meld; having done so, he must take the rest of the discard pile.

The discard comprises one card from the hand (never from a meld). All discards are placed in one pile beside the stock (on the upcard if it is still there). The discard pile must be kept squared up, except as examination is allowed under *Information*.

OBJECT OF PLAY—The principal object of play is to form melds, combinations of three or more cards of the same rank, with or without the help of wild cards. (Sequences are not valid melds in Canasta.)

MELDS—A meld is valid if it contains at least two natural cards of the same rank, ace to four inclusive, and not more than three wild cards. Jokers and twos may never be melded apart from natural cards. A set of three or four black threes (without wild cards) may be melded only in going out.

To count plus, a meld must be laid face up on the table, in a proper turn of the owner. All cards left in the hand when play ends, even though they form melds, count minus.

A player may meld as many cards as he pleases in his turn, of one rank or different ranks, forming new melds or adding cards to previous melds. (But see restrictions on *Going Out.*) All melds of a partnership are placed in front of one member thereof. A partnership may meld a rank already melded by the opponents, but may not make two different melds of the same rank.

A player may add additional cards to a meld of his side, provided that the melds remain valid. He may not add cards to opponents' melds.

CANASTAS—A meld comprising seven or more cards, including at least four natural cards (called a *base*), is a *canasta.* Additional to the point values of the cards, a canasta earns a bonus: 500 for a *natural,* or *pure,* canasta, containing no wild card; 300 for a *mixed* canasta, containing one to three wild cards.

A completed canasta is squared up with a red card on the top to indicate a natural, a black card on top to indicate a mixed. Additional cards may be added to a canasta, to score their point values, but do not affect the bonus except that the addition of a wild card to a natural canasta reduces it to a mixed canasta.

MINIMUM COUNT—Every card has a fixed point value, as follows:

Each joker 50
Each two 20
Each ace 20
Each king, queen, jack, 10, 9, 8.......... 10
Each 7, 6, 5, 4, and black 3............. 5

The first meld made by a side (its initial meld) must meet a minimum count requirement that depends on the accumulated score of that side at the time, as follows:

Accumulated Score
(at beginning of the deal)

Minimum Count

Minus 15
0 to 1,495............................ 50

1,500 to 2,995	90
3,000 or more	120

The count of a meld is the total point value of the cards in it. To meet the minimum, a player may make two or more different melds. If he takes the discard pile, he may count the top card (but no other) toward the requirement. Bonuses for red threes and canastas do not count toward the minimum.

After a side has made its initial meld, either partner may make any valid meld without reference to any minimum count.

TAKING THE DISCARD PILE—The discard pile is *frozen* against a side before that side has made its initial meld. The initial meld unfreezes it for both partners, provided that it is not additionally frozen as below.

The discard pile is frozen against both sides when it contains a red three (turned as upcard) or a wild card (turned or discarded). Such a pile is unfrozen only by being taken. (The lowermost freezing card of the pile is turned sidewise to indicate the freeze.)

At a time when the discard pile is frozen (against his side or both), a player may take it only to meld its top card with a natural pair of the same rank from his hand. Before touching the discard pile, he should show his pair, together with such additional cards as may be necessary if he has to meet the minimum count for an initial meld.

At a time when the discard pile is not frozen against his side, a player may take it: (a) with a natural pair, as above; or (b) to meld its top card together with one matching natural card and one wild card from his hand; or (c) to add its top card to a previous meld of his side. [But see *Variations* on page 141.]

Having taken and melded the top discard legally, the player takes the rest of the pile into his hand, and may then meld all such additional cards as he pleases.

The discard pile may not be taken when its top card is a wild card or black three.

INFORMATION—A player may: (a) examine the discard pile before he has discarded in his first turn; (b) call attention to the correct minimum count requirement if his partner is in the act of making an initial meld; (c) remind his partner to declare red threes or draw replacements; (d) turn the sixth card of a meld crosswise to indicate that only one more card is needed to complete a canasta.

In his own turn to play, a player is entitled to be informed of: (a) the minimum count requirement or score (at the beginning of the hand) of either side; (b) the number of cards held by any player; (c) the number of cards remaining in the stock. If his hand is reduced to one card, he may announce the fact.

GOING OUT—A player goes out when he (legally) gets rid of the last card of his hand, by discard or meld. When any player goes out, play ends and the deal is scored. A player may go out only if his side has melded at least one canasta, or if he completes a canasta in going out. Failing this requirement, he must keep at least one card in his hand.

A player need not make a discard in going out; he may meld all his remaining cards.

A player having only one card in his hand may not take a discard pile comprising only one card.

PERMISSION TO GO OUT—If able to go out, before drawing, or after drawing from the stock, a player may say "Partner, may I go out?" His partner must answer "Yes" or "No" and the answer is binding. Before answering, the partner may obtain the information specified in the second paragraph under *Information*.

A player may not ask "Partner, may I go out?" after having melded any card or having indicated intention to take the discard pile. But a player may go out without asking permission.

CONCEALED HAND—A player goes out *concealed* when he melds his entire hand in one turn, including at least one canasta, without having made a previous meld and without previously having added any card to melds made by his partner. If his partner has not made an initial meld, he must meet the minimum count (without the canasta bonus) if he has taken the discard pile, but need not if he has drawn from the stock.

EXHAUSTING THE STOCK—If a player draws the last card of the stock, and it is a red three, he faces it, he may not meld or discard, and play ends.

If the last card of the stock is drawn, and is not a red three, play continues so long as each player in turn takes the discard. In this period, a player must take the discard if it matches a meld made by his side and the pack is not frozen (except that a one-card hand may not take a one-card discard pile); he need not take it to form a new meld. Play ends when the player in turn cannot take or legally refuses to discard.

SCORING A DEAL—The base score of a side for a deal is determined by totaling all applicable items in the following schedule:

For going out...............................	100
For going out concealed (extra)..........	100
For each red three (see *Red Threes*)......	100
For each natural canasta.................	500
For each mixed canasta..................	300

The point score of a side is the total point values of all cards melded, less the point values of the cards left in both hands.

The score of a side for a deal is the net of its base and point scores. (It may be minus).

SCORING A GAME—The score should be recorded on paper, with one column for each side. Each entry should show the scores of the previous deal, together with the accumulated totals (which determine initial meld requirement).

The side that first reaches a total of 5,000 wins a game. The final deal is played out, even though one or both sides have surely reached 5,000. There is no bonus for winning a game. The margin of victory is the difference of the final totals.

IRREGULARITIES—New Deal. There must be a new deal by the same dealer if he departs in any respect from the laws of correct procedure in dealing, or if he exposes a card other than the correct upcard, or if it is discovered during the deal that the cut was omitted. There must be a new deal if it is discovered, before every player has completed his first turn, that any hand was dealt an incorrect number of cards, that a card is faced in the stock, or that the deck contains a foreign card. (If the error is discovered too late for a new deal, a short hand continues short, a faced card is shuffled in the stock, or a foreign card is discarded from the deck and if it was in a hand the player draws a replacement.)

Drawing Too Many. If a player draws too many cards from the stock he must show the excess cards (if they were not placed in his hand) to all players and replace them on the stock. The next player to draw from the stock may, if he wishes, shuffle it before drawing. If excess cards drawn are placed in the hand, the player must forego drawing in enough successive turns to reduce his hand to the correct number, discarding one card in each turn. Until his hand is correct, he may not meld.

Exposed Card. If a player exposes a card from his hand except as a meld or discard, such card becomes a penalty card and must be left face up on the table. A penalty card counts as part of the hand, and may be duly melded. If not melded, it must be discarded at first opportunity. With two or more penalty cards, the owner may choose which to discard.

Insufficient Count. If a player puts down an insufficient count for an initial meld, he may correct the error by melding additional cards and may rearrange the cards melded. Or he may retract all the cards, in which case the minimum count requirement for his side (during the play of that deal only) is increased by 10 points.

Illegal Meld. Cards melded illegally, e.g., in an effort to go out when the side has no canasta or when partner has answered "No" to "Partner, may I go out?"; or excess wild cards in a meld, must be retracted. The side is penalized 100 points for the offense. The same penalty applies if a player, having put down insufficient count for an initial meld, makes it sufficient with additional cards but retracts one or more of those already exposed.

Failure to Declare a Red Three. If at the end of play a hand is found to contain an undeclared red three the side is penalized 500 points. (This does not apply if a player has had no turn, another before him having gone out on first turn, but the red three still counts 100 minus if his side has not melded.)

Condonement. If a player makes an illegal meld and the error is not called until the next hand has drawn or indicated intention to take the pack, the penalty for illegal meld or insufficient count does not apply. An initial meld of insufficient count stands as sufficient; an incorrect combination is retracted without penalty. But excess wild cards in a meld remain, and are debited against the side (at 50 each if there is question which was the fourth wild card added).

Taking Pack Illegally. A player attempting to take the discard pile without having established his right to do so should be stopped at once. There is no penalty if he can then show a valid claim. But if he has taken the pile into his hand before doing so, the opponents may face his whole hand and reconstruct the pile from it. The offender then picks up his hand and draws from the stock, and his side is penalized 100 points.

Irregularity in Asking. If a player asks "Partner, may I go out?" after melding any card or indicating intention to take the discard pile, he must if possible go out. If a player asks the question at a proper time, but melds any card before receiving an answer, he must if possible go out. If the player then cannot go out, or if he asks, receives the answer "Yes," and then cannot go out, his side is penalized 100 points.

CANASTA CUSTOMS—The discard pile is called "the pack" (by some players, "the deck") and taking it is called "taking the pack." A player who can find no safe discard is "squeezed."

The partner who melds first keeps the melds and red threes for his side.

Score is kept on a regular Bridge scorepad, with "We" and "They" columns.

When a game ends, each side reckons its total score to the nearest hundred, counting 50 or more points as 100. The winners then receive the difference between these net scores. Thus, if a side wins by 5,030 to 3,050, it wins the difference between 50 and 31, or 19 "points" net.

A complete canasta is shoved into a pile, with a red card on top if it is a natural canasta, a black card if it is a mixed canasta.

Two-Hand Canasta

The foregoing rules apply except as follows:

Each player receives 15 cards. A draw from the stock comprises two cards, but only one card is discarded in a turn. A player must have two canastas to go out. The penalties for exposed cards and insufficient meld do not apply.

Cutthroat (Three-Hand) Canasta

Three may play Canasta under the rules for four-hand, with the sole difference that each plays for himself. However, a speedier and more exciting game is produced by modifying the foregoing rules as follows:

PLAYERS—Three, each scoring for himself, but during the play forming sides of two against one.

THE DRAW—In drawing from the stock, a player takes two cards, but then discards only one card.

LONE HAND—The player who first takes the discard pile becomes the *lone hand*. The other two join in partnership against the lone hand, combining their melds and otherwise aiding each other. If a player goes out before the discard pile has ever been taken, he becomes lone hand and the other two score as a partnership.

INITIAL MELD—The initial meld requirement for a player depends on his own score. Hence it may happen that one partner has a higher requirement than the other.

SCORING—A red three counts only for the owner, plus or minus according to whether or not his side has made any meld. The base scores of the partners therefore differ if they have not drawn an equal number of red threes.

All other scores made by the partnership are totaled, and each partner receives the total, plus or minus his own red threes. Game is 7,500.

STOCK EXHAUSTED—If no one goes out, play ends with the discard of the player who drew the last card of the stock. If the discard pile was never taken, each player scores for himself.

Five-Hand Canasta

One side has three players, who take turns sitting out while the other two play the deal against the opponents. A regular four-hand game is played. The player sitting out may not give any advice to his teammates, and may not call attention to irregularities, except in scoring after the play is completed.

Six-Hand Canasta, or Three-Pack Canasta

The rules of four-hand Canasta apply, except as follows:

There may be two partnerships of three players each, seated A B A B A B (each player seated between two opponents), or there may be three partnerships of two players each, seated A B C A B C.

A triple pack is used—three 52-card packs plus six jokers, all shuffled together. Thirteen cards are dealt to each player. When there are three partnerships, game is 7,500. When there are two partnerships, game is 10,000, and when a side reaches 7,000 it needs 150 for its initial meld. Four red threes count only 100 each; five red threes, 1,000 in all; six red threes, 1,200. A side needs two canastas to go out. This game has been largely superseded by Samba and other later forms of Canasta (see following pages).

Variations of Canasta

In the years since Canasta first became popular, there have arisen some variations that have become more popular than the original game. Even in the original game, two variations are generally played: (1) A player may not take the top discard to add it to a completed canasta of his side, even if the pack is not frozen. (2) A player always needs a natural matching pair to take the pack for a meld, but may take an unfrozen pack to add the top card to a meld that is less than a canasta.

Other variations, the first of which was Samba but which later came to include Bolivia, Chilean, Cuban and Brazilian Canasta, and others, incorporate both of the variations stated above plus one or more of the following: (3) Three packs plus six jokers are used. (4) Sequences may be melded and a seven-card sequence ranks as a canasta. (5) Wild cards may be melded and a seven-card meld of wild cards ranks as a canasta. (6) In drawing from the stock a player may take two cards and discard only one. (7) A side needs two canastas to go out.

All the popular variations are described in the following paragraphs.

Samba

Four play in two partnerships, as in Canasta. Three may play. Regular Canasta (page 139) is better for two.

Use a 162-card pack (three full packs plus six jokers). Deal fifteen cards to each player. In drawing from the stock, take two cards and discard one. The discard pile may be taken only with a natural matching pair or, when it is not frozen, to add its top card to a meld (including a sequence meld) that is less than a canasta. It may not be taken to start a sequence meld or to combine with a card from the hand in adding to a sequence meld.

SEQUENCE MELD—Three or more cards of the same unit in sequence (ace high, fourspot low) may be melded. Cards may be added until there are seven cards, at which point the meld becomes a *samba*, or sequence canasta, ranking as a canasta but receiving a bonus of 1,500. A sequence meld may not contain a wild card.

WILD CARDS—Wild cards may not be melded separately and no meld may contain more than two wild cards.

CANASTAS—A side needs two canastas (mixed, natural, or sequence) to go out. A side may have two canastas in the same rank and may at any time combine its melds in the same rank.

SCORING—*Initial meld* requirements are: 15 with a minus score; 50 with 0 to 1,495; 90 with 1,500 to 2,995; 120 with 3,000 to 6,995; 150 over 7,000. *Game* is 10,000, and there is a 200-point bonus for *going out*. No bonus for *concealed hand*. *Red threes* are 100 each unless one side holds all six, in which case they count 1,000, plus or minus. They count minus for a side that has not completed two canastas.

Bolivia

This is the same game as Samba with the following exceptions:

WILD CARDS—Three or more wild cards may be melded. There is no distinction between deuces and jokers. A canasta of seven wild cards, called a *bolivia,* counts 2,500. When the discard pile is topped by a wild card it may not be taken.

GAME—Game is 15,000. The initial meld requirement stays at 150 from 7,000 points up.

GOING OUT—At least one of the two canastas must be a sequence canasta (in this game called an *escalera*).

BLACK THREES—A black three left in the hand when any other player (including partner) goes out counts 100 minus. Black threes melded in going out count 5 each.

Brazilian Canasta

This is the same as Bolivia but with some changes in the initial meld requirements and scoring as follows:

INITIAL MELD—Game is 10,000. From 7,000 to 7,995 the initial meld must be a canasta (mixed or better); from 8,000 to 8,995 it must be worth at least 200 points; from 9,000 to game it must be a natural canasta or better.

DISCARD PILE—May *not* be taken for the initial meld.

CANASTAS—A wild-card canasta counts 2,000. A melded sequence of less than five cards costs a side 1,000 points when the hand ends. In going out, one may add to the ends of a sequence canasta.

RED THREES—One to four count 100 each, five count 1,000, six count 1,200. They count plus if a side has melded *one* canasta, minus if it has not.

GOING OUT—A player must always ask permission of his

partner before going out. He may go out if his side has melded any two canastas.

Chile

This is Three-pack Canasta (162 cards, including six jokers), including either sequences or wild-card melds but not both, with only a one-card draw from the stock and only one canasta required to go out, and other rules as in Canasta.

Cuban Canasta

Use the regular (108-card) Canasta pack but deal thirteen cards to each player. Draw one card in each turn. The discard pile is always frozen (may be taken only by a natural matching pair) and canastas may not contain more than seven cards. Only one canasta is required to go out. Scoring differences are:

Game is 7,500. From 5,000 up, initial meld must be 150.

Red threes count 100 for one, 300 for two, 500 for three, 1,000 for all four. They count minus unless a side has at least one canasta.

Black threes may not be discarded on the first round. Any black threes in the pack when it is taken are discarded and out of play, counting 5 each for the side that took them. All four black threes, discarded or melded, count 100.

Wild cards may be melded and a canasta of wild cards counts: 4,000 for seven deuces; 3,000 for four jokers and three deuces; 2,000 for any other combination of seven wild cards. *Sequences may not be melded.* A discard pile topped by a wild card may not be taken.

Going out earns a 100-point bonus.

Italian Canasta

Italian Canasta follows the rules of Samba except as follows:

DISCARD PILE—After the deal and before a card is turned each player replaces his red threes. Then the top card is turned. A number of cards equal to its rank (counting jack 11, queen 12, king 13, ace or joker 20) are counted off the stock to begin the discard pile. They are turned face down, and the upcard is placed face up on them. The discard pile may be taken only by a natural pair from the hand (it is "always frozen").

WILD CARDS—Deuces may be melded as an independent

rank, with or without the aid of jokers as wild cards. A side that has melded deuces may not meld deuces as wild cards elsewhere until the canasta of deuces is completed.

INITIAL MELD—The initial meld must meet the required count without aid of any wild card. The requirements are:

Total Score	Minimum Count
0 to 1,495	50
1,500 to 2,995	90
3,000 to 4,995	120
5,000 to 7,495	160
7,500 to 9,995	180
10,000 or more	200

GOING OUT—A wild-card canasta does not count as one of the two canastas required to go out. The bonus for going out is 300.

RED THREES—When a side has no more than three red threes, they count 100 each; four or more, 200 each.

SCORING—Seven deuces count 3,000; a mixed canasta of deuces, 2,000; but these bonuses go only to the side that goes out; opponents having deuce melds score only the point value of the cards. Extra bonuses: for five pure canastas, 2,000; for five canastas including a mixed, 1,000; for ten canastas of any kind, 2,000.

Game is 12,000.

Uruguay

Uruguay follows the rules of Canasta except for the following:

WILD CARDS—Three or more wild cards, up to seven, are a valid meld. A canasta of wild cards counts 2,000.

TAKING THE PACK—The discard pile may be taken only by matching its top card with a natural pair from the hand. (Or, as is commonly said, "the pack is always frozen.")

Hollywood Canasta

Follow the rules of Samba, except:

Each meld must include at least three natural cards. One wild card may be used in a sequence canasta, and a mixed sequence canasta counts 1,000, a natural sequence canasta 1,500. A canasta of wild cards counts 2,000. No canasta may be extended beyond seven cards.

The discard pile may always be taken by a natural matching pair, except black threes. A deuce may be taken by a pair of deuces, a joker by a pair of jokers. When the pack is not frozen, the top card (unless it is a wild card) may be taken to lay off on a meld of less than seven cards.

Pennies from Heaven

Several variations of Canasta, including Mexicana (see below) are called by this name, but usually the game is for six players, in two partnerships of three players each, following the rules of Canasta with the following exceptions:

Use four packs plus eight jokers (216 cards). Deal thirteen cards to each player, then deal each player a packet of eleven cards, face down, which he may add to his hand when he has completed his first canasta. Draw two cards from the stock, discard one card per turn.

Sevens may not be discarded until each side has completed a canasta of sevens (natural or mixed). A seven may not be discarded in going out. No canasta may contain more than seven cards.

Red threes count 100 each; if all eight are held by one side they count 1,000. They count minus for a side that has not completed a canasta of sevens.

Wild cards may be melded (jokers and deuces together) but the discard pile may not be taken when topped by a wild card.

The initial meld must count: 15 when minus; 0-495, 50; 500-995, 90; 1,000-1,495, 120; 1,500 or more, 150. *To go out,* a side must have a canasta of sevens (1,500), one of wild cards (1,000), one natural (500) and one mixed (300). Game is 20,000.

Mexicana

The basic rules of Canasta are followed (sequences and wild cards may not be melded; only one card per turn is drawn from the stock), plus the following special rules:

A triple pack is used, with six jokers (162 cards). Each player is dealt thirteen cards. When a player makes the initial meld for his side, he draws the top thirteen cards of the stock and adds them to his hand.

A canasta of sevens (natural or mixed) counts 1,000. The discard pile may not be taken when it is topped by a seven.

To go out, a side must have two canastas, plus at least as many red threes as it has canastas.

Oklahoma or Arlington

Two, three or four may play, each for himself. A double pack (104 cards) is used, with or without a joker, which if used is wild. In any case, all deuces are wild. Ace ranks high or low.

PRELIMINARIES—The players draw, and low deals first (the joker, if used, is low). Thereafter the winner of the previous hand deals. Each player receives thirteen cards, dealt one at a time. The next card is turned up and placed beside the stock. Eldest hand, and then each player in turn after him, may become the first player by taking this card; if all refuse, eldest hand draws the top of the stock and play proceeds as in Rummy.

THE PLAY—When a deuce (or the joker) is melded, the player must name the card it represents. There is no trading for deuces, but the player who laid down the joker may reclaim it by substituting the card it represents. No other player may do this. A player may lay off only on his own groups and sequences, and may not add to any group that already contains four of a kind.

To take the top card of the discard pile, a player must take the entire discard pile and must immediately use the top card in a meld, or lay it off on one of his previous melds. (He may also take it to trade for the joker in a meld of his own.)

The hand ends when a player in turn melds his last card but one and discards his last card. *A player may not discard ♠Q if there is any other card he can discard, or unless it puts him out.*

SCORING—Each player is credited with the point value of each card he has melded, and is charged with the point value of each card left in his hand, as follows:

Card	If melded	If left in hand
Each ace	+20	−20
Each K, Q, J, 10, 9, or 8	+10	−10
—except ♠Q	+50	−100
Each 7, 6, 5, 4, or 3	+5	−5
Joker	+100	−200
Each deuce	Value of Card represented	−20

(A deuce representing ♠Q counts only +10)

The player who goes out receives a bonus of 100 points.

A player's net score for the deal is added to (or subtracted from) his score. The game ends when, at the end of any hand, a player has 1,000 points. If two or more players reach 1,000 on the same hand, the highest score wins the game. The winner receives a bonus of 200. Each player's score is then figured to the nearest 100 and each settles separately with each other.

BLOCKED GAME—If a player who draws the last card of the stock discards without going out, the hand ends and is scored, no one receiving the bonus of 100 for going out.

GOING OUT ALL AT ONCE—If a player who has not previously melded goes out in one turn (except the first), 250 is added to his score but does not count toward reaching the game of 1,000.

500 RUM

From this popular form of Rummy have been developed the new game of Canasta and several other variants. The distinctive feature of 500 Rum is that each player scores the value of the sets he melds, in addition to the usual points for going out and for cards caught in other players' hands. Other names for 500 Rum are Pinochle Rummy and Michigan Rum.

NUMBER OF PAYERS—Two to eight. Best for three, four or five. Four may play as partners (see Persian Rummy, on next page).

THE PACK—52 cards. Five or more should use a double pack.

RANK OF CARDS—Ace (high or low), K, Q, J, 10, 9, 8, 7, 6, 5, 4, 3, 2, A (high or low).

VALUES OF CARDS—Ace, 15, except in the sequence 3-2-A, when ace counts as 1; face cards, 10 each; other cards, pip value.

THE SHUFFLE AND CUT—Draw for deal, low dealing first; ace is low in the draw. Dealer shuffles and the player at his right cuts.

THE DEAL—Seven cards to each player except in the two-hand game, in which each player receives thirteen cards.

OBJECT OF PLAY—To score points by laying down and laying off cards as in regular Rummy (in groups of three or four of a kind, and in sequences of three or more cards of the same suit).

THE PLAY—The undealt portion of the cards, face down, is the stock; its top card is placed beside it to start the discard pile. Each player in turn, beginning with eldest hand, may draw the top card of the stock; or may draw any card from the discard pile provided he takes with it all cards on the discard pile above it, and also provided that he at once uses the card so drawn, either by laying it down in a set or by laying it off on a set already on the table. Cards taken with the top discard may be melded in the same turn.

Each player in turn, after drawing and before discarding, may lay down any matched set on the table in front of him, or may lay off any card which matches a set already on the table; but such cards laid off are also kept on the table in front of the player.

Sequences may not "go around the corner"—A, K, Q or A, 2, 3 may be melded, but not K, A, 2.

SCORING—When any player gets rid of all his cards, play immediately ends. Each player's score is then figured as follows: He is credited with the point value of all cards he has shown on the table; from this figure is subtracted the point value of all cards remaining in his hand. The difference is added to or subtracted from his score, as the case may be. *Example.* The cards he has shown total 87 points, and the cards left in his hand total 90 points; 3 points are subtracted from his previous net score.

The first player whose score reaches +500 wins the game and collects from each other player the difference between their final scores. If two or more players reach 500 on the same hand, the one with the highest score is the winner.

When a player lays off a card, he keeps it on the table in front of him for convenience in scoring later, but must state to which showing combination it is added; thus, if ◇ 9, 10, J are on the table, and also ♤ Q, ♡ Q, ♧ Q, a player putting down the ◇ Q in front of him must state which set it becomes part of: if he makes it part of the diamond sequence, any player may later add ◇ K to that sequence.

IRREGULARITIES—See page 128.

Partnership 500 Rum

Four play, two against two as partners, partners facing each other across the table. The rules are exactly as in 500 Rum, except that partners try to help each other to form matched sets and to go out. When any player goes out, play ends and the score of each partnership is figured as a unit. The game is over when either side reaches 500.

Persian Rummy

The same game as Partnership 500 Rum, with the following exceptions:

The Pack: 56 cards, including the standard 52 cards plus

four jokers. Such a pack may be constructed by taking two standard packs which are identical in back design and color; use the jokers and extra cards from both packs; the remaining 52 cards form a standard pack which may be used in other games in which no joker is required.

Values of cards and of matched sets. Each joker counts 20. Jokers may not be used in sequences, but only in groups of three or four jokers. Any group of four of a kind, laid down all at once, counts double its face value; thus, four jokers laid down at once count 160; three jokers laid down count 60, and the fourth joker when added counts only 20 more; four sixes put down at once count 48, but three sixes count only 18 and the fourth six adds only 6. If a player gets rid of all his cards, his side scores a bonus of 25.

Game. A game ends after two deals. The side with the best score for the two deals receives a bonus of 50 points and wins the difference between its final score and its opponents'.

Queen City Rum

The rules are as in regular Rummy (page 126), with seven cards dealt to each player, with the following special rules:

A player may not meld until he can go rummy. When he goes out he may meld seven or eight cards; he need not discard.

The winner collects the point value of *his own* hand from each other player (not the value of this opponents' hands, and not double).

Gin Rummy

This has become the most popular two-handed variant of the Rummy family. It is the favorite among all games with the motion picture, radio and theatrical world.

NUMBER OF PLAYERS—Two. Three may participate in the same game, usually with one sitting out while the other two play. Four or more, in pairs up to almost any number, may play in a partnership game (see the rules on page 155), but this is done by playing separate two-hand games and combining scores.

THE PACK—52 cards. Two packs should be used, so that while one player deals the other shuffles for the next deal.

RANK OF CARDS—K (high), Q, J, 10, 9, 8, 7, 6, 5, 4, 3, 2, A.

VALUE OF CARDS—Face cards, 10 each; ace, 1; other cards their pip value.

THE SHUFFLE AND CUT—One pack is shuffled and spread, and each player draws a card; if he draws one of the four cards at either end, he must draw again. If the cards drawn are otherwise of the same rank the suits rank: spades (high), hearts, diamonds, clubs. The player drawing the high card has choice of cards and seats, and whether or not he will deal first. Either player may shuffle, the dealer having the right to shuffle last. Non-dealer must cut the pack.

THE DEAL—Dealer gives the cards, one at a time, face down, alternately to his opponent and to himself until each has ten cards; the next card, called the *upcard*, is placed face up in the center of the table, and the remaining cards, called the *stock*, are placed face down beside it.

OBJECT OF PLAY—To form *matched sets*, consisting of three or four of a kind, or of sequences of three or more cards of consecutive rank in the same suit.

THE PLAY—Non-dealer plays first, and the turn to play alternates thereafter. In each turn, a player must draw either the upcard (top card of the discard pile) or the top card of the stock, and then must discard one card (which may not be an upcard he has drawn in the same turn) face up on the discard pile.

On the first play, if non-dealer does not wish to take the upcard he must so announce and dealer may have the first turn by drawing the upcard; if dealer does not wish the upcard, non-dealer draws the top card of the stock and play proceeds.

KNOCKING—Each *hand* begins when a legal deal is completed and ends when either player *knocks*.

A player may knock in any turn, after drawing and before discarding, if the value of the unmatched cards in his hand (after he discards) will be 10 points or less. He need not knock when able to do so. Having knocked, he discards one card face down and spreads his hand, arranged into matched sets and unmatched cards. The opponent then spreads his hand, removes from it any unmatched sets, and *lays off* whatever cards he has that match the knocker's matched sets.

The point values of the two players' unmatched cards are then compared, and the result of the hand is scored (see Scoring, below).

Neither of the last two cards in the stock may be drawn;

if the player who draws the fiftieth card discards without knocking, his opponent may not take the discard and the hand is a draw. The same dealer deals again.

SCORING—If the knocker's count is less than his opponent's, the knocker wins the hand; the difference in counts is scored to his credit.

If the opponent ties or beats the knocker, he has *undercut* him; he wins the hand, and scores 25 points plus the difference in counts, if any.

However, if the knocker has a count of zero (has all ten of his cards matched in sets) he is *gin;* his opponent may not lay off, and the knocker wins the hand even if the opponent can reduce his own count to zero, and the knocker receives 25 points plus the difference in counts, if any.

A running total of each player's score is kept, with a line drawn under his score every time he wins a hand. *Example.* A player wins the first hand by 11 points; he scores 11 and draws a line under it. The same player wins the next hand by 14 points; he writes down 25 and draws another line.

The winner of each hand deals next.

GAME—The player first scoring 100 points or more wins the game. He adds to his score 100 points game bonus. If his opponent has not won a hand during that game, he doubles his entire score, including the game bonus. Each player then adds to his score 25 points for every hand he has won (called a *line* or *box* bonus). The two players' total scores are then determined and the player with the higher score wins the difference between his score and his opponent's.

The winner of each game has choice of cards and seats for the next game, and deals the first hand of the next game.

VARIANT SCORING—Some players score only 10 points for undercut, and only 20 points for gin bonus or box bonus, and permit a player to lay off when his opponent goes gin.

IRREGULARITIES—(Condensed, by permission, from the Laws of Gin Rummy by Walter L. Richard, C. E. Van Vleck and Lee Hazen.)

New Deal. A deal out of turn may be stopped at any time before the upcard is dealt; thereafter it stands as a correct deal.

There must be a new deal by the same dealer if it is found, before the completion of the deal, that the pack is imperfect or that a card is faced in the pack; or if a card is exposed in dealing, or if a player has looked at the face of a card.

Other occasions for a new deal are covered in laws governing other irregularities.

Irregular hands. If either player's hand is discovered to have an incorrect number of cards before that player has made his first draw, there must be a new deal.

After the first draw, if it is discovered that both players have incorrect hands, there must be a new deal. If one player's hand is incorrect and the other player's hand is correct, the player with the correct hand may decide either to have a new deal or to continue play. If play continues, the player with the incorrect hand must correct his hand by drawing without discarding, or by discarding without drawing, and may not knock until his next turn to play.

After a knock, a player with too few cards is charged 10 points for each card missing, and may not claim the undercut bonus; if the knocker's opponent has more than ten cards, the hand may not be corrected, the offender may not claim an undercut bonus, and can lose or tie but may not win the hand.

If the player who knocks has an incorrect number of cards, the penalty for an illegal knock applies.

Imperfect pack. When two packs are being used, a card from the other pack found in the stock is eliminated and play continues. If it is discovered, after the knock, that the pack is incomplete, the deal stands. Discovery that the pack is imperfect in any way has no bearing on any score that has been entered on the score sheet.

Premature play. If non-dealer draws from the stock before dealer has refused the upcard, the draw stands without penalty as his first play. If a player draws from the stock before his opponent has discarded, the draw stands as his proper play.

Illegally seeing a card. If a player drawing in turn sees any card to which he is not entitled, every such card must be placed face up next to the discard pile. The offender may not knock until his next turn to play, unless he is gin. The non-offender has the sole right to take any of the exposed cards until first thereafter he draws from the stock; then the offender has the same right until first thereafter he draws from the stock; when each player has drawn from the stock, the exposed cards are placed in the discard pile.

If a player drawing out of turn sees a card to which he is not entitled, the rule given in the preceding paragraph applies, except that the offender may never take such cards, but may draw only his opponent's discard or the top card of the stock in each turn.

Exposed card. A card found exposed in the stock, or in the other pack or away from the table, is shuffled into the stock and play continues. Accidental exposure of a card in a player's hand is not subject to penalty. An exposed card becomes a discard when the holder indicates intent to discard it; when his opponent has seen and can name such a card, the holder may not thereafter knock in that turn.

Illegal knock. If a player knocks with a count higher than 10, but his opponent has not exposed any cards before the error is discovered, the offender must leave his hand face up on the table until his opponent has completed his next play. However, if the knocker's hand is illegal only with respect to the count of his unmatched cards, his opponent may accept the illegal knock as legal.

If the knocker has more than 10 points, and the error is discovered after the opponent has exposed any of his own cards but before he has laid off any cards, the opponent may choose which of the following penalties to apply: To make the knocker play the rest of the hand with all his cards exposed; or to permit the offender to pick up his hand, in which event the offender may not score for any undercut or gin bonus in that hand.

If the knocker has an incorrect number of cards, his opponent may demand a new deal; or may require the offender to play with his hand exposed and to correct his hand on his next play or plays, either by drawing without discarding or by discarding without drawing.

If a player, after knocking, inadvertently discards a card which makes his knock illegal, he may replace that discard with a discard which makes his knock legal.

Looking back at discards. Players may agree in advance that looking back at discards will be permitted. In the absence of such agreement, a player who looks back at a covered discard loses his right to his next draw.

Picking up wrong discards. If a player inadvertently picks up the wrong discard, he may correct or he may be made to correct the error, if attention is called to it prior to his opponent's next discard.

Hollywood Gin or Simultaneous Play

Two play, but each hand is scored as though they were playing three different games. The result of the first hand won by each player is scored once, being credited toward Game 1. The result of the second hand won by a player who has already scored in Game 1 is scored twice, being credited to him as a second score in Game 1 and as his first score in Game 2. The result of the third hand won by a player who has already scored in Games 1 and 2 is scored to his credit in all three games. Each subsequent hand won by that player is scored to his credit in all three games.

When a player reaches 100 points in any game, he wins that game but play continues until all three games have been decided and subsequent scores are entered only in the remaining game or games.

Each game is scored independently and each player receives all bonuses to which he is entitled in that game. A player who was shut out in one game enters his first score in the first game still uncompleted.

Oklahoma Gin

In Oklahoma Gin the rank of the upcard fixes the maximum number of points with which a player may knock in that deal. Thus, if the upcard is a five, the knocker must have 5 points or less. Face cards count 10. Some play that an ace calls for a gin hand, not merely a count of 1. A usual added rule is that when the upcard is a spade all scores accruing from that deal are doubled.

Gin Rummy for Three Players

There are two methods for playing Gin Rummy with two players active and one inactive in each hand; and there is one method by which all three players may be active in every hand.

FIRST METHOD—Each player cuts; lowest stays out the first hand, next lowest deals. At the end of each hand the loser goes out and the idle player takes his place. Each plays for himself, hands he wins being credited to his individual score, and the idle player may not advise either of the active players except to give information as to the laws in case of an irregularity. Game ends when a player reaches 100 or more, and after game and box bonuses have been added, each player pays the difference in scores to each player having a higher score. If one player is shut out, he pays an additional 100 to the winner of the game only.

SECOND METHOD—Each player draws a card; high man is "in the box" and the two others are partners against him throughout the game. The partner drawing the second-highest card deals the first hand and the other partner sits out, but may consult on the play, the active partner having the final decision. When the active partner loses a hand, the idle partner takes his place. One score is kept for the man in the box, another score for the partnership; if the man in the box wins he collects in full from each opponent, and if the partnership wins each collects in full from the man in the box.

THIRD METHOD—Each player draws a card; high deals, next-highest is at his left. Ten cards are dealt to each of the three players. Eldest hand plays first; if he refuses the upcard, the player at his left may take it. Thereafter, each player in turn may draw either of his opponents' previous discards, unless one of them has already been taken.

An individual score is kept for each player. The winner of each hand scores the difference between his count and the combined counts of the other two players.

There is no undercut bonus; if the knocker is tied, the player who ties him wins the hand and 20 points are deducted from the knocker's score.

The other two players may lay off only on the knocker's hand, and only on the original matched sets (*Example:* If knocker has ♡ 9, 8, 7, and one opponent lays off ♡ 6 on it, the other opponent may not lay off ♡ 5.) The bonus for going gin is 40. When only three undrawn cards remain in the stock, and no one has knocked, the hand ends in a draw.

Game does not end until a player reaches 200, after which bonuses are added as in two-handed Gin Rummy (page 151) and each player pays the difference in scores to any player having a higher score.

Partnership Gin Rummy

FOR FOUR PLAYERS—Draw for partnerships, as in Contract Bridge (page 20). Partners sit facing each other at the table. One member of each side cuts for deal; both members of the side cutting the low card deal the first hand; thereafter the winners of each hand deal the next.

Each dealer deals to the opponent on his right for the first hand; thereafter players alternate opponents.

Only one score is kept for each side, so that if one member of a partnership wins his hand by 12 points and the other member loses his by 10 points, that side wins the hand by 2 points and will eventually receive the box bonus.

When there has been a knock in the play of one hand,

either player in the other hand may delay play until he learns the result. When one hand is finished, the idle player may advise his partner (after his partner's opponent has knocked) as to the best way of matching his hand, or laying off, and as to any irregularity and the laws governing it. If a partner gives any information other than this, his partner's opponent may claim a new deal if he does so before his next draw or discard.

Drawn hands are not replayed. Game does not end until one side reaches 125 points, but all other scoring is the same as in two-handed play (page 151).

FOR SIX OR MORE PLAYERS IN EVEN NUMBERS—Half the total number of players form one partnership against the other half. All partners sit on one side of the table, and each plays against the opponent facing him, never changing opponents during the game. One partner draws for deal on each side, and all members of the side drawing the lower card deal the first hand. Thereafter, all members of the winning side deal the next hand.

Each player plays a regular two-handed game against the player facing him. The results of all these two-hand matches are amalgamated to determine the winning side of each deal.

Game does not end until one side reaches 150 points, if there are three or four players on each side; 175 points if there are five players; 200 points if there are six players.

A player whose hand is finished may advise any of his teammates, but only if he has not seen the hand of any opponent.

Drawn hands are not replayed.

Round-the-Corner Gin Rummy

This form of Gin Rummy may be played in any variant of that game, with the following differences in procedure:

Ace may rank high or low in a sequence and sequences may go around the corner (A-2-3, A-K-Q, K-A-2, etc.). As an unmatched card, an ace counts 15 points.

If the knocker goes gin but his opponent can reduce his own count to zero, neither player scores on that hand.

Game ends when one player reaches 125 points. In any partnership game, it takes 25 points more to end the game than when regular Partnership Gin Rummy is played (see above).

Players may at all times inspect the previous discards.

Knock Rummy, or Poker Rum

NUMBER OF PLAYERS—Two to five.

THE PACK—52 cards.

THE SHUFFLE, CUT AND DEAL—Follow the laws of Rummy (page 126). When two play, each receives ten cards; when three or four play, seven cards; when five play, six cards.

RANK OF CARDS—K (high), Q, J, 10, 9, 8, 7, 6, 5, 4, 3, 2, A.

VALUES OF CARDS—Each face card counts 10 points, each ace 1 point, other cards their pip value.

THE PLAY—Drawing and discarding proceed as in Rummy, but there is no laying down or laying off. Any player, after drawing but before discarding, may knock, ending the hand. He then discards, separates his matched sets from his unmatched cards, and announces the count of his unmatched cards. Each other player then separates his matched sets from his unmatched cards and announces his count.

SCORING—The hand with the low count wins the difference in counts from each other player plus 25 points if he goes rum. If any other player ties the knocker for low count, he wins instead of the knocker. If the knocker does not have the low count, he pays a penalty of 10 points plus the difference in counts to the player with the low count, who wins the hand.

Tunk, or Tonk

This is a form of Knock Rummy ("tunk" means "knock"). It is played in several different variations.

Two to four players use a single pack, five or more use a double pack. Deuces are wild. A group may have no more than four cards and must include two natural cards. A sequence may be three cards or more.

Seven cards are dealt to each player and an upcard is turned. Each player in turn draws from the stock, or the top discard, and then discards. Only the player at the dealer's left, whose turn comes first, may take the first upcard.

Before discarding, the player may tunk if his unmatched cards count 5 or less. He spreads his hand, separating matched and unmatched cards. Each other player then has one turn to draw, meld, lay off on the tunker's melds, and discard. (If all the tunker's cards were matched, no one may lay off on his hand.)

After each player has had his turn, the count of each player's unmatched cards is scored against him. (A deuce counts only 2 points.) If the tunker does not have the lowest count, he is charged double his count. When a player's score reaches 100 he is out of the game and play continues until there is only one player left, the winner.

At the break—when there are not enough cards left in the stock to give each player a draw after a tunk—the hand is re-dealt and there is no score. (*Variation:* After the break a player may tunk if all his cards are matched. Play ends; there are no further draws, and no laying off, and the deal is scored.)

Contract Rummy

(ALSO CALLED LIVERPOOL RUMMY, JOKER RUMMY, PROGRESSIVE RUMMY, COMBINATION RUMMY, SHANG-HAI RUMMY, KING RUMMY, OR ZIONCHECK)

This is one of the most popular Rummy games for three or more players. There are many forms of the game, differing in minor details but alike in one essential respect: A series of four, five or more deals is played, there being a different requirement for going out in each deal. One of the most popular variants is given here.

NUMBER OF PLAYERS—Three to eight. Each plays for himself.

THE PACK—For three or four players, a double pack with one joker (105 cards in all). For five or more players, a triple pack with two jokers (158 cards in all). All the cards are shuffled together, and should be, but need not be, identical in back design and color.

RANK OF CARDS—A (high or low), K, Q, J, 10, 9, 8, 7, 6, 5, 4, 3, 2, A (high or low). (*Variant.* Some play that the ace may be high only.)

VALUES OF CARDS—Ace, joker and other wild cards, if any, 15; each face card, 10; each other card, its pip value.

THE DRAW, SHUFFLE AND CUT—Draw for deal from a spread pack; low deals first, ace being low. If a double pack is used, dealer shuffles; if a triple pack is used, dealer and one other player each shuffle a portion of the pack, dealer having the right to shuffle each portion last, and the portions are then combined. The player at dealer's right cuts. When the pack is too thick for dealer to handle, he may take the top portion of it and deal as far as it will go, and then resume dealing with the remaining portion.

THE DEAL—Each game consists of seven deals, the turn to

deal passing from player to player to the left. Cards are dealt face down, one at a time in clockwise rotation beginning at the dealer's left. In each of the first four deals, each player receives ten cards; in each of the last three deals, each player receives twelve cards. The remainder of the pack is put in the center as the *stock,* with the top card placed face up to found the *discard pile.*

OBJECT OF PLAY—To get rid of all one's cards, by laying down groups of three or more of a kind (regardless of suit) and sequences of four or more cards of the same suit, in accordance with the rules of the deal, as follows:

First deal. The basic contract is two groups, which a player in turn must lay down at the same time before he can lay off any other cards.

Second deal. Basic contract, one group and one sequence.

Third deal. Basic contract, two sequences.

Fourth deal. Basic contract, three groups.

Fifth deal. Basic contract, two groups and one sequence.

Sixth deal. Basic contract, one group and two sequences.

Seventh deal. The basic contract is three sequences, but no cards may be laid down until some player can lay down his entire hand, matched in sets, to form the basic contract. This ends the game.

It should be noted that the basic contract in the first deal requires six cards, in the second deal seven cards, and so forth, increasing by one card each time.

When two or more sequences are required, they must be in different suits (or, if in the same suit, not in consecutive order, as ♡ 2, 3, 4, 5, 7, 8, 9, 10; but not ♡ 2, 3, 4, 5, 6, 7, 8, 9, which counts as only one sequence.)

THE PLAY—Each player in turn, beginning with eldest hand, must draw either the top of the discard pile or the top card of the stock, and must then discard; between drawing and discarding, *provided he has laid down the basic contract,* he may lay off any cards which match a set already on the table, but may not lay down any more matched sets.

If the player in turn does not want the top of the discard pile, any other player, in order of rotation to his left, may claim that card and must also draw the top card of the stock, as a penalty card, without discarding; the player in turn then draws the top card of the stock and play proceeds.

When ace counts as either high or low, an ace may be laid off as low card on a sequence which already includes the ace as high card, and vice versa.

WILD CARDS—Each joker may be used to stand for any card named by its holder in forming a group or a sequence. When a joker has been laid down as part of a sequence, any other player (provided he too has laid down the basic contract) may take the joker into his hand by trading for it the card it represents. If more than one player is able to do this, the one next in turn to play has precedence.

(*Variant.* Many players designate other cards to be wild; as, deuces wild, or nines wild. A player may not trade for such additional wild cards as he may for a joker.)

When a wild card has been used in a sequence, any card not already represented in that sequence may be laid off on it, and the wild card moves to either end (for example, if ◇ 9, ♣ 2, ◇ 7, ◇ 6 are shown, deuces being wild, the ◇ 8 may be added and the ♣ 2 moved to either end); except that no sequence may contain more than fourteen cards.

SCORING—In each deal, play ceases when any player gets rid of his last card, and every other player is charged the pip value of each card remaining in his hand. The player having the lowest score at the end of the seventh deal is the winner.

IRREGULARITIES—Irregularities are covered by the rules of Rummy (page 128).

Continental Rummy

Played in many different forms, but always with the same basic requirements, Continental Rummy is one of the most popular Rummy games for large groups.

NUMBER OF PLAYERS—2 to 12.

THE PACK—Two or more 53-card packs (the standard 52-card plus one joker) are shuffled together; five or fewer players use a double pack, six to eight players a triple pack, nine to twelve players a quadruple pack.

RANK OF CARDS—A (high or low) K, Q, J, 10, 9, 8, 7, 6, 5, 4, 3, 2, A (high or low).

THE SHUFFLE, CUT AND DEAL—Same as in Rummy (page 126), except that each player receives 15 cards, dealt as many as three at a time. The winner of each deal becomes the next dealer.

OBJECT OF PLAY—To go out by forming sequences (groups do not count) in accordance with the following requirements:

A player may not lay down any cards until he can go out all at once with five 3-card sequences; or three 4-card and one 3-card sequence; or one 5-card, one 4-card and two 3-card sequences. Two or more of these sequences may be in the same suit, but a sequence may not "go around the corner."

The Play—Each player in turn draws either the top card of the stock, or the top card of the discard pile, and then discards, as in Rummy, until some player goes out. Any joker is wild (may represent any card its holder designates). Many play with deuces also as wild cards.

Scoring—The winner of the game collects from each other player: one point (or chip, or similar counter) for game; plus two points for each joker used in the winner's hand; plus one point for each deuce (if deuces are wild) used as a wild card.

Variants—There are many, both in play and in scoring, including the following bonus payments which are used in some localities: For going out without drawing a card, 10 points; for going out after drawing only one card, 7 points; for going out without using any joker (or deuce, when deuces are wild), 10 points; for having all fifteen cards of the same suit, 10 points.

Irregularities—The rules of Rummy apply (page 128).

Going down illegally. If a player lays down a hand which does not conform to the requirements stated above, he must leave his hand face up on the table and play proceeds with his hand exposed. Any collections he has made are returned. Any other player who has exposed his hand may pick it up.

PANGUINGUE, OR PAN

NUMBER OF PLAYERS—Any number up to about fifteen. Best for six, seven, or eight.

THE PACK—Eight packs, each stripped to 40 cards by throwing out the eights, nines and tens. (In some localities, as few as five packs are used.) Chips are used for settlement.

RANK OF CARDS—The cards in each suit rank: K (high), Q, J, 7, 6, 5, 4, 3, 2, A. The jack and seven are in sequence.

THE DRAW—A portion of the pack is shuffled and spread face down. Each player draws a card. Lowest card deals the first hand. Other players may take places at random. If two or more players tie for low, they draw again.

ROTATION—The rotation of dealing and playing is to the *right*, not to the left as in most games. Eldest hand is therefore the player at dealer's right. The winner of each hand becomes eldest hand for the next, and the player at his left deals.

THE SHUFFLE—The player at dealer's left shuffles. Before the first deal, the eight packs are shuffled together. After each hand, the discards are shuffled with a packet from the foot (bottom of the stock), to which they are then restored.

THE DEAL—The dealer gives each player ten cards, in two rounds of five at a time, beginning with eldest hand. For the deal, he should take from the top of the pack only such cards as he needs, as nearly as he can estimate, taking more if needed or returning any excess to the top of the pack. After all hands are complete, the rest of the pack is placed face down on the table to form the *stock*. The stock is usually cut in two portions; the *head* is used in play, and the *foot* is set aside to be used if the head is exhausted. The top card of the stock is turned face up and set beside it to start the *discard pile*.

GOING ON TOP—Before play begins, each player beginning with eldest hand declares whether he will stay in the play or retire. In the latter course, he pays a forfeit, usually two chips. He is said to *go on top* for the reason that the forfeits are by custom stacked on the foot of the pack. Hands discarded by retiring players are not returned to the stock, but are held separate, so that they may not be drawn in play. The "tops" (chips thus deposited) go to the player who goes out.

THE PLAY—Each player in turn to the right must take the top card of the discard pile or draw the top card of the stock. He may take from the discard pile only if the card (1) was drawn from the stock by the preceding player, and (2) can be immediately melded by the taker. When a player draws from the stock, he must immediately meld the card or discard it (he may not put it in his hand and discard another, unless the drawn card matches a meld of his right-hand opponent who has already melded ten cards—see page 164). To complete his turn, a player discards one card face up on the pile.

After drawing and before discarding, a player may meld as many sets as he holds, or add to his existing melds.

The object of play is to meld eleven cards, and the first player to do so wins the game.

MELDS—Each meld (or *spread*) must comprise at least three cards; it may comprise as many as eleven. The melds may be classified for convenience as *sequences* and *sets*. (Sequences are colloquially called *stringers* or *ropes*.)

Sequence. Any three cards in sequence of the same suit, as ♡ Q J 7.

Set. Three cards of the same rank and of different suits, as ♤ 4, ♡ 4, ♧ 4; or of the same suit, as ♧ Q Q Q. In addition, any three aces or any three kings form a valid set regardless of suit, as ◇ A, ◇ A, ♧ A. (Aces and kings are called *non-comoquers*.)

CONDITIONS—Certain melds are called *conditions*. On melding a condition, the player immediately collects chips from every other player. All threes, fives and sevens are *valle* (pronounced "valley") *cards*, that is, "cards of value." Cards of other rank are *non-valle*. The conditions are:

1. Any *set* of valle cards, not in the same suit. 1 chip.

2. Any *set* of valle cards, in the same suit. 4 chips in spades, 2 chips in any other suit.

3. Any *set* of non-valle cards, in the same suit. 2 chips in spades, 1 chip in any other suit.

4. Any *sequence* of 3, 2, A, in the same suit. 2 chips in spades, 1 chip in any other suit.

5. Any *sequence* of K, Q, J, in the same suit. 2 chips in spades, 1 chip in any other suit.

INCREASING—A player may add one or more cards to any of his melds, provided that the character of the meld is preserved. To a set of different suits may be added *any* card of the same rank; to a set of the same suit, another of the same rank and suit. When cards are so added to a condition, the player collects the value of the original condition for each additional card, except that for addition to a set of three valle cards in the same suit the payment is only 2 chips in spades, 1 chip in any other suit.

By addition of cards, one meld may be split into two, provided that each comprises a valid meld in itself. *For example:* ◇ J 7 6 5 may be made into two melds by the addition of ◇ Q, 4. If splitting a meld creates a condition, it is duly collected. A player may take a card from one of his melds to complete a new meld, provided he leaves a valid meld. *Example:* From ♣ 7 6 5 4 either the 7 or 4 may be borrowed, but not 6 or 5.

FORCING CARDS—If the top of the discard pile can be added to a meld of the player to whom it is available, he is forced to take it and meld it, upon demand of any other player.

GOING OUT—When any player shows eleven cards in melds, he collects 1 chip from every other player and also collects all over again for each condition in his cards. (Some play that a hand which has made no meld when another wins must pay 2 chips.)

When a player has no card left in his hand, having melded ten cards and needing only to pick up one card and meld it, to bring his meld up to eleven cards, the player at his left may not discard a card that can be added to any of his melds, thereby putting him out—unless the player at the left holds no safe card.

IRREGULARITIES—*Wrong number of cards.* If a player finds that he has more or less than ten cards, before he has made his first draw, dealer must withdraw the excess cards and put them with the discarded hands of retired players, or must serve the short hand with additional cards from the center of the pack. If, after a player's first draw, his hand is found to be incorrect, he must discard his hand and retire from that deal, and must return all collections he has made for conditions, but must continue to make due payments to others for conditions and winning.

Foul meld. If a player lays down any spread not conforming to the rules, he must make it valid on demand. If he cannot do so, he must return any collections made in consequence of the improper spread and legally proceed with his turn. If he has already discarded, he must return all collections he has made on that hand, discard his hand, and retire from the play until the next deal, but must continue to make due payments to others for conditions and winning. However, if he has made the meld valid before attention is called to it, there is no penalty.

Conquian, or Coon-Can

This was the original type of Rummy played in the United States. It is a two-hand game. The name Coon-Can was applied also to the first two-pack Rummy game (see page 130).

The pack has 40 cards (a regular pack stripped of all tens, nines, and eights). Jack and seven are in sequence. Ace counts only low in a sequence—A-2-3, not A-K-Q.

Each of the two players is dealt ten cards. The remaining cards form the stock; no upcard is turned.

Melds ("spreads") are as in regular Rummy—three or four of a kind, or a sequence of three or more cards of the same suit.

Non-dealer turns up the top card of the stock. He does not put it in his hand but must immediately meld it with cards from his hand, or discard it. Each player in turn thereafter must either take the top discard and meld it, or turn up the top card of the stock and meld or discard it. When he takes and melds a discard, he must then discard from his hand. If a player can add the discard to one of his previous melds, his opponent may force him to take it and do so, then discard.

After turning up the top card of the stock and before discarding it, a player may meld or lay off from his hand if he wishes.

A player may shift his own melds around as long as only valid melds remain. If he has melded ♡ J 7 6 and ♡ 5 is drawn or discarded, he may add it to the sequence, remove the jack, and meld three jacks.

The game ends when a player has melded exactly eleven cards. Therefore a player may have no card left in his hand but continue to play because he needs another melded card to go out. Each deal is a separate game, and if the stock is exhausted before either player has melded eleven cards the next game counts double.

HEARTS (BLACK LADY)

Hearts is one of the foremost of games in giving opportunity for skill in the play of the cards.

NUMBER OF PLAYERS—Three to seven; best for four. Each plays for himself. Two players may play Domino Hearts. More than seven should play Cancellation Hearts.

THE PACK—52 cards.

RANK OF CARDS—A (high), K, Q, J, 10, 9, 8, 7, 6, 5, 4, 3, 2.

THE DRAW—Draw or cut; low deals first and thereafter the deal passes to the left.

THE SHUFFLE AND CUT—Any player may shuffle, dealer last. The player at dealer's right cuts.

THE DEAL—The cards are dealt one at a time as far as they will go equally; any remaining cards are placed on the table, face down, and are taken in by the player who wins the first trick; no one may look at them during the play.

THE PASS—After looking at his hand, each player selects any three cards and passes them face down to his right-hand neighbor. The player must pass the three cards before looking at the three cards he receives from his left. (*Variant.* The cards may be passed to left instead of right. In some circles a second round of passing takes place between players sitting opposite each other.) In six- and seven-hand play, only two cards are passed.

THE PLAY—Eldest hand makes the opening lead. Each hand must follow suit to a lead if able; if unable, a hand may discard any card. But the player dealt the ♤ Q must discard it at his first opportunity. A trick is won by the highest card of the suit led. The winner of a trick leads to the next. (There is no trump suit. Hearts are sometimes called "trumps" but do not actually have the privilege of a trump suit.)

Variants. Some play the rule that hearts may not be led

until the third trick. The rule that the ♤ Q must be discarded at first opportunity is often set aside in social play.

OBJECT OF PLAY—To avoid winning in tricks any heart or the ♤ Q (called *Black Lady* or *Black Maria*).

SCORING—A separate account is kept for each player. At the end of each hand, the points taken in tricks by each player are totaled and entered in his column. The counting cards are:

Each heart counts. 1
The ♤ Q counts. 13

When a table breaks up, all columns are totaled, and each player settles with every other on the difference of their totals. One way to determine the payments is to determine the average of all scores and the difference by which each player exceeds or falls below the average: *Example:*

PLAYER	FINAL TOTAL	DIFFERENCE FROM AVERAGE
W	42	+3
X	71	+32
Y	19	—20
Z	24	—15
	4) 156 (39 average	

Since the object of play is to take the *least* points, Y and Z collect 20 and 15 points respectively, W paying 3 and X 32.

If desired, the individual scores may be kept as running totals, so that a player may see at a glance how he stands relative to the others. The aggregate of all scores at any time must be a multiple of 26.

SCORING VARIANTS—*Variant No. 1.* Each player pays one chip for each heart, thirteen chips for ♤ Q, and lowest score for the deal takes all. Players that tie split the pool, leaving any odd chips in the pool for the next deal.

Variant No. 2 (Sweepstakes). Each player pays one chip for each heart, thirteen chips for ♤ Q. If one player alone scored 0, he takes the pool; if two or more players made 0 they split the pool. If every hand was *painted* (took one point or more), the pool remains as a *jack* for the next deal, or until it is eventually won.

IRREGULARITIES—(See also General Laws, page 14.)

Misdeal. If dealer exposes a card in dealing, or gives one player too many cards, another player too few, the next player in turn deals.

Play out of turn. A lead or play out of turn must be re-tracted if demand is made before all have played to the trick; after all have played, a play out of turn stands as regular without penalty.

Quitted tricks. Each trick gathered must be placed face down in front of the winner and tricks must be kept separate. If a player so mixes his cards that a claim of revoke cannot be proved, he is charged with all 26 points for the deal, regardless of whether the alleged revoke was made by him or another player.

Revoke. Failure to follow suit when able, or to discard the ♤ Q at first opportunity (where this rule is in force), constitutes a revoke. A revoke may be corrected before the trick is turned and quitted; if not discovered until later, the revoke is established, play is immediately abandoned, and the revoking hand is charged with all 26 points for the deal. If revoke is established against more than one player, each is charged 26 points. But the revoke penalty may not be enforced after the next ensuing cut after the deal in which the revoke occurred.

Incorrect hand. A player discovered to have too few cards must take the last trick (if more than one card short he must take in every trick to which he cannot play).

Omnibus Hearts

This variant adds two features to Black Lady whereby a player may score *plus.* The play of the cards takes on height-ened interest, since it combines nullo play (to avoid gathering hearts and the ♤ Q) with positive play to win plus scores.

NUMBER OF PLAYERS—Four to six. Best for four, each play-ing for himself.

THE PLUS CARD—The hearts and ♤ Q are minus cards, as in Black Lady, but in addition the ◇ 10 counts ten plus for the player winning it in tricks. (*Variant.* In some localities, ◇ J instead of ◇ 10 is the plus card.)

TAKE-ALL, OR SLAM—A player who wins all fifteen counting cards—the thirteen hearts, ♤ Q and ◇ 10—scores 26 plus (instead of 16 minus).

In all other respects Omnibus Hearts follows the rules of Black Lady.

Cancellation Hearts

NUMBER OF PLAYERS—Seven to ten.

THE PACK—Two full packs of 52 cards shuffled together.

THE DEAL—The cards are dealt around as far as they will go evenly. Any remaining odd cards are placed face down for a *widow*.

THE PLAY—No cards are passed before the play. Eldest hand makes the opening lead, and the rules of play are as at four-hand Hearts, with the additions:

The widow is added to the first trick.

Cancellation. Two like cards in the same trick cancel each other, and neither can win the trick. If all cards played to a trick are paired, the trick goes to the next winner of a trick.

SCORING—Same as in four-hand Hearts.

Hearts Without Black Lady

Hearts may be played without scoring ♤ Q as a counting card, there being only 13 points in play. In this variant, the passing of cards before play is omitted, each playing his original cards. Settlement is usually by the Howell Method: For each heart taken, the player puts up as many chips as there are players besides himself in the game; he then takes out of the pool as many chips as the difference between 13 and the number of hearts he took. *Example:* In a four-hand game, a player who won 7 hearts puts in 21 chips and takes out 6.

Domino Hearts

NUMBER OF PLAYERS—Two to seven.

THE PACK—52 cards.

THE DEAL—Each player receives six cards, dealt one at a time. The remainder of the pack is placed face down in the center of the table, forming the *stock*.

THE PLAY—Eldest hand makes the opening lead. Rules of play are as at four-hand Hearts, with the difference that a hand unable to follow suit to the lead must draw cards from the top of the stock until he can play. After the stock is exhausted, a hand unable to follow suit may discard. Play continues until all cards have been won in tricks, each player dropping out as his cards are exhausted. If a player wins a trick with his last card, the turn to lead passes to the first active hand on his left. The last survivor must keep all cards remaining in his hand.

SCORING—Same as in four-hand Hearts, but because of the

hazard involved it is usual to count only the hearts, not the ♤ Q.

Spot Hearts

A variation in which the various hearts are settled for according to their denominations, ace being worth 14 counters, king 13, queen 12, jack 11, and the others worth their spot value, *i.e.*, tens 10, nines 9, etc.

Auction Hearts

The same as "Hearts without Black Lady," except that players bid after the deal for the privilege of naming the suit to be avoided. In bidding, a player names the number of counters he will put up as a pool, if allowed to name the suit. Bidding begins with eldest hand, and rotates to the left, each player being allowed one bid only. Each player must bid higher than the preceding bid or must pass.

The highest bidder puts up his pool and names the suit. He leads first, and thereafter play proceeds as in the regular game.

When the hands are played out, each player adds one counter to the pool for each card he has taken of the forbidden suit. The player taking no card of forbidden suit wins the pool; if two players take no card of forbidden suit, they divide the pool, leaving an odd counter, if any, for the next pool, which is a *jack*, as at sweepstakes. If more than two players take no card of the suit, or one player takes all thirteen or each player takes at least one, no player wins. The deal passes, and the successful bidder on the original deal names the suit to be avoided, without bidding. The play proceeds as before, and at the end of the play of the hand each player puts up a chip for each card of forbidden suit he has taken. If no player wins on this deal, a new deal ensues, and so on, until the pool is won.

SPITE AND MALICE

NUMBER OF PLAYERS—Two.

CARDS—Two packs. Pack A is a standard 52-card pack. Pack B is a standard 52-card pack plus four jokers. The packs should be of different back designs or colors.

RANK OF CARDS—K (high), Q, J, 10, 9, 8, 7, 6, 5, 4, 3, 2, A (low).

PRELIMINARIES—Pack A is shuffled and divided into two 26-card packets, which become the *pay-off piles* of the two players. Each player turns up the top card of his pay-off pile; the higher card designates the first player, and if the cards are the same rank the pay-off piles are shuffled and new cards turned up.

Pack B is shuffled by the first player's opponent, who deals a five-card hand to each player (one at a time, face down) and puts the remainder of Pack B in the center as the *stock*.

OBJECT OF THE GAME—To get rid of one's pay-off pile.

THE PLAY—Each available ace must be played immediately to form a *center stack*. There may be no more than four center stacks at one time. Each available two must be played, if possible, on an ace in a center stack. Center stacks are built up in ascending order, regardless of suit—any deuce on any ace, any three on any two, etc. Both players play to center stacks.

Each player may have four *side stacks*. These are discard piles. A player may play only to his own side stacks and only from his hand. Any card may start a side stack. Side stacks are built downward, regardless of suit (any five on any six), or with like cards (any queen on any queen). When there are already four center stacks, a deuce from the hand may be played on a three in a side stack, and an ace on a deuce.

The top card of a pay-off pile may be played only to the center. When it is played, the next card is turned up. A card from the hand or from the top of a side stack may be played

171

to the center. A card from the hand may be played to a side stack, but only one such card in turn. When a player plays to a side stack his turn ends and his opponent's turn begins. Cards may not be moved from one side stack to another, or to fill a space.

A player may also end his turn by saying so, when he cannot, or does not wish to, play.

RULES OF PLAY—Each joker is wild and may be played in place of any card except an ace. If a joker becomes available at the top of a side stack, it may be played to the center.

At the beginning of each turn, a player draws enough cards from the stock to restore his hand to five cards.

When any center stack is built up through the king, it is shuffled into the stock. A new center stack is then started.

SCORING—The player who first gets rid of all the cards in his pay-off pile wins, his margin being the number of cards in his opponent's pay-off pile. If there are cards left in both pay-off piles and neither player can or will play, the winner is the player who has fewer cards in his pay-off pile and he wins the difference; but it is never legal to count the cards in a pay-off pile.

FIVE HUNDRED

This was the favorite social game of the United States for more than ten years between 1904 and 1920. It became less popular than Bridge but is still played by millions. The game was devised and introduced in 1904, as a service to card-players, by the United States Playing Card Co., which held the copyright for 56 years but never charged anyone for its use.

NUMBER OF PLAYERS—Two to six. A good three-hand game. Four may play in two partnerships, or with three active play-ers plus one player (the dealer) who sits out each game. Five may play in two partnerships, three against two (see page 179), or may cut to decide which three or four play the first game while the other sits out. Six play in two partnerships of three each (see page 179).

THE PACK—For two or three players, 33 cards—A, K, Q, J, 10, 9, 8, 7 in each suit, plus a joker. [Two may also use a 24-card pack—see page 179.] Four players use a 43-card pack, A (high) to 5 (low) in each suit, plus ♡ 4 and ◇ 4 and the joker. Five players use the regular 52-card pack plus the joker. For six players there is a special 63-card pack with spot cards numbered 11 and 12 in each suit, ♡ 13 and ◇ 13, and the joker. By agreement the joker may be omitted.

RANK OF CARDS—The joker is always the highest trump. Sec-ond-best is the jack of trumps (*right bower*); third-best is the jack of the other suit of same color as the trump (*left bower*). The rank in trumps is: Joker (high), J (right bower), J (left bower), A, K, Q, 10, 9, 8, 7. In each plain suit the rank is: A (high), K, Q, (J), 10, 9, 8, 7.

The bidding denominations rank: no-trump (high), hearts, diamonds, clubs, spades.

DRAWING—Cards are drawn from a pack spread face down, for first deal. Lowest card is the first dealer. In drawing for deal only, ace ranks low, below the two, and the joker is the lowest card of the pack.

SHUFFLE AND CUT—Any player may shuffle. Dealer has the right to shuffle last. The pack is cut by the player at his right; the cut must leave at least four cards in each packet.

THE DEAL—Each player in rotation to the left, beginning with the player at the dealer's left, is dealt ten cards, face down. Dealer gives each player three cards, then deals a widow of three cards (two cards, if the joker is not used), then deals each player four cards, then three cards.

BIDDING—Each player in turn, beginning with the player at dealer's left, has one opportunity to bid. He may pass or bid; if there has been a previous bid, his bid must be higher than any previous bid. Each bid must name a number of tricks, from six to ten, together with a denomination, which will establish the trump suit (as, "Six spades"). To overcall a previous bid, a player must bid more tricks or the same number of tricks in a high-ranking denomination. (*Optional rule:* If the Original or Inverted Schedule is used, as shown on page 175, a bid overcalls the preceding bids if its scoring value is higher or if it requires a greater number of tricks for the same scoring value.)

(*Nullo bid:* Some permit the bid "Nullo," which is a contract to lose all the tricks at no-trump. The nullo bid has a scoring value of 250; on the Avondale Schedule it overcalls eight spades or lower and is overcalled by eight clubs or higher. If nullo becomes the contract, in a partnership game the contractor's partner or partners abandon their hands and the contractor plays alone against the others. If he wins a trick he (or his side) is set back the 250 points and each opponent scores 10 for each trick the contractor takes.)

If all players pass, the deal is abandoned without a score. (*Optional rule:* A passed deal is played at no-trump, each player for himself. Eldest hand leads first. Each trick won counts 10 points. As there is no contract, there is no setting back.)

THE PLAY—The high bid becomes the contract. In three-hand play, the two other players combine in temporary partnership against the contractor.

The contractor takes the widow into his hand, without showing it, and then discards any three cards face down, without showing them.

The contractor makes the first lead. The leader at any

TABLES OF SCORING POINTS
GAME OF FIVE HUNDRED

AVONDALE SCHEDULE

TRICKS	6	7	8	9	10
♠	40	140	240	340	440
♣	60	160	260	360	460
♦	80	180	280	380	480
♥	100	200	300	400	500
No Trump	120	220	320	420	520

Original Schedule

If Trumps Are	6 tricks	7 tricks	8 tricks	9 tricks	10 tricks
Spades	40	80	120	160	200
Clubs	60	120	180	240	300
Diamonds	80	160	240	320	400
Hearts	100	200	300	400	500
No Trump	120	240	360	480	600

If reverse order of suit values is used, table of points is as follows:

Inverted Schedule

If Trumps Are	6 tricks	7 tricks	8 tricks	9 tricks	10 tricks
Clubs	40	80	120	160	200
Spades	60	120	180	240	300
Hearts	80	160	240	320	400
Diamonds	100	200	300	400	500
No Trump	120	240	360	480	600

NOTE—The Avondale Schedule is recommended because it contains no two bids of same numerical value and more nearly equalizes the value of the suits.

time may lead any card. Each other hand must follow suit if able; if unable to follow suit, the hand may play any card. A trick is won by the highest trump, or, if it contains no trump, by the highest card of the suit led. The winner of a trick leads to the next. Each of the contractor's opponents takes in and keeps the tricks he wins.

THE JOKER—When there is a trump suit, the joker is the highest trump; it belongs to the trump suit, must be played if necessary to follow suit, and may be played only when a card of the trump suit can legally be played. At no-trump contracts (or nullo, if played), the joker is a suit by itself but also is the highest card of any suit and wins any trick to which it is legally played. The holder of the joker may not play it when he can follow suit to the suit led, but if he cannot follow suit and plays the joker he wins the trick. If a player leads the joker at a no-trump (or nullo) contract, he must specify the suit others must play to follow suit, but the joker wins the trick.

SCORING—If the contractor wins as many tricks as he bid, he scores the number of points for in whichever scoring table is being used (see page 175). There is no credit for extra tricks over the contract, except that if the contractor wins all ten tricks he scores a minimum of 250 (more, if his bid was for more).

If the contractor fails to make the contract, the value of his bid is deducted from his score. It is possible for a player to be set back until he has a minus score; he is then said to be *in the hole* (from the common practice of drawing a ring around a minus score).

Whether the contract is made or defeated, each opponent of the contractor scores 10 for each trick he himself has taken.

GAME—The player or side first to reach a total of 500 points wins the game. A player or side that goes 500 in the hole loses the game; if one player in a three-hand game becomes minus 500 he cannot win the game but continues to play until the game is won, and if he is first to reach 500 no one wins the game. If the contractor and an opponent reach 500 on the same deal, the contractor wins.

In a three-hand game, if the contractor does not reach 500 but both his opponents do, the first opponent to reach 500 wins. If the contractor could not reach 500 by making his bid, the opponent first to reach 500 may claim the game as

soon as the tricks he has won bring him to 500. At the time
of making the claim he must show his remaining cards. If he
does not have the 500 he claimed, play continues; all his
remaining cards become exposed cards (see *Irregularities*).

[An optional alternative is to require 1,000 or 1,500 for
game. The scoring is speeded up by awarding points for
cards won in tricks: 1 for each ace, 10 for each face card
or ten, the pip value for each lower card, nothing for the
joker. These points do not affect the question of whether the
contractor makes his bid, which depends on the number
of tricks won. He scores his points, extra, if he makes his
bid; the opponents always score them.]

IRREGULARITIES—*New Deal*. There must be a new deal by
the same dealer if a card is found exposed in the pack; if
the dealer gives the wrong number of cards to any hand; or
if, before the last card is dealt, attention is called to the fact
that the cut was omitted or that the dealer departed in any
way from the prescribed method of dealing (as by dealing
batches of 3-3-4 or 4-3-3, or laying out the widow at any
time but after the first round).

Bid out of turn. In three-hand play, there is no penalty
for a pass or bid out of turn; the call is void, and the player
may make any legal call in his proper turn. In partnership
play, a bid (not a pass) out of turn is void and that side
may make no further bid (though a bid made made previously by partner of the offender is not canceled).

Wrong number of cards. If, during the bidding, two hands
(excluding the widow) are found to have the wrong number
of cards, there must be a new deal by the same dealer. If the
widow and one hand are incorrect, they must be rectified; another player draws out the excess cards and gives them to the
short hand, and the player whose hand was incorrect is
barred from bidding.

If, during the play, the contractor and an opponent are
found to have incorrect hands, or if there is one incorrect
hand due to an incorrect pack, there must be a new deal by
the same dealer. If two opponents have incorrect hands, the
contractor's being correct, the bid is deemed to have been
made and the opponents may not score. The contractor may
continue play in an effort to win all the tricks, and he is
deemed to win all the final tricks to which the short hand cannot play. If the opponents' hands are correct, the contractor's
hand and his discard incorrect, the bid is lost, but the deal is

played out to determine how many tricks are to be credited to each opponent.

Exposed card. A card is deemed exposed if it is dropped face up on the table, held so that a partner sees its face, or named by the owner as being in his hand. An exposed card must be left face up on the table and played at the first legal opportunity thereafter. But there is no penalty against a contractor playing alone for exposing cards, except in case of a corrected revoke.

Lead or play out of turn. A lead out of turn must be retracted on demand of an opponent, if the demand is made before the trick is completed; and cards played to it may be retracted without penalty. The card led in error is treated as an exposed card; and if it was the offender's partner's turn to lead, an opponent may require him to lead a named suit, or not to lead the suit of the exposed card.

If a player plays out of turn, not as leader, his card is deemed exposed.

If an error in leading or playing out of turn is not noticed until the trick is gathered, the trick stands as regular.

Revoke. Failure to follow suit to a lead when able is a revoke. A revoke may be corrected at any time before the next ensuing lead, otherwise it stands as established. When a revoke is corrected, the incorrect card is deemed exposed, including a case where it belongs to a contractor playing alone. If an established revoke is claimed and proved before the cut for the next deal, and the revoking hand was on the contracting side, the contract is scored as lost; if the revoking hand was an opponent, the contract is scored as made, and the opponents score nothing.

Illegal information. If a player gives information illegally to his partner, or looks at a trick after it is gathered and quitted, or if the contractor's discards are looked at by him after the opening lead, or by another player at any time: The opponent at the right of the dealer may name the suit to be led the next time the offender or his partner has the lead.

Error in score. A proved error in recording scores must be corrected on demand made before the first bid (not pass) of the next deal after that to which the error pertains. In any other case, recorded scores may not be changed.

Four-Hand Five Hundred

The four-hand game is played with fixed partnerships, partners sitting opposite each other. The pack is 42 or 43 cards, made by discarding the twos, threes, and black fours from a 52-card pack, and adding joker if desired; often it is not. Each player receives ten cards and the remaining cards go to the widow. If one side's score reaches minus 500, its opponents win the game. All other rules are as in the three-hand game, except that two always play against two.

Two-Hand Five Hundred

The pack and the deal are the same as in the three-hand game, except that the hand at dealer's left is dealt face down on the table and is dead. With these ten cards out of play, the bidding is largely guesswork. Not to be left "at home" by a bold opponent, a player is bound to be forward in bidding and to speculate on buying just what he needs from the widow. If one player's score reaches minus 500, the other wins the game.

The two-hand game may also be played with a 24-card pack, ninespot low; the widow is four cards, no extra hand is dealt, and the rules otherwise are as in three-hand.

Five-Hand Five Hundred

Five players use the regular 52-card pack, usually with the joker added, so that each player receives ten cards and there is a three-card widow as in three-hand.

After the bidding, the high bidder may select any other player to be his partner; if he bid for eight or more tricks, he may name any two partners. (Some play that the high bidder selects his partner by naming a card, as in Call-Ace Euchre, page 186).

Six-Hand Five Hundred

For six players there is available a 62-card pack that includes spot cards numbered 11 and 12 in each suit and 13 in each of two suits; the joker may be added, making a 63-card pack and permitting a deal of ten cards to each player and three to the widow. There are two sides of three partners each, the partners being seated alternately so that each has an opponent on his right and left.

EUCHRE

NUMBER OF PLAYERS—From two to seven. Best for four, two against two as partners. The rules for four-hand will therefore be given first.

Four-Hand Euchre

THE PACK—32 cards (A, K, Q, J, 10, 9, 8, 7 of each suit), or 28 cards (7's omitted), or 24 cards (7's and 8's omitted). Joker is sometimes added.

RANK OF CARDS—The highest trump is the jack of the trump suit, called *right bower*. The second-highest trump is the jack of the other suit of the same color as the trump, called *left bower*. (*Example:* If diamonds are trumps, right bower is ◇ J and left bower is ♡ J.) The remaining trumps, and also the plain suits, rank as follows: A (high), K, Q, (J), 10, 9, 8, 7.

THE DRAW—Draw cards for partners and deal. The two lowest play against the two highest, and lowest card deals first. In drawing, the cards rank: K (high), Q, J, 10, 9, 8, 7, A. Players drawing equal cards must draw again. Partners sit opposite each other.

THE SHUFFLE AND CUT—Dealer has the right to shuffle last. The pack is cut by the player at his right. The cut must not leave less than four cards in each packet.

THE DEAL—The cards are dealt to the left, beginning with eldest hand. Each player receives five cards. Dealer may give a round of three at a time, then a round of two at a time, or may give two, then three; but he must adhere to whichever plan he commences. Turn to deal passes to the left.

THE TURN-UP—On completing the deal, dealer places the rest of the pack in the center of the table and turns the top card face up. Should the turn-up be accepted as trump, regardless of by whom, dealer has the right to exchange the turn-up for any card in his hand. In practice, the turn-up is not taken into his hand but is left on the pack until played; dealer signifies his exchange by placing his discard face down underneath the pack.

MAKING THE TRUMP—Commencing with eldest hand, each player to the left has the option of passing or of accepting the turn-up for trump. An opponent of dealer accepts by saying "I order it up." Partner of dealer accepts by saying "I assist." Dealer accepts by making his discard; his acceptance is called *taking it up.*

Dealer signifies refusal of the turn-up by removing the card from the top and placing it (face up) partially underneath the pack; this is called *turning it down.* When all four players pass in the first round, each hand in turn, commencing with eldest, has the option of passing again or of naming the trump suit. The rejected suit may not be named. Declaring the other suit of the same color as the reject is called *making it next;* declaring a suit of opposite color is called *crossing it.* If all four players pass in the second round, the cards are *bunched* (mixed together for the shuffle) and the next dealer in turn deals.

Once the trump is fixed, either by acceptance of the turn-up or declaration after it is rejected, the bidding ends and play begins.

PLAYING ALONE—The player who fixes the trump suit has the option of playing alone, without help of his partner's cards. If he wishes to exercise this option, he must declare "alone" distinctly at the time he makes the trump. His partner then turns his cards face down and does not participate in the play.

THE PLAY—The opening lead is made by eldest hand, or by the player at his left if partner of eldest hand is playing alone. Each hand must follow suit to a lead if able; if unable, the hand may trump or discard at will. A trick is won by the highest card of the suit led, or, if it contains trumps, by the highest trump. The winner of a trick leads to the next.

OBJECT OF PLAY—To win at least three tricks. If the side that made the trump fails to get three tricks, it is said to be *euchred.* Winning all five tricks is called a *march.*

SCORING—The following table shows all scoring situations:

Partnership making trump wins 3 or 4 tricks	1
Partnership making trump wins 5 tricks	2
Lone hand wins 3 or 4 tricks	1
Lone hand wins 5 tricks	4
Partnership or lone hand is euchred, opponents score	2

GAME—5, 7 or 10 points as agreed. In 5 point game a side is said to be *at the bridge* when it has scored 4 and opponents have scored 2 or less.

MARKERS—A widespread method of keeping score is by use of small cards lower than those in play. When game is 5 points, each side uses a threespot and a fourspot as markers. To indicate score of 1, place the four face down on the three, leaving one pip thereof exposed. Score of 2: Place the three face down on the four, leaving two pips thereof exposed. Score of 3: Place the three face up on the four. Score of 4: Place the four face up on the three. In higher point games a two-spot and three-spot are frequently used as markers to keep score.

RUBBERS—Many Euchre games are scored by *rubber points,* as in Whist. The first side to win two games wins the rubber. Each game counts for the side winning it; 3 rubber points if the losers' score in that game was 0 or less; 2 rubber points if the losers' score was 1 or 2; and 1 rubber point if the losers scored 3 or more. The winners' margin in the rubber is 2 points bonus, plus the winners' rubber points, minus the losers' rubber points.

IRREGULARITIES—*Misdeal.* There may be a new deal by the same dealer if a card is exposed in dealing; a card is faced in the pack; or if the pack is found imperfect. When a pack is found imperfect, previous scores stand.

A deal by the wrong player may be stopped before a card is turned up; if the error is not noticed until later, the deal stands.

Error in bidding. A player who *orders it up* when he is partner of dealer, or *assists* when he is an opponent of dealer, is deemed to have accepted the turn-up for trump. If a player names for trump the suit of the turn-up after it has been turned down, his declaration is void and his side may not make the trump.

Declaration out of turn. If a player makes a declaration (or turn-down) other than a pass, out of turn, it is void and his side may not make the trump.

Incorrect number of cards. If any hand is found to have too many or too few cards, and the error is discovered before the first trick is quitted, there must be a new deal; if the error is not noticed until later, play continues and the side of the erroneous hand may not score for that deal.

If dealer has accepted the turn-up and plays to the first trick before discarding, he must play with the five cards dealt him and the turn-up card is out of play.

Lone hand. A hand playing alone does not incur penalty for lead or play out of turn or exposing a card, but must correct the error on demand if it is noticed in time.

Lead out of turn. If a hand leads out of turn and all other hands play to the trick before the error is noticed, the trick stands. But if any hand has not played, the false lead must be taken back on demand of any player and becomes an exposed card. Any cards played to the incorrect lead may be retracted without penalty. An opponent of the incorrect leader may name the suit to be led at the first opportunity thereafter of the offender or his partner to lead; such call must be made by the hand that will play last to the trick.

Exposed cards. A card is deemed exposed if it is led or played out of turn; dropped face up on the table except as a regular play in turn; played with another card intended to be played; or named by a player as being in his hand. An exposed card must be left face up on the table and must be played at the first legal opportunity.

Quitted tricks. Each trick as gathered must be turned face down, and the tricks must be kept separate so that the identity of each can be determined. Quitted tricks may not be examined for any purpose until the end of play. If a player turns up a quitted trick at any previous time, the opponents may call a lead from his side.

Revoke. Failure to follow suit to a lead when able is a revoke. A revoke may be corrected before the trick is quitted, and if it is corrected any opponent who played after the revoke may retract his card and substitute another. If a player so mixes the tricks that a claim of revoke against his side cannot be proved, the claim must be considered proved.

Upon proof of established revoke, the non-revoking side has the option of scoring the hand as played or of taking the revoke penalty. The revoke penalty is 2 points, which may be either added to the score of the non-revoking side or subtracted from the score of its opponents. If the revoke was made by the opponents of a lone hand, the penalty is 4 points.

Railroad Euchre

Railroad Euchre is the name given to any number of variants designed to speed up the scoring. Some of the features added in various localities are:

Joker. The joker is added and ranks as the highest trump.

Defending alone. Either opponent of a lone player may call *alone* and defend alone against him. Euchre of a lone hand by a lone opponent counts 4.

Calling for best. A lone player or defender may discard any one card and call for his partner's best card as a replacement.

Laps. Points scored in excess of those necessary to win game are counted toward the next game.

Slam. A side is credited with two games if it reaches game before the opponents have scored a point.

Three-hand (Cutthroat) Euchre

The two other hands combine in play against the maker of trump. The scoring:

Maker of trump wins 3 or 4 tricks. . . . 1
Maker of trump wins 5 tricks. 3
Maker of trump is euchred, each
opponent scores 2

All other rules are as in four-hand. In applying laws on irregularities, making of trump is deemed a lone hand and the other two a partnership.

Two-hand Euchre

Reduce the pack to 24 cards by discarding the sevens and eights. Rules are as in four-hand, except that the declaration *alone* does not exist and score for *march* is 2 points. Laws on irregularities omit penalties for errors that do not damage the opponent, e.g., exposure of cards, lead out of turn.

Auction Euchre

NUMBER OF PLAYERS—Five, six or seven.

THE PACK—*Five-hand.* 32 cards, as in four-hand. *Six-hand.* 36 cards, the usual pack with sixes added. *Seven-hand.* 52 cards. In each instance, the joker may be added if desired, ranking as the highest trump.

RANK OF CARDS—Same as in four-hand.

THE DRAW—Players draw cards and the lowest card is the first dealer. Second-lowest sits at his left, and so on.

THE SHUFFLE AND CUT—Same as in four-hand.

THE DEAL—*Five-hand and six-hand.* Same as in four-hand, but after the first round deal two cards face down for a widow. *Seven-hand*. Give each hand seven cards, a round of three cards at a time, then a round of four, or vice versa. After the first round, deal three cards face down for a widow (or four cards if the joker is used).

THE BIDDING—Each player in turn, commencing with eldest hand, may make a bid or pass. There is only one round of bidding. Highest bidder names the trump suit. Each bid names a number of points, and must be higher than the preceding bid.

THE WIDOW—Maker of trump may take the widow in his hand and discard an equal number of cards, unless he has contracted to play without the widow.

PARTNERS—*Five-hand*. Maker of trump chooses his partners after seeing the widow. Bid of 3 tricks entitles him to one partner; bid of 4 or 5 tricks, to two partners. He may choose any he pleases, regardless of where he sits. *Six-hand*. Usually played by set partnerships of three against three, partners sitting alternately. *Seven-hand*. Maker of trump chooses his partners after seeing widow. Bid of 4 or 5 tricks entitles him to one partner; bid of 6 or 7, to two partners.

THE PLAY—Same as in four-hand.

SCORING—The following tables show the various numbers that may be bid and the obligation of each bid.

Five-hand

3..maker must win 3 tricks with help of one partner.
4..maker must win 4 tricks with help of two partners.
5..maker must win 5 tricks with help of two partners.
8..maker must play alone and win 5 tricks, using widow.
15..maker must play alone and win 5 tricks, without widow.

Six-hand

3,4,5..side making trump must win number of tricks named (widow taken by maker of trump).
8..maker must play alone and win 5 tricks, using widow.
15..maker must play alone and win 5 tricks without widow.

Seven-hand

4,5..maker must win number of tricks named with help of one partner.
6,7..maker must win number of tricks named with help of two partners.
10..maker must play alone and win 7 tricks, using widow.
20..maker must play alone and win 7 tricks, without widow.

If the side making trump wins the number of tricks bid, it scores the value given in the table. There is no credit for winning more tricks than necessary. If the side making trump is euchred, the opponents score the value of the bid. In six-hand partnership play, only two accounts need be kept, one for each side. But with five or seven players, the full amount to which a side is entitled is credited to each member individually.

IRREGULARITIES—Same as in four-hand.

Call-Ace Euchre

This is a variant in the matter of determining partnerships, with four, five, or six players. Trump is made as in four-hand, by acceptance of the turn-up or declaration after it is rejected. The maker of trump calls a suit, and the holder of the best card in that suit becomes his partner, but must not reveal the fact until the card is duly played.

Napoleon (Nap)

NUMBER OF PLAYERS—Two to six.

THE PACK—52 cards.

RANK OF CARDS—A (high), K, Q, J, 10, 9, 8, 7, 6, 5, 4, 3, 2.

THE DRAW—Lowest card deals first, the ace ranking below the two.

THE SHUFFLE AND CUT—Dealer has the right to shuffle last. The pack is cut by the player at his right. The cut must leave at least four cards in each packet.

THE DEAL—Each player receives five cards, dealt in a round of three at a time, then a round of two at a time, or first two and then three.

BIDDING—Each player in turn, commencing with eldest hand, may make one bid or may pass. A bid is the number of tricks, out of five, that the player thinks he can win if he names the trump; a bid of all five is called *Nap*. (*Variant*. A bid of Nap can be overcalled by *Wellington*, and that in turn by *Blucher*. These latter are also bids to win five tricks but increase the penalties if the bidder fails.)

THE PLAY—Highest bidder indicates the trump by making the opening lead, which must be a trump. A player must follow suit to a lead if able; if unable, he may trump or discard at will. A trick is won by the highest card played of the suit led, or, if it contains a trump, by the highest trump. The winner of a trick leads to the next.

SCORING—There is no credit for extra tricks won by the bidder or by his opponents beyond what are needed to make or defeat the bid. If the bidder makes his bid, he collects from each other player; if he is defeated, he pays every other player.

BID	BIDDER WINS	BIDDER LOSES
Less than 5	1 for each trick	1 for each trick
Nap	10	5
Wellington	10	10
Blucher	10	20

The usual way of scoring is to distribute an equal number of chips to all players before the game and then settle in chips after each deal.

IRREGULARITIES—*Misdeal.* If a misdeal is called for any of the usual causes (see General Laws, page 14), the same dealer redeals.

Incorrect number of cards. A player dealt the wrong number of cards must announce the error before making any bid or pass, otherwise he must play on with the incorrect hand. A short hand cannot win a trick on which it has no card to play. If bidder's hand is correct, an opponent's incorrect, bidder does not pay if he loses but collects if he wins. If bidder's hand is incorrect, all others correct, bidder does not collect if he wins but pays if he loses.

Play out of turn. There is no penalty for a lead or play out of turn by bidder, but the error must be corrected on demand if noticed before the trick is turned and quitted, otherwise the trick stands. If an opponent of bidder leads or plays out of turn, he must pay three chips to bidder and may collect nothing if bidder loses

Revoke. Failure to follow suit to the lead when able is a revoke. If a revoke is detected and claimed before settlement for the deal, play is abandoned and settlement made at once. A revoking bidder must pay all opponents as though he had lost. A revoking opponent must pay bidder the full amount he would have collected had he won, the other opponents paying nothing.

POOLS—Pools are sometimes made by each player's putting up an equal number of counters; and each dealer in turn adding a certain number of counters. The pool may be further increased by requiring a player revoking to contribute five counters; and for a lead out of turn, three. The first player taking five tricks on a Nap bid wins the pool. A player bidding Nap and failing to take five tricks must double the pool.

WIDOW—Five cards may be dealt, face down, on the table as an extra hand, 2-3 or 3-2 at a time, just before dealer helps himself. The player who takes the widow must bid Nap and discard five cards, face down.

PEEP NAP—Variant of Pool Nap. One card only is dealt to the widow, usually on the first round. By adding one counter to the pool, any player may look at this card before bidding or passing, highest bidder taking the card without paying a counter. He must discard one card to reduce his hand to five cards.

SIR GARNET—This is a popular variety of Nap. An extra hand of five cards is dealt, the dealer giving the cards for it just before he deals to himself in each round.

Each player in turn to the left, instead of making the usual bid, may pick up the widow and place it with the five cards originally dealt to him. From these ten he picks out any five he likes, discarding the others without showing them. He is then obliged to play Nap, but if he fails he loses double as much as he would have lost without the widow.

The ordinary Nap declaration wins ten counters from each player if it succeeds, but pays only five to each if it fails. In Sir Garnet, the loser of a Nap that takes the widow loses ten to each adversary.

Spoil Five, or 45

(Also called Five Fingers)

NUMBER OF PLAYERS—Two to ten, as individuals. Best for five or six.

THE PACK—52 cards.

RANK OF CARDS—Ace of hearts is always third best trump.

As trumps: Spades and clubs, 5 (high), J, ♡ A, A, K, Q, 2, 3, 4, 6, 7, 8, 9, 10. Diamonds and hearts, 5 (high), J, ♡ A, ◇ A (if diamonds are trumps), K, Q, 10, 9, 8, 7, 6, 4, 3, 2.

When not trumps: Spades and clubs, K (high), Q, J, A, 2, 3, 4, 5, 6, 7, 8, 9, 10. Diamonds and hearts K (high), Q, J, 10, 9, 8, 7, 6, 5, 4, 3, 2, A (except in hearts). "Low in black, high in red."

THE SHUFFLE AND CUT—First jack deals (see page 109), dealer may shuffle last, and the player at dealer's right cuts.

THE DEAL—Five cards to each player—three, then two, or two, then three, in rotation to the left, beginning with eldest hand. The next card is turned for trump.

ROBBING THE TRUMP—Player holding ace of suit turned for trump may exchange any card in his hand for card turned, if he wishes; if not, he must request dealer to turn down trump card, thus announcing that he holds ace, otherwise he loses right to exchange ace for trump card, and his ace becomes lowest trump, even if it be the ace of hearts. If an ace is turned, dealer may discard at once and take the ace into his hand after the first trick; or may play with his original hand, announcing his intention.

OBJECT OF PLAY—To win tricks.

THE PLAY—Eldest hand leads any card. Each player in turn, if able to follow suit, must either do so, or trump; if unable to follow suit, a player may play any card.

A player is not required to follow suit with the 5 or jack of trumps or ♡ A when a lower trump is led.

A trick containing a trump is won by the highest trump played; any other trick is won by the highest card of the suit led. The winner of each trick leads to the next.

SCORING—Each player puts one chip in the pool. The pool may be taken by the first player to win three tricks in any deal. If a player continues to play after winning three tricks, he must win all five tricks (in which case he gets the pool plus one chip from each other player); if he does not win all five tricks, he does not get the pool.

After any hand in which the pool is not won, each player puts in another chip for the next deal.

IRREGULARITIES—(See also General Laws, page 14.)

Misdeal (deal passes to the player at dealer's left): If too many or too few cards are dealt on any round; if dealer exposes a card in dealing; if the deal is commenced with an uncut pack (provided a new deal is demanded before the deal is completed); if dealer counts the cards on the table or in the pack.

Irregular hand. A hand with an incorrect number of cards is dead, and the other players continue play; but if a player has won three tricks with an irregular hand before it is discovered he wins the pool.

Revoke; illegal exposure of a card after any player has won two tricks; robbing the trump when not holding the ace. The offender's hand is dead and he does not receive cards until the pool in progress is won; but he must still add to the pool when other players do.

Forty-Five

Variation of Spoil Five, for two, four (two against two), or six (three against three) players. Game is scored by points: side taking three or four tricks scores 5 points; five tricks, 10 points. Sometimes each trick counts 5 points, and score of side taking fewest tricks is deducted from that of side taking most tricks. Thus three tricks count 5; four tricks, 15; five tricks, 25 points; 45 points is game.

Auction Forty-Fives

This form of Spoil Five and Forty-Five is the national game of Nova Scotia. The number 45 no longer figures in it.

NUMBER OF PLAYERS—Four, two against two as partners, or six, three against three as partners, seated alternately.

PRELIMINARIES, RANK OF CARDS, AND PLAY—As in Spoil Five.

BIDDING—Eldest hand bids first and the turn passes to the left. Bids are in multiples of 5 points and the highest bid is 30. Each bid must be higher than the preceding bid, except that dealer may beat the previous bid without going over, by saying "I hold"; if he does, each player who did not previously pass gets another turn and dealer again may take the bid without going over. A side having 100 points or more may not bid less than 20.

DISCARDING AND DRAWING—The high bidder names the trump, then each player discards as many cards as he wishes and dealer restores his hand to five cards from the top of the pack. The player at the left of the high bidder leads first.

SCORING—Each trick won counts 5 and the highest trump in play counts an additional 5, making 10 in all for the trick it wins. If the high bidder's side makes its bid, it scores all it makes; if it fails, the amount of the bid is subtracted from its score. The opposing side always scores whatever it wins in tricks. A bid of 30 (for all five tricks) is worth 60 if it is made and loses 30 if it fails. Game is won by the first side to reach 120.

ALL FOURS OR HIGH-LOW-JACK

All Fours, a game of early English origin, was once known to virtually every card-playing American; it has survived principally in the game of Auction Pitch, which is still among the most popular games played in the United States. There are many varieties and the rules have changed greatly over the years, but the essential feature always is the scoring of high, low, jack, and the game.

Auction Pitch, or Set Back

NUMBER OF PLAYERS—Two to seven; most often played by three to five players, most popular for four. Each plays for himself.

THE PACK—52 cards.

RANK OF CARDS—A (high), K, Q, J, 10, 9, 8, 7, 6, 5, 4, 3, 2.

THE DRAW—High deals and has choice of seats; other players may sit where they please, and in case of any question the higher card drawn has preference.

THE SHUFFLE AND CUT—Any player may shuffle, dealer last, and player to dealer's right cuts, leaving at least five cards in each packet.

THE DEAL—Three cards at a time, in rotation, beginning with eldest hand, until each player has six cards. After each hand, the deal passes to the left.

OBJECT OF THE GAME—To be the first player to reach a total of 7 points. Points are scored as follows:

High. One point for holding the highest trump in play.

Low. One point for being dealt the lowest trump in play, no matter who wins it in a trick. (*Variant.* Many play that Low counts for the player winning it.)

Jack. One point for winning the trick on which the jack of trumps is played, no matter to whom it was dealt.

Game. One point for winning in tricks scoring cards to the greatest value, each ten counting 10 points, each ace 4, each king 3, each queen 2, each jack 1.

If the trump jack is not in play, no one counts it. If two or more players tie for game, no one counts the point for game.

THE BIDDING—Eldest hand bids first. Each player in rotation may either bid or pass; the lowest bid is two, and each successive bid must be higher than any preceding bid, except that the dealer may become the maker for the amount of the last preceding bid without bidding over. However, if any player bids four he is said to *smudge*, and the bid cannot be taken away from him.

THE PLAY—The *pitcher* (highest bidder, or dealer if he assumes the contract at the highest preceding bid) leads to the first trick. The suit of the card he leads *(pitches)* becomes the trump suit. On a trump lead, each other hand must follow suit if able; on any other lead, a player may either follow suit or trump, as he prefers. When unable to follow suit, a player may play any card—he need not trump. The player of the highest trump, or the highest card of the suit led if the tricks contains no trump, wins the trick and leads first to the next trick.

SCORING—When all six tricks have been played, the points due each player are ascertained. Usually a score is kept with pencil and paper. Each player except the pitcher always scores whatever points he makes. The pitcher scores whatever points he makes if his score at least equals his contract; but if he has not scored as many points as he bid for, he is *set back* by the amount of his bid (the number of points he bid is deducted from his score). Thus a player may have a net minus score, being "in the hole," in which case his score is shown on the score sheet with a ring around it.

The first player to reach a plus score of 7 points wins the game. The pitcher's score is counted first, so that if he and another player reach 7 on the same hand, the pitcher wins even though the other player has a higher total score. If two players other than the pitcher could reach 7 on the same hand, the points are counted in this order: High, Low, Jack, Game.

Smudge. A player who smudges and who makes his contract by winning all 4 points wins the game immediately, unless he was in the hole before he made his bid, in which case he receives only the 4 points.

IRREGULARITIES—*Misdeal.* See General Laws, page 14. It is a misdeal if an ace, jack or deuce is exposed in dealing. Since the deal is an advantage, a misdeal loses the deal.

Revoke (failure to follow suit or trump, when able to follow suit). A play once made cannot be withdrawn, so a revoke stands and play continues to the end. If the pitcher revokes, he cannot score and is set back the amount of his bid, while each other player scores what he makes. If any player except the pitcher revokes, all players except the revoker score what they make (including the pitcher, even if he does not make his bid). The revoking player cannot score, and has the amount of the bid deducted from his score.

Error in bidding. An insufficient bid, or a bid out of turn, is void and the offender must pass in his turn to bid.

Error in pitching. Once the pitcher plays a card, the trump cannot be changed.

If a player pitches before the auction closes, he is assumed to have bid four and play proceeds; except that any player in turn before him who has not had a turn to bid may himself bid four and pitch, whereupon the card illegally pitched, and any card played to it, must be withdrawn.

If the wrong player pitches after the auction is closed, the pitcher may require that card and any card played to it to be withdrawn; and, when first it is the offender's turn to play, the pitcher may require him to play his highest or lowest card of the suit led or to trump or not to trump; except that if the pitcher has played to the incorrect lead, it cannot be withdrawn and the pitcher must immediately name the trump, which he must then lead the first time he wins a trick.

SETTLEMENT—The winner of the game receives one counter from each other player who score is one or more, and two counters from each other player whose score is zero or who is in the hole. (*Variant.* Some play that the winner receives an additional counter from each player for each time that player has been set back.)

Smudge

One of the most popular forms of Auction Pitch, formerly called Smudge, is usually termed simply Pitch by those who play it.

This variant is the same as the game described under the heading Auction Pitch, except that winning all four points in one hand constitutes a smudge by any player, whether he is the pitcher or not, and wins the game immediately regardless of that player's previous score. The dealer is not permitted to take the contract unless he bids more than any previous bid. Low is scored by the player winning it in a trick, and not necessarily by the player to whom it was dealt. In case of a misdeal, the same player deals again.

It is customary for every player to start with a score of 7. When a player is set back, the points he bid are added to his score; points he makes are subtracted from his score; and the first player to reach zero is the winner of the game.

Auction Pitch with a Joker

Any variant of Auction Pitch may be played with the 53-card pack including the joker. In this event there are 5 points in play, the joker counting as one point to the player who wins it in a trick. The joker is the lowest trump in the play, but does not score for Low, that point going to the holder of the lowest natural trump card. If the joker is pitched, it is a spade. Game is won by the first player to reach 10 points.

In counting points to determine the winner of the game, they count in order: High, Low, Jack, Joker, Game. However, the pitcher's points are always counted first.

Sell-Out

In one of the most popular early forms of Auction Pitch, eldest hand has the right to "sell" the right to pitch. Eldest hand may either assume the contract himself for a bid of four, or give each player, beginning at his left, one bid as in Auction Pitch. Eldest hand may then *sell* to the highest bidder, in which case that player becomes the pitcher and eldest hand immediately scores the amount of the bid; or eldest hand may become the pitcher at the highest bid made, in which case the high bidder immediately scores the amount of his bid. A player is not permitted to make any bid high enough to put eldest hand out if he sells, and eldest hand is required to sell if he would put the high bidder out by refusing to do so. Game is 7 points.

Cinch

Once the most popular game of the All Fours family, Cinch (also called High Five, or Double Pedro) eventually gave way to Auction Bridge and finally to Contract Bridge among serious card players.

NUMBER OF PLAYERS—Four; each may play for himself, but

Cinch is almost always played two against two as partners, who face each other across the table.

THE PACK—52 cards.

RANK OF CARDS—In trumps, A (high), K, Q, J, 10, 9, 8, 7, 6, 5 (Right Pedro), 5 of same color as trumps (Left Pedro), 4, 3, 2. In each other suit, A (high), K, Q, J, 10, 9, 8, 7, 6, 5 (except in suit of same color as trumps), 4, 3, 2.

THE SHUFFLE AND CUT—All players draw, and in a partnership game the two high play against the two low; high has choice of cards and seats. Any player may shuffle, dealer last, and the player to dealer's right cuts, leaving at least four cards in each packet.

The deal passes, after each hand, to the left.

THE DEAL—Three at a time, in rotation beginning with eldest hand, until each player has nine cards.

THE BIDDING—Eldest hand bids first and each player has one turn to bid (or pass). Each bid must overcall the last preceding bid. The highest possible bid is fourteen, all the points in play.

DRAWING AND DISCARDING—The high bidder names the trump, and then each player discards all cards but trumps from his hand. Dealer then gives to each player in rotation enough cards to fill his hand out to six cards. Dealer then discards and *robs the pack* (looks through the undealt cards and selects whichever he pleases to fill his own hand out to six cards).

Each player but dealer must discard all cards but trumps (though there is no prescribed penalty for failure to do so), and if a player is forced to discard a trump (through having seven or more trumps in his hand) any trump he discards must be shown to the other players, after which it is out of play.

A player may change his discard until he has looked at any card dealt to him in the draw, but thereafter his discard may not be changed and if he has discarded a trump it must be shown, after which it is a dead card. However, if such a card is a scoring card discarded in error by an opponent of the high bidder, it is later scored for the high bidder's side.

OBJECT OF PLAY—To win in tricks the scoring cards, each of which counts for the side or player winning it, as follows: High, 1; Low, 1; Jack, 1; ten of trumps (Game), 1; each Pedro, 5; making a total of 14 points which may be scored.

THE PLAY—The high bidder leads first; he may lead any card. Each hand must follow suit to a trump lead, if able; on any other lead, a player may follow suit or trump, as he prefers. If unable to follow suit, a hand may play any card. Any trick containing a trump is won by the highest trump played; any other trick is won by the highest card of the suit led.

SCORING—If the bidding side wins at least as many points as it bids, the side with the higher count scores the difference between the two counts; thus, either the bidding or the non-bidding side may score. If the bidding side does not make its contract, the non-bidding side scores 14 plus the number of points by which the bidding side fell short. *Examples.* The bid is 6, bidding side wins 6 points, opponents win 8 points: opponents score 2 points for the hand. The bid is 8, bidding side wins 7 points, opponents win 7 points: opponents score 15 points.

Game is won by the first player or side to reach 51 points.

IRREGULARITIES—*New deal by the same dealer:* if a card is found faced in the pack; or, on demand of an adversary, if a card is faced in dealing; or if the shuffle or cut was improper, provided attention is called to it before the deal is completed.

Misdeal (loses the deal, which passes to the left): if dealer gives too many or too few cards to any player in any round, and the fact is discovered before the first bid is made.

Incorrect hand. A player with too few cards must play on; a player with too many cards must offer his hand, face down, and an opponent draws out the excess, which are shuffled into the stock.

Bid out of turn. Neither member of the offending side may bid thereafter, but any bid previously made stands.

Lead or play out of turn. The card must be withdrawn upon demand of an opponent if neither opponent has played to the trick. The card played in error is subject to call. If the lead out of turn was made when it was the offender's partner's turn to lead, the offender's right-hand opponent may require the offender's partner to lead or not to lead a trump.

Revoke. Play continues, but the offending side may not score in that hand and, if the offender is an opponent of the bidder, the bidder cannot be set.

Seven-Up

All Fours, or Old Sledge

NUMBER OF PLAYERS—Two or three, or four as partners, two against two.

THE PACK—52 cards.

RANK OF CARDS—A (high), K, Q, J, 10, 9, 8, 7, 6, 5, 4, 3, 2.

THE DRAW—High deals and has choice of seats; in a partnership game, the two high play against the two low.

THE SHUFFLE AND CUT—Any player may shuffle, dealer last, and the player at dealer's right cuts, leaving at least five cards in each packet.

THE DEAL—Three at a time to each player, in rotation beginning with eldest hand, until each player has six cards. The next card is turned up and placed on top of the undealt cards (stock), and if it is a jack the dealer scores one point immediately.

MAKING THE TRUMP—If eldest hand stands, the suit of the turn-up card becomes trump and eldest hand leads to the first trick. If eldest hand begs, dealer may say "Take it," whereupon eldest hand scores one point for gift; or dealer may run the cards (give three more cards to each player) and turn up another card. If this is of a different suit from the first turned card, it becomes trump without further option, and if it is a jack, dealer again scores one. However, if the second card turned is of the same suit as the first, that card and the three cards dealt to each player are laid aside, and dealer runs the pack again, continuing to do so until a new suit turns up or until there are enough cards to go around; in the latter case, there is a new deal by the same dealer.

There may also be a new deal by the same dealer if, when the second trump is turned, any player suggests "Bunch." If no other player insists that the hand be played, the same dealer deals a new hand.

If the cards have been run, once the trump is decided each player discards enough cards to bring his hand down to the original six.

THE PLAY—Eldest hand leads first. Each player in turn, if able to follow suit, must either follow suit or play a trump. The winner of each trick leads to the next.

SCORING—At the start of the game, each player has seven

counters, and each time he scores a point he puts one counter in the pool. In addition to the points for turn of jack and for gift, the following score:

High. One point for being dealt the highest trump in play.

Low. One point for being dealt the lowest trump in play.

Jack. One point for winning the trick containing the jack of trumps.

Game. One point for winning in tricks the greatest total in counting cards, each ten counting 10, each ace 4, each king 3, each queen 2, and each jack 1. In case of a tie for game, in two-hand play non-dealer scores it; in three- or four-hand play, no one scores it.

The first player to get rid of all his counters wins the game; if the winner is not determined until the end of a hand, and two or more players are able to go out, the points are counted in this order: High, Low, Jack, Game. Some play that 10 points, instead of 7, constitute game.

IRREGULARITIES—*Misdeal.* If dealer gives any player an incorrect number of cards, he loses the deal, which passes to the next player in turn. If dealer exposes a card, the player to whom it is dealt may decide to let the deal stand or to have a new deal by the same dealer. If a card is faced in the pack there is a new deal by the same dealer.

Revoke. The offender cannot score for Jack or Game, and each opponent scores one point if the jack is not in play; two points if the jack is in play.

California Jack

NUMBER OF PLAYERS—Two.

THE PACK—52 cards.

RANK OF CARDS—A (high), K, Q, J, 10, 9, 8, 7, 6, 5, 4, 3, 2.

THE SHUFFLE AND CUT—Cut for deal, high dealing; dealer shuffles the cards and his opponent cuts.

THE DEAL—Either one or three at a time, to each player alternately beginning with eldest hand, until each has six cards. The remaining cards are squared and turned face up in the center of the table, serving as a *stock*. The top card is the trump suit for that deal.

THE PLAY—Eldest hand leads first; the card led loses the trick to a higher card of the same suit or to a trump, but wins the trick otherwise. The winner of each trick leads to the next. The second player to each trick, if able to follow suit, must either follow suit or trump; if unable to follow suit he may play any card. The winner of each trick draws the top card of the stock, and the loser takes the next card; since the top card of the stock is always exposed, an object of play frequently is to win or lose a trick depending on whether the player wishes to draw the top card of the stock or take his chances on what the next card will be. When the stock is exhausted, the last six cards of each player's hand are played out until all cards have been played.

SCORING—One point each is scored for winning in tricks High (ace of trumps), Low (deuce of trumps), Jack of trumps, and Game (the greatest number of points in counting cards, each ten counting 10, each ace 4, each king 3, each queen 2, each jack 1).

The first player to score 10 points wins the game; if both players reach 10 in the same hand, the points count in order: High, Low, Jack, Game.

IRREGULARITIES—Non-dealer may call for a new deal by the same dealer in case of any irregularity in dealing. If a card of the stock is exposed during the deal, or is found face down after the stock has been turned up, there is no penalty and the card is merely restored to its proper position.

The penalty for a revoke is one point, deducted from the offender's score.

Shasta Sam

Shasta Sam is the same game as California Jack except that the stock is kept face down so that the winner of each trick does not know what card he will draw. Before the deal, a card is cut or turned from the pack to determine the trump suit for that deal.

PINOCHLE

Two-hand Pinochle

This is the original game of the Pinochle family and is still among the most popular two-hand card games played in the United States.

NUMBER OF PLAYERS—Two. The variants once played by three or four players have been superseded by Auction Pinochle and by several Partnership Pinochle games.

THE PACK—The 48-card Pinochle pack, ace high and 9 low in each of the four suits, with two cards of each denomination in each suit. Less often, the 64-card Pinochle pack is used, with 7 low in each suit.

RANK OF CARDS—A (high), 10, K, Q, J, 9.

THE SHUFFLE AND CUT—Cut or draw from a shuffled pack, high dealing first and having choice of seats. If both draw cards of the same rank, they cut again. Non-dealer may shuffle, then dealer shuffles and non-dealer cuts, leaving at least five cards in each portion of the pack. Dealer completes the cut.

THE DEAL—12 cards to each player, non-dealer first, dealt three or four cards at a time. The next card is turned up and placed on the table; it is the *trump card* and every card of its suit is a trump. The remainder of the pack is placed, face down, so as to cover half of the trump card; these cards from the *stock*. (When the 64-card pack is used, each player receives 16 cards.)

OBJECTS OF PLAY—To win tricks, so as to score the value of counting cards taken in on tricks; and so as to *meld* (German: "announce") certain combinations of cards having values in points.

The values of cards taken in on tricks are:

Each ace 11
Each ten 10

Each king	4
Each queen	3
Each jack..	2
Last trick	10

Nines (and 8s and 7s, when the 64-card pack is used) have no point value.

The values of the melds are:

A-K-Q-J-10 of trump (flush, or sequence)..150	
K-Q of trump (royal marriage)...........	40
K-Q of any other suit (marriage).........	20
Dix (lowest trump; pronounced *deece*).....	10

Class B

♠ A—♡ A—♦ A—♣ A (100 aces)........	100
♠ K—♡ K—♦ K—♣ K (80 kings)......	80
♠ Q—♡ Q—♦ Q—♣ Q (60 queens)......	60
♠ J—♡ J—♦ J—♣ J (40 jacks).........	40

Class C

♠ Q—♦ J (pinochle).............	40

(The dix is the nine of trumps if the 48-card pack is used; the seven of trumps if the 64-card pack is used.)

THE PLAY—Each trick consists of a lead and a play. Non-dealer makes the first lead; thereafter the winner of each trick leads to the next. When a trump is led, it wins the trick unless the opponent plays a higher trump; when any other suit is led, the card led wins unless the opponent plays a higher card of the same suit or a trump. The leader may lead any card, and his opponent may play any card; it is not necessary to follow suit.

After each trick, each player draws a card from the top of the stock to restore his hand to 12 cards; the winner draws first.

MELDING—Upon winning a trick, and before drawing from the stock, a player may meld any one of the combinations which have value, as previously described. He makes his meld by placing the cards face up on the table, where they remain until he wishes to play them, or until the stock is exhausted. Melding is subject to the following restrictions:

1. Only one meld may be made in a turn;

2. For each meld, at least one card must be taken from the hand and placed on the table;

3. A card once melded may be melded again only in a different class, or in a higher-scoring meld of the same class.

To illustrate these rules: A player may not put down
♠ K Q ♦ J and score both for the marriage and for the
pinochle; only one meld may be made in any turn. He may
put down ♠ Q and ♦ J, 40; and after winning a subsequent
trick he may add the ♠ K and score for the marriage. A
player may meld trump K-Q, 40; and add A-J-10 for 150;
but he may not first meld ♠ A K Q J 10 for 150 and later
score for a royal marriage, even if he adds another king or
queen of spades. A player may not meld ♦ K Q and then
meld another marriage in diamonds by adding another ♦ K
or another ♦ Q. He would need an entirely different K-Q
of diamonds.

Once a card has been melded and placed on the table, it
may be played to a trick as though it were in the holder's
hand; but when it has been played, it may no longer be used
to form a new meld.

Melding the dix. If the dealer turns a dix as the trump
card, he scores 10 points immediately. Thereafter a player
holding a dix may count it merely by showing it upon winning a trick. He may count the dix and make another meld
in the same turn. The holder of the dix has the right to exchange it, upon winning a trick, for the trump card.

THE PLAY-OFF—The winner of the twelfth trick may meld
if able; then he draws the last face-down card of the stock.
He shows this card to his opponent. His opponent draws
the trump card (or the dix, if the exchange has been made).
The winner of the preceding trick now leads and the rules of
the play are as follows: Each player must follow suit to the
card led if able, and must win if able when a trump is led.
A player who cannot follow suit must trump if he has a
trump. In this manner the last twelve tricks are played, after
which the players agree on the points respectively taken in
by the cards.

SCORING—Score may be kept with pencil and paper, or chips
may be used. If chips are used, there may be a central pile
from which each player draws sufficient chips to represent
the number of points he scores; or each player may be provided with chips representing 1,000, from which he removes
the appropriate chips as he scores points.

Melds are scored when they are made; score for cards
taken in tricks is added after the play is complete and the
cards are counted. In this count, 7 points or more count as
10. *Example:* 87 points count as 90; if one player scores 126

and the other 124, or if each scores 125, they count only 120 each; the other 10 points are lost.

GAME—Every deal may constitute a game, the player who scores the most points winning; no points are carried over to the next deal.

Another method is to make 1,000 points the game. When one player has scored 1,000 or more, and the other player less than 1,000, the former wins the game. If at the end of the play of any hand each player has 1,000 or more, play continues for a game of 1,250, even if one player has, for example, 1,130 while the other has only 1,000. If both players go over 1,250 at the end of the play of the hand, play continues for a 1,500-point game, etc. However, this seldom happens because either player has the right, during the play, to "declare himself out."

DECLARING OUT—At any point in the play a player may *declare himself out*. At that point, play ceases and his tricks are counted; if in fact he has 1,000 points or more, he wins the game even if his opponent has more; if the claimant has fewer than 1,000 points, he loses the game. If the game has been increased to 1,250 points, or 1,500 points, etc., a player may declare himself out when he believes that his score has reached that figure. (*Variant 1*. After declaring himself out, a player must win a trick before his cards are counted, and if in the meantime his opponent also declares himself out, the first to win a trick is the one to have his cards counted and to win or lose the game depending on whether or not his total is sufficient for game. *Variant 2*. The same as variant 1, except that the claimant's cards are not counted to verify his claim until he wins a trick on a lead from his own hand.)

IRREGULARITIES—(See also General Laws, page 14.)

Misdeal. The same dealer redeals. There must be a new deal if, before both players have played to the first trick, it is discovered that either player was dealt too many cards. Before playing to the first trick, the non-dealer may call for a new deal if any of his own cards or those of the pack are exposed in dealing, or if either player has too few cards.

There is no penalty for an *exposed card. A lead out of turn* must be withdrawn on demand of the non-offender.

Incorrect hand, discovered after the first trick: A player with too few cards draws, on his next turn, sufficient cards to restore his hand to 12 cards; if he has too many cards, he does not draw from the stock until he has the correct number. A player may not meld so long as he has an incorrect number of cards in his hand.

In drawing, if a player draws out of turn he must give the card to his opponent and then show his opponent the card he draws. If a player draws more than one card the excess is restored to the top of the stock, but all cards he drew must be shown to his opponent.

Stock incorrect. If finally three cards remain in the stock (two face-down cards plus the trump card) and if each player has the correct number of cards: The winner of the last trick draws the top card of the stock. The loser of the last trick, without looking at the face-down card, may decide whether to draw the face-down card or the trump card. Whichever card he chooses to draw, the other must be shown but is out of play and does not count for either player.

A *revoke* may occur only after the stock is exhausted. A revoke is failure to follow suit, trump, or win a trump trick, by a player able and required by law to do so. When every deal constitutes a game, a player who revokes loses the game. When game is 1,000 points, the player who revokes scores nothing for the cards he takes in, while his opponent scores for whatever cards he takes in; but play may continue after the revoke so that the offender may limit the number of points scored by his opponent.

In melding, if a player scores fewer points than he is entitled to, he may correct the score at any time before he has played or picked up any of the melded cards. If a player scores too many points when he melds, he must correct the score if his opponent so demands before drawing from the stock.

Three-hand Pinochle

A Pinochle game on the order of the two-hand game was once played by three players, usually with a 64-card pack, each player receiving twelve cards in the deal and playing in turn. Game was 1,000, as in the two-hand game. This variant has been superseded by Auction Pinochle (page 214).

Partnership Pinochle

The basic game of Partnership Pinochle will be described first, but two games developed from it have become more popular than the basic game; Partnership Auction Pinochle (page 207) and Double-pack Pinochle (page 209).

NUMBER OF PLAYERS—Four, two against two as partners.

THE PACK—The 48-card Pinochle pack.

THE DRAW—The two players drawing the highest cards play as partners against the other two. If two players cut cards of identical rank, they draw again.

RANK OF CARDS—A (high), 10, K, Q, J, 9. Of duplicate cards played to the same trick, the one played first ranks higher.

THE SHUFFLE AND CUT—Any player may shuffle the cards, the dealer last. The player at dealer's right cuts.

THE DEAL—Dealer gives three cards at a time to each player in rotation, including himself, except that he turns up his last card as the *trump card*. Every card of its suit is a trump.

THE TRUMP CARD—Each player in turn, beginning with eldest hand, has the right to exchange the dix (nine of trumps), if he has it, for the trump card. The trump card, or the dix exchanged for it, becomes part of the dealer's hand, so that each player has 12 cards. If the dealer turns a dix as the trump card, he scores 10 for it; each original holder of a dix scores 10 for it, whether or not he exchanges it for the trump card.

MELDING—Following the exchange for the trump card, each player shows on the table in front of him any melding combinations he holds, scoring them in accord with the tables and rules on pages 200-201, and, instead of doubling the value of a single combination, the following scores are counted for double combinations:

Double pinochle	300	All 8 kings	800
All 8 jacks	400	All 8 aces	1000
All 8 queens	600	Double flush	1500

Having shown and scored their melds, all players pick up their hands. No meld finally counts unless the side making it wins at least one trick in the play; if either member of that side wins a trick, both members score their melds.

THE PLAY—The eldest hand leads to the first trick; he may lead any card. Each player in turn must follow suit if able; must play any trump in his hand if unable to follow suit; if able must beat the highest card previously played to a trump lead. If unable to play according to these requirements, a player may play any card. The winner of each trick leads to the next. (*Variant*. Some play that each player in turn must try to win every trick, whether in trump or not, heading the highest card previously played to the trick even if it belongs to his partner.)

SCORING—A single score is kept for each partnership. The partnership is credited with the points both partners score in melds (provided the side wins at least one trick) plus the value of cards taken in on tricks won by the partnership. Cards may be counted as in two-hand Pinochle (A-11, ten-10, K-4, Q-3, J-2), but most players simplify the count by scoring 10 for each ace or ten taken in, and 5 for each king or queen taken in, jacks and nines counting nothing. Other players simplify still further by counting 10 points each for ace, ten, or king and nothing for any lower card. In every method the winner of the last trick scores 10 points and the total points by cards are 250.

GAME—The first side to score 1,000 points, in melds and cards, wins the game. Any player may claim the game at any time he believes that his side has scored 1,000 points or more; play then ceases and the cards are counted to verify the claim. If the claimant's side has 1,000 points or more, it wins the game regardless of how many points the other side had; if the claimant's side has fewer than 1,000 points, it loses the game. It may not count its melds in the current deal as part of its total unless it has won a trick after melding. If at the end of play in any deal both sides have reached 1,000 or more, play continues to 1,250; if the same thing happens again it continues to 1,500; and so on.

IRREGULARITIES—See also General Laws, page 14). *Misdeal.* There must be a new deal by the same dealer if more than one card is exposed in dealing. If the dealer neglects to turn the trump card, either opponent may decide either that there will be a new deal, or that a card be drawn face down from the dealer's cards to serve as the trump card.

Incorrect hand. If one player has too many cards and another too few, and if it is discovered before these players have looked at their cards, the player with too few cards draws the excess from the player with too many. If it is not discovered before the players have looked at their hands, they proceed to meld; after the melding is completed, the player with too few cards draws the excess from the unmelded cards of a player with too many; the cards so drawn may not be used in melding.

If a player revokes (fails to follow suit, trump, or play over on a trump lead, when able) or when he leads out of turn or exposes a card, his side may not score anything for cards taken in in that deal, but does not necessarily lose its melds.

Partnership Auction Pinochle

Twelve cards are dealt to each player, but a trump card is not turned. Each player in turn, beginning with eldest hand, may either bid or pass. The lowest bid is 100. When a player has passed, he may no longer bid; until then, he may bid each time his turn comes provided he overcalls the last previous bid. Bids are made in multiples of 10 points.

The highest bidder names any trump he wishes, and the players meld. Play then proceeds as in Partnership Pinochle, with the eldest hand leading to the first trick no matter who made the highest bid. A side which wins any trick may count the melds of both partners.

Scoring. If the bidding side, in melds and cards, scores at least the amount of its bid, it scores all the points that it makes; if it scores less than its bid, the amount of its bid is deducted from its score even if it causes that side to have a net minus score. The non-bidding side always scores all the points it makes. The first side to reach 1,000 points wins the game; there is no declaring out, because the score of the bidding side is always counted first and both sides cannot reach 1,000 on the same hand.

The widow. Some prefer to deal only 11 cards to each player, and a widow of four cards which goes to the highest bidder. The highest bidder looks at the widow, but does not show it; he may then keep one card for himself and give one card, face down, to each other player as he chooses. (*Variant.* Others play that the highest bidder puts all four cards of the widow into his hand, discards any four cards face down, and play proceeds with only 11 cards in each hand. The discard is counted among the bidder's tricks.)

Partnership Pinochle for Six or Eight

Six players form two partnerships of three each, sitting alternately (A-B, A-B, A-B). Eight players form two partnerships of four each, sitting alternately. A double Pinochle pack (96 cards) is used, and the cards are dealt out four at a time, so that each player has 16 cards in the six-hand game and 12 cards in the eight-hand game.

The rules of Partnership Pinochle (with the last card turned as trump) or of Partnership Auction Pinochle (with players bidding for the trump) are followed.

Instead of the scores for certain standard melds, as shown on page 201, multiples of these melds are scored as follows:

8 aces (two of each suit)................1000
8 kings (two of each suit)................ 800
8 queens (two of each suit)............... 600
8 jacks (two of each suit)............... 400
Double pinochle 300
Two kings and two queens of same suit...... 300
Double flush 1500
Triple pinochle 600
Three kings and three queens of same suit.... 600
Quadruple pinochle 1200
Four kings and four queens of same suit.....1200
12 aces (three of each suit)..............2000
12 kings (three of each suit)..............1600
12 queens (three of each suit)............1200
12 jacks (three of each suit)............. 800
Triple flush 3000
15 of same denomination, as 15 aces, etc.....3000

Firehouse Pinochle

This is the game from which Check Pinochle was derived. It is a four-hand partnership game, with 12 cards dealt to each player and bidding for trump. Eldest hand bids first, and each player has exactly one bid (or may pass). The minimum bid is 200, and a player does not need any specific holding to bid. The high bidder names the trump and leads first. Game is won by the first side to reach 1,000 points, and the score of the bidding side is counted first.

Check Pinochle

This is a Partnership Auction Pinochle game in which there are special bonuses, paid in checks (chips), for unusual melds and for making or defeating the bid.

Four play, two against two, using a regular 48-card Pinochle pack. Each is dealt 12 cards, and no trump is turned. The bidding begins with the player at dealer's left. The minimum bid is 200. None of the first three players may bid unless he holds a marriage; if they all pass, the dealer must bid 200, and may bid more if he holds a marriage. Until he has once passed, a player may continue to bid in turn so long as he overcalls the previous bid.

The high bidder names the trump; then all players may meld, according to the table on page 215. The high bidder leads any card, and play proceeds as in Partnership Pinochle (page 204).

Game is 1,000, and the score of the bidding side is counted first. Every hand is played out. A side loses its meld unless it wins a trick.

CHECK AWARDS—Each player collects from one of his opponents:

For melding: round trip, 5 checks; flush, 2 checks; 100 aces, 2 checks; 80 kings, 60 queens, or 40 jacks, 1 check; double pinochle, 2 checks.

For making contract: 200-240, 2 checks; 250-290, 4 checks; 300-340, 7 checks; 350-390, 10 checks; and 5 checks more for each series of 50 points.

For defeating opponents' contract: twice the number of checks for making contract.

For slam (winning all 12 tricks): 5 checks.

For winning game: 10 checks, plus 1 check for each 100 points (or fraction thereof) by which winners' score exceeds losers'; plus 5 checks if losers have a net minus score.

IRREGULARITIES—*Bidding without a marriage.* The opponents, after consultation, may elect: (a) to abandon the deal; or (b) to assume the contract at the highest or lowest bid they made during the auction, or (c) to require the offending side to assume the contract at the highest bid it made during the auction.

Revoke. A revoke (failing to follow suit or trump when required and able to do so) becomes established when the offending side leads or plays to the next trick; previous tricks stand, but all other cards go to the non-offending side.

Double-Pack Pinochle

The most popular form of Partnership Pinochle, this game arose in the 1940's and produced two innovations: A double pack, with no nines or lower cards; and bidding in which a player can tell his partner something about his hand.*

NUMBER OF PLAYERS—Four, two against two as partners.

---

* These rules are based on those prepared by Richard Setian of Philadelphia.

THE PACK—80 cards, four each of A, 10, K, Q, J (ranking in that order) in each suit. The pack is made by mixing together two regular 48-card Pinochle packs, discarding all nines.

THE DRAW—Each player draws a card from the pack. The two highest are partners against the two lowest, and the highest deals. There is no rank of suits, and if two or more players draw cards of the same rank they draw again to determine the order among themselves only. High card deals. [Example: A draws an ace, B and C draw kings, D draws a jack. B and C draw again; the higher will be A's partner, the lower D's partner. A deals.]

THE DEAL—Dealer shuffles the pack and offers it to his right-hand opponent, who cuts it approximately in half. The entire pack is dealt, four or five cards at a time, giving each player twenty cards. The turn to deal passes to the left.

THE BIDDING—(a) Beginning with the player at dealer's left, each player in turn may make a bid, announce a meld, or pass. Having once passed, a player may not reënter the auction.

(b) The minimum bid is 500. Bids are made in multiples of 10 and each bid must be higher than any previous bid. [*Note:* It is customary to drop the extra zero at the end of every score and bid, for example, 50 instead of 500, 51 instead of 510, etc.]

(c) Before any player has bid, each player in turn may announce the amount of his meld, without giving any other information as to the nature of his hand, as by announcing 100, 400 (or 10, 40), etc. He may announce more or less than the actual amount.

(d) In making a bid, a player may state that it is based on a flush or on a long suit and may also announce a meld, as by bidding 500 and announcing a flush and 100 meld. He may not name a particular suit, or say he has two long suits, or give any information as to the playing strength of his hand. If a player announces a flush or long suit before any bid has been made, he is deemed to have bid 500. If a player announces a meld in points after a bid has been made, he is deemed to have overcalled the previous bid by 10 points for each 100 points or fraction of 100 points that he announces. [*Example:* Last bid was 500; if next player announces 100 meld he has bid 510, if he announces 140 meld he has bid

520.] NOTE: In some games only bids and passes are permitted, no announcements.

(e) If all four players pass (or announce melds) but no one bids, the hands are thrown in and the next dealer deals.

MELDING—The high bidder names the trump suit; once named, it cannot be changed. Each player then melds, scoring as follows:

Sequences

A-K-Q-J-10 of trumps (flush) 150
K-Q of trumps (royal marriage) 40
K-Q of any other suit (marriage) 20
(No extra score for duplicated sequence;
double flush counts only 300.)

Groups

Four aces (one of each suit) 100
Double aces (two of each suit) 1000
Triple aces (three of each suit) 1500
Four kings (one of each suit) 80
Double kings (two of each suit) 800
Triple kings (three of each suit) 1200
Four queens (one of each suit) 60
Double queens (two of each suit) 600
Triple queens (three of each suit) 900
Four jacks (one of each suit) 40
Double jacks (two of each suit) 400
Triple jacks (three of each suit) 600
(A quadruple group counts simply as
two doubles; sixteen aces count 2000.)

Pinochles

Pinochle (♠Q & ◇ J) 40
Double pinochle 300
Triple pinochle 450
Quadruple pinochle 3000

A card that is part of a meld under one heading may be counted as part of a meld under another heading but may not be counted as part of another meld under the same heading.

A side's melds do not count unless that side later wins a scoring trick. A worthless trick, such as four jacks, does not make the meld count.

THE PLAY—The high bidder leads. He may lead any card.

Each player after him in turn must follow suit if able. If a trump is led he must play over if able. If he cannot follow suit he must trump if able. Of duplicate cards played to the same trick, the one played first ranks higher. The winner of each trick leads to the next.

SCORING—Cards won in tricks may be scored in either of two ways, to be agreed upon before the game begins: (a) aces, tens and kings 10 each; or (b) aces and tens 10 each, kings and queens 5 each. Other cards count nothing. Last trick counts 20. Total to be won in cards is 500.

If the bidding side, in melds and cards, makes at least the amount of its bid, it scores all it makes; if it makes less than its bid, the whole amount of the bid is subtracted from its score. Its opponents always score whatever they made.

Game is 3,550, and the score of the bidding side is counted first.

IRREGULARITIES—*Misdeal.* There must be a new deal by the same dealer: (a) If the pack was not properly shuffled or was not cut and if a player calls attention to the fact before looking at any card dealt to him and before the last card is dealt. (b) If more than one card is exposed in dealing. (c) As provided in the paragraphs on *Wrong Number of Cards* and *Illegal Information.*

Wrong Number of Cards. If one player has too many cards and another too few: (a) If the error is discovered before either player has looked at his hand, the player with too few cards draws the excess from the player with too many. (b) If either player has looked at his hand, any player may require a new deal; or, by mutual agreement, after all players meld, the player with too few cards draws the excess from the player with too many and may then change his meld. (c) If the error is discovered after the first lead, it is a misdeal.

Illegal Information. If a player during the bidding gives unauthorized information, as by naming a suit or saying that he has two long suits, the opponents may claim a misdeal. (They may consult before deciding, but may not show or describe their hands.)

Incorrect Bid. A bid in turn may not be changed. A bid out of turn counts as a pass. An insufficient bid in turn must be replaced by a sufficient bid or a pass, if attention is drawn to it before the next player bids or passes; after that it stands without penalty.

Incorrect Meld. (a) If a claimed meld does not contain

the proper cards, and the error is discovered before the first lead, the player may correct it by substituting correct cards, or withdraw it. (b) After the first lead, all claimed and undisputed scores stand and no correction may be made for a meld later found to have been erroneous; but this does not prevent correction of an error in writing down an agreed score.

Lead or Play Out of Turn. If a player leads or plays out of turn, and the opponent at his left plays before attention is drawn to the error, it stands as regular without penalty. If attention is drawn to the error in time, the card is withdrawn without penalty and the turn reverts to the rightful player.

Revoke. (a) A player revokes if he fails, when able, to follow suit, trump, or play over on a trump lead, as required by law. A revoke may be correct before the revoker or his partner has played to the next trick, and if it is corrected the opponents may withdraw and replace cards they have played in the interval; a card played by the revoker's partner may be changed only to avoid a second revoke.

(b) A revoke not corrected in time becomes established. Play ceases. Neither side scores for points taken in cards. The amount of the bid is subtracted from the score of the revoking side (regardless of which side made the high bid). The opposing side scores its melds, whether or not it won a point in play.

(c) The tricks taken in should be stacked so that their order is apparent. They may be examined when a revoke is claimed, and if an opponent of the claimant has mixed them so that the fact cannot be clearly established, the claim must be allowed.

Wipe-Off

This is Double-pack Pinochle with the proviso that a side must score 200 or more in cards to count either its meld or its cards.

Three-hand Double-Pack Pinochle

There are two methods of dealing:

(a) 25 cards to each player and 5 to a widow; the high bidder must announce the trump *before* seeing the widow.

(b) 26 cards to each player and 2 to a widow; the high bidder may announce the trump *after* seeing the widow.

Game is 4,550. The minimum bid is 500, and if the first

two pass, dealer must bid 500. There are no announcements of melds or suits in the bidding. Each player melds, and must win a scoring trick to make his meld count. The high bidder gets the widow cards and must discard that many cards before picking up his meld; his discard counts for him, but he must still win a trick to score his meld. Any irregularity in discarding is a revoke.

The high bidder may concede defeat before leading, in which case each opponent scores his meld plus 100, while the bidder is set back the amount of his bid.

Six-hand Triple-Pack Pinochle

Six play in two partnerships of three each; each player has an opponent at his right and left. Three regular Pinochle packs, without the nines, are mixed together, making a pack of 120 cards. Each player is dealt 20 cards, and the rules of Double-pack Pinochle apply, except that game is 4,550, the minimum bid is 750, and the last trick counts 30. Most of the extra melds made possible by the triple pack do not count extra; if a player should hold twenty aces, five of each suit, the value would be 2,500 (1,500 for triple aces plus 1,000 for double aces). However, quintuple pinochle counts 4,000 and all six pinochles count 5,000 (more than enough for game, if the side is not 500 in the hole).

Auction Pinochle

This is the most popular form of Pinochle for three players, and is even better for four, each for himself.

NUMBER OF PLAYERS—Three players receive cards in the deal; these are the active players. If four play, the dealer receives no cards; if five play, the dealer and the player second from his left receive no cards. These are the inactive players, who participate in the settlement but not in the bidding or play.

THE PACK—48 cards (Pinochle pack).

RANK OF CARDS—A (high) 10, K, Q, J, 9.

THE DRAW—Draw or cut for deal and seats; lowest deals first, next lowest sits at his left, etc. There is no rank of suits, and players cutting equal cards cut again.

THE SHUFFLE AND CUT—Dealer shuffles the pack and the player at his right cuts, leaving at least five cards in each packet.

THE DEAL—Three or four cards at a time to each active player in turn, beginning at the dealer's left; a widow of three cards is dealt at the end of the first round of dealing. All cards are dealt, either 3-widow-3-3-3-3, or 4-widow-4-4-3. Each active player receives 15 cards.

THE BIDDING—Each active player in turn, beginning with eldest hand, bids or passes. Having once passed, a player may no longer bid. Eldest hand must start by bidding at least 300; each successive bid, in multiples of 10, must be higher than any preceding bid. When two players have passed the auction is closed, the highest bid is the *contract*, the player making it is the *Bidder*, and the other two players are his *opponents*. (*Variant*. In many games the compulsory first bid by eldest hand is 250, not 300.)

THE WIDOW—If the contract is 300, the Bidder may concede defeat without looking at the widow, in which case his loss is reduced (see *Concessions*). If the bid is anything more than 300, or if the bidder of 300 does not wish to concede, he turns up the three cards of the widow so that all players may see them, and then adds them to his hand.

MELDING—The Bidder names the trump suit and lays out his melds, which are scored in accordance with the following table.

Class A

A-K-Q-J-10 of trump (flush, or sequence)....150
K-Q of trump (royal marriage)..............40
K-Q of any other suit (marriage)...........20
Dix (lowest trump; pronounced *deece*)......10

Class B

♠ A—♡ A—◇ A—♧ A (100 aces)........100
♠ K—♡ K—◇ K—♧ K (80 kings)........80
♠ Q—♡ Q—◇ Q—♧ Q (60 queens).......60
♠ J—♡ J—◇ J—♧ J (40 jacks)...........40

Class C

♡ Q—◇ J (pinochle)......................40

No card may be used twice in melds of the same class, but the same card may be used in two or more melds of different classes.

BURYING—Only the Bidder may meld. Then the Bidder *buries* (discards) three cards face down in front of him; they count for him as a trick won in play. The Bidder may not bury any card he has used in a meld. However, he may change the trump suit, the melds, and the cards he buries as often as he wishes before he leads to the first trick; thereafter he may make no change.

OBJECTS OF THE GAME—The Bidder seeks, with melds and by taking counting cards in tricks, to score at least as many points as he bid. His two opponents combine against him to prevent his making his contract.

Cards taken in count for the side winning them as follows: each ace, 11; each ten, 10; each king, 4; each queen 3; each jack, 2; winning last trick, 10. Some simplify the count by scoring 10 each for aces and tens, and 5 each for kings and queens, nothing for jacks or nines. Others simplify still further by scoring 10 for aces, tens and kings and nothing for other cards. Under any system, the total points scored for cards is 250.

THE PLAY—Having melded and buried, the Bidder restores his melds to his hand and leads to the first trick; he may lead any card. A trick consists of one card played by each player. The highest card of the suit led, or the highest trump if the trick contains any trump, wins the trick; of identical cards, the one played first outranks the other. Each player in turn must follow suit if able, and if a trump was led he must try to win the trick if able. If he cannot follow suit but has a trump, he must play a trump but need not try to win the trick if it has previously been trumped.

The winner of each trick leads to the next.

SETTLEMENT—In Auction Pinochle every deal is a complete game and the players settle in full before the next deal. Settlement may be made with chips, or a score may be kept with pencil and paper. The Bidder collects if his melds plus the value of the cards he takes in equal or exceed the amount of his contract; he can never win more than he bid. He pays if the points he scores fall short of his bid.

In settlement, the Bidder pays to or collects from every other player in the game, including the inactive fourth and fifth players if any, and including the *kitty* when the bid is 350 or more.

THE KITTY—A separate score is kept, and a separate pile of chips is maintained, for an imaginary extra player called the kitty. The kitty solely collects when a minimum bid of 300 is forfeited, and pays or collects the same as an opponent when the bid is 350 or more. Every player in the game owns an equal share of the kitty, must chip in to supply any deficit when kitty cannot pay what it owes, and shares equally in any surplus remaining in the kitty when the game breaks up or when a player leaves the game.

VALUES OF BIDS—Every contract has a value in units, or chips. The usual schedule of values is as follows:

Units (or Chips)

BID	BASIC VALUE	VALUE IF SPADES ARE TRUMP
300-340	3	6
350-390	5	10
400-440	10	20
450-490	15	30
500-540	20	40
550-590	25	50
600 or more	30	60

(*Variant.* Several other schedules of unit values are in common use. These are: (a) the basic value doubles for each step above 350, so that 450 is worth 20; 500, 40; 550, 80; etc. This schedule, however, tends to bring the value of an unusually big hand far out of proportion to the values of normal hands. (b) 300 is worth 1 chip; 350, 2 chips; 400, 4 chips; 450, 6 chips; etc., adding two chips for each step; these values apply when diamonds or clubs are trumps, spades count double and hearts count triple. (c) One unit or chip is added for every additional 10 points bid, so that 350 is worth 5, 360 worth 6, 370 worth 7, etc.)

CONCESSIONS—When the compulsory 300 bid is passed out, the Bidder may forfeit without looking at the widow, in which case he pays the basic unit value (3 chips) to the kitty but nothing to the other players.

Having intentionally looked at any card in the widow, the Bidder may concede defeat, in which case there is no play but the Bidder pays the basic unit value of his bid to each opponent. This is called a *single bete*.

The opponents, by agreement, may concede the Bidder's contract without forcing him to play. In this event the Bidder collects from every other player the value of his bid.

Once the Bidder leads to the first trick, the deal stands as though played out, even if either side later concedes.

DEALS PLAYED OUT—If the Bidder, having led to the first trick, makes his contract he collects from each other player;

if he fails to make his contract, he pays every other player twice what he would have collected if he had won; this is called a *double bete*.

INACTIVE PLAYER—An inactive player should not look at the widow or any hand, or give advice or comment on any matter of judgment in bidding, play, or concession. If he has not intentionally looked at the widow or any hand, he may draw attention to an irregularity, such as a revoke or a play out of turn.

IRREGULARITIES—(See also General Laws, page 14.)

Misdeal. Obligatory if the dealer exposes more than one card of any player's hand, or any card of the widow; may be demanded, before the widow has been dealt, if the pack was not properly shuffled and cut. The same dealer deals again.

Exposure of the widow—If, before the auction closes, a player sees any card of the widow, he is barred from the bidding. If he exposes any card of the widow, the deal is called off and the next player in turn deals; the offender must pay to each other player the unit value of the highest bid last made prior to his offense.

Incorrect hand. If discovered before proper exposure of the widow, the hand with too few cards draws, face down, from the hand or widow with too many; if discovered, after proper exposure of the widow, the Bidder makes his contract if his own hand is correct and if his own hand is incorrect he is bete (double bete if he has led). If the widow has too few cards, there must be a new deal by the same dealer.

Exposure of one card. By the Bidder, no penalty. By an opponent, or by a player who becomes an opponent: The Bidder may require or forbid him to play that card at his first legal opportunity to do so.

Exposure of more than one card. If more than one card held by an opponent becomes exposed, the Bidder makes his contract.

Insufficient bid. Void. If the offender had previously passed, no penalty; if he had not previously passed, he must substitute any sufficient bid.

Impossible bid. A bid of less than 300, or more than 650, or any bid which is not a multiple of ten points, is void without penalty.

Improper burying. If the Bidder leads before burying, or buries a card he has melded, he is double bete.

Bidder failing to announce trump. Any player may ask at any time what suit is trump. A player has no redress if he revokes through ignorance of what is trump, even if the Bidder failed to announce it.

Illegal information. After either opponent has played to the first trick, neither opponent may ask or state the bid, the melds, or how many points either side has or needs, and if an opponent does so the contract is made.

Looking at turned cards. If a player turns and looks at any played cards after his side has played to the next trick, play ceases and the other side wins. However, the Bidder may look at the cards he buried until he has played to the second trick.

Trick appropriated in error. Must be restored if claimed before it is covered by cards taken in on a subsequent trick.

Revoke. Any failure to follow suit, trump, or play over on a trump lead, when able to do so, loses the hand. If the bidder revokes he is double bete; if an opponent revokes the bid is made.

Lead out of turn. By a defender, the Bidder makes his contract. By the Bidder, no penalty but the proper leader may choose to treat it as a correct lead.

Claim or concession. If either side claims victory, play ceases and all unplayed cards plus last trick go to the other side. If either side concedes defeat, the concession is binding; except that an opponent may suggest to his partner that they concede, and if the partner does not agree play continues.

Error in count or meld. If the Bidder showed his melds on the table, and an incorrect point value was agreed upon for it, correction may be made at any time before settlement is completed. *Example:* Bidder's contract is 350. Bidder shows ♠ A K Q J 10 9 and ◇ K Q J. The agreed value is 210; Bidder plays and takes in 134. Then he remembers that the melds he showed actually should have been counted as 220. If he has not actually paid the other players, he is deemed to have made the contract.

Chances of Finding a Desired Card in the Widow

PLACES OPEN	CHANCES	APPROXIMATE ODDS
1	961 out of 5456	5-1 against
2	1802 out of 5456	2-1 against
3	2531 out of 5456	even
4	3156 out of 5456	3-2 for
5	3685 out of 5456	2-1 for

It must be remembered that there are two cards of every suit and denomination. Having one ◇ A in the hand, it is 10-1 against finding the other ◇ A in the widow.

Principal Auction Pinochle Conventions

As a rule the opponents should use the following methods, it being always understood that the usual play is not made when more points might be scored by a different play.

1. "An ace calls for an ace." When the opponent at Bidder's left leads an ace, the other opponent is expected to play the other ace of the suit on the trick if he holds it.

2. "Smear on partner's tricks." One should *fatten* (German, *schmier*) a trick won by partner by playing a high-scoring card on it, reserving his lowest cards for tricks won by Bidder.

Auction Pinochle Etiquette

Active players should never intentionally break the laws of the game (as, by making a facetious bid out of turn or by bidding after having previously passed) even when there is no penalty.

No player should remark or intimate that a card in the widow would have helped (or failed to help) his hand.

Auction Pinochle for 1,000 Points

Three or four play; when four play the dealer receives no cards. The deal and bidding are as described on page 209, except that the lowest possible bid is 100. The Bidder takes the widow, shows it and adds it to his hand; he then names the trump and all players meld what they can. The Bidder lays away three cards, which may not include any card he melded, and then leads to the first trick; he need not lead a trump. Each player plays for himself and scores what he makes in melds and cards, provided he wins at least one trick to make his meld good. If the Bidder does not score as much as he bid, he is set back by the amount of his bid; but the Bidder does not need to win a trick to make his meld good, since the cards he lays away count as a trick for him. The first player to reach 1,000 points wins the game, the Bidder's points are counted first, the eldest hand's points next. Irregularities are treated as on pages 218-219; but after an irregularity such as a revoke, play continues though the offender cannot score.

Sixty-Six

NUMBER OF PLAYERS—TWO.

THE PACK—24 cards (A, K, Q, J, 10 and 9 of each suit).

RANK OF CARDS—A (high), 10, K, Q, J, 9.

THE DEAL—Each cuts, and high shuffles, offers the pack for a cut, and deals six cards to each, three at a time, beginning with his opponent. The thirteenth card is turned up for trump and laid beside the *Stock* (undealt cards).

OBJECT OF THE GAME—To score 66 points as follows:

Marriage in trumps (K and Q announced) . . 40 points

Marriage in any other suit

    (K and Q announced) . . . . 20 points

Each ace (taken in on tricks) . . . . 11 points

Each ten (taken in on tricks) . . . . 10 points

Each king (taken in on tricks) . . . . 4 points

Each queen (taken in on tricks) . . . . 3 points

Each jack (taken in on tricks) . . . . 2 points

Winning last trick . . . . 10 points

The player who first reaches 66 scores 1 game point. If he reaches 66 before his opponent gets 33 (*schneider*) he scores 2 game points; if before his opponent gets a trick (*schwarz*) he scores 3 game points. If neither player scores 66, or each has scored 66 or more without announcing it, neither scores in that hand, 1 game point being added to the score of the winner of the next hand.

If a player *closing* gets 66 or more, he scores the same as if the game had been played out. If he fails, his opponent scores 2 points. Should a player close before his opponent has taken a trick, and fails to score 66, his opponent scores 3 points.

THE PLAY—Non-dealer leads first. It is not necessary to follow suit. The higher card of the suit led, or a trump played to a plain-suit lead, wins the trick. The winner of the trick draws the top card of the stock (his opponent taking the next card) and leads for the next trick.

Either player holding the nine of trumps may exchange it for the trump card at any time, provided he has previously won a trick, unless the nine is the last card in the stock. A marriage (see *Object of the Game*) is announced by showing cards composing it and leading one of them. Non-dealer may declare a marriage on his first lead, and score it when he wins a trick. Marriages may be announced only in leading them unless a player by showing a marriage makes his score 66 or more.

When the stock is exhausted or closed, the non-leader on each trick must follow suit if able. Marriages may still be scored.

CLOSING—Either player may *close* when he has the lead, either before or after drawing, by turning down the trump card. Thereafter no cards are drawn, and the last trick does not score 10.

If either player announces, during play, that his score is 66 or more, the play immediately stops and the game is "closed."

GAME—Seven game points.

IRREGULARITIES—As in Pinochle (page 203).

Three-hand Sixty-Six

Dealer takes no cards, and scores as many game points as are won on his deal by either of the players. If neither scores 66, or both score 66 or more but fail to announce it, dealer scores 1 game point and active players nothing. Game is 7 game points. A dealer cannot score enough to win game. His 7th point must be won when he is an active player.

Four-hand Sixty-Six

Use the 32-card pack (A, 10, K, Q, J, 9, 8, 7 of each suit).

Eight cards are dealt to each player—three, then two, then three, in rotation to the left, beginning with eldest hand. Last card is turned for trump and belongs to dealer.

Eldest hand leads, and each succeeding player in turn must not only follow suit, but must win the trick if possible. Having no card of the suit led, a player must trump or overtrump if he can.

Scoring is the same as in the two-hand game, except that there are no marriages. A side counting 66 or more, but less than 100, scores 1 game point; over 100 and less than 130, 2 points; if it takes every trick (130), 3 points. If each side has 65, neither scores, and 1 game point is added to the score of the winners of next hand.

Game is 7 game points. In some localities the ten of trumps counts 1 game point for the side winning it in addition to its value as a scoring card. If one side has 6 game points and wins the ten of trumps on a trick, that side scores game immediately.

BEZIQUE

The original game of Bezique is the ancestor of American Pinochle (page 200), which, as well as other descendants of Bezique—notably Rubicon Bezique and Six-Pack Bezique—have become more popular than the parent game.

NUMBER OF PLAYERS—Two. For three- and four-hand Bezique, see page 225.

THE PACK—64 cards; two 32-card packs shuffled together.

RANK OF CARDS—A (high), 10, K, Q, J, 9, 8, 7.

THE SHUFFLE AND CUT—After a preliminary shuffle by either player, each lifts a portion of the pack and shows the bottom card. Low deals first; if cards of the same rank are shown, the players cut again. Each player may then shuffle, dealer last. Non-dealer cuts about half the pack and dealer completes the cut.

THE DEAL—Eight cards to each player, dealt 3, 2, 3, non-dealer receiving cards first. The next card is turned and its suit is the trump suit; the undealt cards are placed face down, partly covering the trump card, and become the *stock*.

OBJECT OF PLAY—To show and score for certain *declarations* and to win tricks containing aces and tens, called *brisques*.

SCORING—If dealer turns a seven as the trump card, he scores 10; thereafter either player, upon winning a trick, may exchange a trump seven for the trump card, or merely declare a trump seven, and score 10. The other declarations are:

Marriage (K, Q of the same suit),
  in trumps 40
  in any other suit.................... 20
Sequence (A, K, Q, J, 10 of trumps)........ 250
Bezique (♠ Q and ◇ J)................... 40
Double Bezique 500
Any four aces........................... 100

Any four kings............................	80
Any four queens..........................	60
Any four jacks............................	40

Each brisque (ace or 10) taken in counts 10; winning the last trick counts 10.

All points except brisques are scored as soon as made, using special scoring devices or chips. After the play ends, brisques and last trick are counted and scored.

THE PLAY—Non-dealer leads first; thereafter the winner of each trick leads to the next. Any card may be played to the lead. The card led wins the trick unless a higher-ranking card of the same suit is played to it, or unless a trump is played to the lead of a plain suit.

After winning a trick, a player may make any declaration by placing the cards face up on the table in front of him and leaving them there until he wishes to play them, which he may do at any time. After making his declaration, if any, the winner of the trick draws the top card of the stock and his opponent draws the next card of the stock, to restore each hand to eight cards.

A player may declare and show more than one declaration in a turn, but may score for only one of them at that time, scoring any other of them (or a new declaration) the next time he wins a trick.

A card may not be used twice in the same declaration, but may be used in different declarations. *Example:* Spades being trumps, ♤ Q may be used in a marriage, sequence, bezique and four queens; but, four queens having been declared and one of them having been played, another queen may not be added to the three still on the table and another 60 scored. Four different queens would be required.

The K, Q of trumps may be declared as 40, and the A, J, 10 added at a later turn to score 250; but if the entire sequence is declared at once, the K, Q may no longer be declared as 40.

Bezique may be declared as 40 and a second bezique added for 500, but if double bezique is declared at once it counts only 500.

When the stock contains only one face-down card, the winner of the previous trick takes it but may not declare; his opponent takes the exposed trump. Each player picks up any cards still exposed on the table. The winner leads and in the play of the last eight cards each player must follow suit to the card led, if able; and must win the trick, if able.

GAME—1,500 points; if both players reach 1,500 on the same deal, the higher score wins. Some play 1,000 points as the game; some play that each deal represents a game.

IRREGULARITIES—The latest Bezique laws are those applying to Six-Pack Bezique (page 226), and may be applied to regular Bezique as well.

Bezique Without a Trump

This is the same as regular Bezique (page 223) except that no trump card is turned; the first marriage declared establishes the trump suit, and there is no count for the seven of trumps.

Three-hand Bezique

A 96-card pack is used (three 32-card packs shuffled together). The player to dealer's left leads to the first trick, and thereafter the winner of each trick leads to the next; all three play to each trick, in clockwise rotation. Only the winner of the trick may declare. The triple bezique counts 1,500; a player having counted 500 for double bezique may add the third and count 1,500.

Game is usually set at 2,000.

Four-hand Bezique

A 128-card pack is used (four 32-card packs shuffled together). Each may play for himself, or two against two as partners, who face each other across the table. All four play to each trick, in clockwise rotation.

In the partnership game, the winner of each trick may declare, or may pass the privilege to his partner (whereupon if his partner cannot declare, the winner of the trick cannot declare). Partners may not consult on which shall declare. A player may put down cards from his own hand to form declarations in combination with cards previously declared by his partner and still exposed on the table, but he may not declare any combination his partner could not legally declare (see above). That is, if one partner has declared a sequence the other partner may not add a trump king to the queen in the sequence and score for a marriage.

After the last card of the stock has been drawn, each player in turn must beat the highest card previously played to a trick, even if it was his partner's.

Double Bezique counts 500 and triple Bezique 1,500 only if all the cards come from the hand of the same player.

Game is usually set at 2,000 points.

Six-Pack Bezique

(ALSO CALLED CHINESE BEZIQUE; SEE RUBICON BEZIQUE, PAGE 230)

The favorite game of Winston Churchill (and a game at which he was one of the earliest expert players), Six-Pack Bezique is one of the most popular games of the fashionable world. It is fast, high-scoring, exciting.

NUMBER OF PLAYERS—Two.

THE PACK—Six 32-card packs, all shuffled together. It does not matter if they differ in back design or color (32-card packs are available economically in sets of three packs).

RANK OF CARDS—A (high), 10, K, Q, J, 9, 8, 7 in each suit.

THE SHUFFLE—Both players shuffle, trading portions until all cards of all six packs are thoroughly mixed.

THE CUT—Each player lifts a portion of the pack and shows the bottom card. The player cutting the high card has choice of seats and whether or not to deal; since the deal is a disadvantage, he invariably chooses not to deal. If the players cut cards of the same rank, regardless of suit, they cut again.

The dealer then lifts off a portion of the pack; if this portion contains exactly 24 cards, dealer scores 250. Non-dealer then estimates the number of cards lifted off; if his estimate is correct, he scores 150. The remainder of the pack is toppled over, all cards face down, at the side of the table so that cards may easily be slid off the top of it; this is the *stock.*

THE DEAL—Dealer, using the portion lifted off the pack, gives one card at a time to each player, starting with his opponent, until each has 12 cards. If cards remain undealt, they are restored to the stock; if there are not enough cards to give each player twelve, a sufficient number of cards is taken from the stock to complete the deal.

OBJECT OF THE GAME—To score points by showing certain *declarations,* sometimes called *melds,* as in Pinochle, and by winning the last trick.

DECLARATIONS—The following combinations have scoring value:

Sequence (A, K, Q, J, 10 in trumps)..........	250
in any other suit......	150

Marriage (K, Q) in trumps......................	40
in any other suit.............	20
Bezique—♠ Q—◇ J, if spades are trumps	
◇ Q—♠ J, if diamonds are trumps	
♡ Q—♣ J, if hearts are trumps	
♣ Q—♡ J, if clubs are trumps.......	40
Double bezique (two such queens and jacks)....	500
Triple bezique (three such queens and jacks)....	1500
Quadruple bezique (four such queens and jacks).	4500
Any four aces..............................	100
Any four kings.............................	80
Any four queens............................	60
Any four jacks.............................	40
Four aces of trumps........................	1000
Four tens of trumps........................	900
Four kings of trumps.......................	800
Four queens of trumps......................	600
Four jacks of trumps.......................	400

Winning the last trick scores 250.

Carte Blanche, which is having no king, queen or jack in the 12 cards originally dealt, scores 250. The entire hand must be shown. Thereafter, each time the holder draws a card he may show it before putting it into his hand, and if it is not a face card he again scores 250; but as soon as he draws a face card, or puts any drawn card into his hand without showing it, he may no longer score for carte blanche.

In many circles, carte blanche is not counted.

Variant. Originally, the spade queen and diamond jack counted as bezique no matter what suit was trump, and no other queen-and-jack combination ever counted as Bezique; many players still follow this rule in playing Six-Pack Bezique.

THE PLAY—When the dealing is completed, non-dealer leads any card; dealer may play any card to it (it is not necessary to follow suit). The card led wins unless a higher card of the same suit is played, or unless a trump is played to a plain-suit lead.

No points are scored for cards won in tricks; therefore the tricks are not gathered in, but are left face up in a pile.

The winner of each trick may show and score any one declaration; then each player draws one card from the top of the stock, to restore his hand to 12 cards, the winner of the previous trick drawing first. The winner then leads to the next trick.

THE TRUMP SUIT—The suit of the first marriage declared

becomes trump. If a sequence is declared before a marriage, the suit of the sequence becomes trump. The same suit may not become trump in two consecutive deals. A marriage in the trump suit of the previous deal may be declared before the new trump is established, counting 20. (*Variant.* When it is played that ♠ Q and ♦ J always constitute bezique, regardless of the trump, the same suit may become trump in two or more consecutive deals.)

METHOD OF DECLARING—A player makes a declaration by placing the counting cards face up on the table in front of him and leaving them there, except that any such card is available for play as though it were in the player's hand.

Every declaration is scored when it is made. Since the scoring is fast, it is customary to use special counting devices to record each player's score, or to use a pile of chips in at least three colors, representing 10, 100 and 1,000 each. As a player scores, he takes the appropriate amount of chips from the pile.

The same card may be counted in a declaration more than once. *Example.* A player puts down ♠ A, ♡ A, ♦ A, ♦ A and counts 100. He plays one of the aces. If it wins a trick, or the next time the player wins a trick, he may put down another ace and score 100 again.

However, no more than the cards necessary to any one declaration may be on the table at one time. *Example.* A player declares four queens of trumps, counting 600. He has in his hand another queen of trumps, but he may not add it to the four on the table and score another 600. He must play one of the four on the table; then, if he wins that trick or a subsequent one, he may add the queen from his hand.

A marriage may be declared, then A-J-10 of the suit may be added and a sequence scored; but if the entire sequence is scored at one time, the count for marriage is lost.

If double bezique is declared at one time, it counts 500; but if a single bezique is declared it counts 40, and when a second bezique is added (both cards of the first bezique being on the table) the full 500 is counted, making the total score for the two 540. Likewise a third may be added for a count of 1,500, provided all cards of the double bezique are still on the table; and a fourth bezique may be added for 4,000, provided all cards of the triple bezique are still on the table.

Only one declaration may be scored in one turn, but more than one declaration may be announced in one turn. *Example.* Hearts are trumps; a player who has ♡ K on the table puts down ♡ Q and ♣ J, declaring "40 (for bezique) and 40 to score (for the marriage of ♡ K, Q)." The next time he wins a trick he may score the additional 40. A player may have several unscored declarations pending at the same time. He may select the order in which such declarations are scored, and he is not required to score a combination unless he chooses, whether or not the necessary cards are on the table.

A player who has a declaration still unscored should announce it after every trick, whether he wins the trick or not.

THE FINAL PLAY—No declaration may be scored after the last two cards of the stock have been drawn. Each player picks up any cards he has on the table and the winner of the previous trick leads. In the play of the final twelve cards, the non-leader must, if able, follow suit to the card led, and must win the trick if he can.

GAME—Each deal constitutes a game, and the player with the higher score is the winner. The winner adds 1,000 to his score. If the loser has failed to reach 3,000, it is a *rubicon* and the winner scores all the points made by both players, even if the winner's score was less than 3,000. *Example.* The winner scores 2,700; the loser 2,600. The winner scores 2,700 + 2,600 + 1,000 for game, a total of 6,300. In computing the final scores it is customary to disregard any fraction of 100 points.

IRREGULARITIES—Incorrect deal. May be rectified by mutual agreement, but either player may demand a new deal. There must be a new deal if either player is dealt too many cards and it is discovered before a card is played.

Incorrect hand. If it is discovered at any time that each player has more than 12 cards, there must be a new deal. If it is discovered, after both players have drawn from the stock, that a player has fewer than 12 cards, play continues and the player with fewer cards than his opponent cannot win the last trick. If one player has too many cards and his opponent the right number, the offender is rubiconed but his score cannot be counted as more than 2,900. If the play is not completed, there is no score for last trick.

Exposed card. Non-dealer may demand a new deal if one of his cards is exposed in dealing. There must be a new deal if a card of the pack is found exposed before a play has been made; if discovered thereafter, the card is shuffled into the stock.

Illegal draw. If a player, in drawing, sees a card he is not entitled to, his opponent at his next draw may look at the two top cards of the stock and select either.

Lead out of turn. Must be withdrawn on demand, but may not be withdrawn without permission.

Odd number of cards in stock. The last card is dead.

Error in declaring. If a player shows and scores for cards which do not in fact constitute the declaration claimed, the score stands unless the opponent demands correction before playing to the next trick.

Error in scoring. May be corrected at any time before the final score for the deal has been agreed.

Revoke. If a player fails to play according to law after the stock is exhausted, his opponent scores last trick.

Imperfect pack. If discovered before the final score has been agreed, the deal is void; except that if the imperfection consists of a shortage due to cards found on the floor or in the vicinity of the table, the deal stands and such cards are dead.

Looking back at played cards is permitted. Counting the stock to see how many cards remain is permitted.

Eight-Pack Bezique

In some circles, Bezique played with eight 32-card packs is supplanting the six-pack game.

The eight-pack game is exactly the same as the six-pack game, described on the preceding pages, except for the increased number of cards and the following differences:

In the deal, each player receives 15 cards.

Single Bezique counts 50, double bezique 500, triple bezique 1,500, quadruple bezique 4,500 and quintuple bezique 9,000.

Five trump aces count 2,000, five trump tens 1,800, five trump kings 1,600, five trump queens 1,200 and five trump jacks 800.

The loser is rubiconed if he fails to reach 5,000.

Rubicon Bezique

This is the forerunner of Six-Pack and Eight-Pack Bezique. Two play, using four 32-card packs shuffled together, 128 cards in all. In the deal, 9 cards are dealt to each player. No trump is turned, the first marriage declared being the trump suit.

A sequence in a non-trump suit (called a "back door")

counts 150; triple bezique counts 1,500, quadruple bezique 4,500, last trick 50. There is no count for the seven of trumps.

Carte Blanche is scored as explained under Six-Pack Bezique (page 227) but counts only 50 each time.

The same cards may be used more than once in the same declaration, as explained under Six-Pack Bezique; but there is no additional count for four of a kind in the trump suit.

Each player gathers in his tricks as he wins them, but brisques are not counted except to break a tie or to permit a player to escape being rubiconed. If either player counts brisques, both count them.

Each deal is a game, the player with the higher score adding 500 for game. All fractions of 100 points are disregarded, unless they are necessary to determine the winner. If the player with the lower score has fewer than 1,000 points, including his brisques, he is *rubiconed;* the winner receives a bonus of 1,000 instead of 500; plus all his own points, plus all the loser's points, plus 320 for all the brisques.

Irregularities may be governed by the laws of Six-Pack Bezique.

Chouette

Three or more play Rubicon, Six-Pack or Eight-Pack Bezique, as follows: All three cut; high is "in the box" and has choice of seats; next-highest is "captain" and plays against the man in the box; the third and other players are partners of the captain and may consult with him, the captain making the final decision.

If the man in the box wins the game he collects in full from every opponent and remains in the box; the captain retires and the next player in order of precedence becomes captain.

When the man in the box loses a game he pays every opponent in full and retires, becoming lowest in order of precedence; the previous captain is now in the box and the player who would have replaced him, had he lost, becomes captain.

SKAT

Skat, the most popular game of Germany, has been carried by German emigrants to other countries, where they have won many converts to it. Many rate it among the most scientific of all games.

NUMBER OF PLAYERS—Three, four, or five, but only three play at a time.

THE PACK—32 cards (A, K, Q, J, 10, 9, 8, 7 of each suit).

RANK OF CARDS—When there is a trump suit, the four jacks are always the four highest trumps, ranking as follows regardless of which suit is trump: ♣ J (high), ♠ J, ♡ J, ◇ J. The remainder of the trump suit, and also non-trump suits, rank in order: A (high), 10, K, Q, 9, 8, 7. When there is no trump suit the cards in every suit rank: A, K, Q, J, 10, 9, 8, 7.

THE DRAW—In home play, positions at the table should be decided by lot in any agreed manner. In tournament play seats are assigned under direction of the Skatmeister (referee).

SHUFFLE AND CUT—The last shuffle must be made by dealer, and the pack is cut by the player at his right.

THE DEAL—One participant is appointed by agreement to keep score. The player at his left deals first. The deal then rotates clockwise around the table. It is desirable to terminate play only at a time when all players have dealt the same number of times.

Cards are dealt only to three players. With four at the table, the dealer does not give cards to himself. With five at the table, dealer omits himself and the third player to his left. In any event the first packet of cards is dealt to the player adjacent to dealer at his left.

The rule of the deal is "3-skat-4-3." That is, a round of three cards at a time is dealt. Then two cards are dealt face down in the center the table, constituting a *skat*, or *blind*.

Then a round is dealt four at a time, and finally a round three at a time.

DESIGNATION OF PLAYERS—The player adjacent to dealer at his left is called forehand or leader, the other two players in order being middlehand and rearhand (or endhand). He who finally wins the right to name the trump is then called the Player, and the other two become the opponents.

BIDDING—The leader is entitled to name the trump unless another player makes a bid which the leader is unwilling to equal. Leader does not specify how high he is willing to bid. Middlehand begins by making a bid. If leader is willing to bid the same amount he says "I hold" or "Yes." To win the right to name trump middlehand must increase his bid to an amount that leader is unwilling to meet. When a player wishes to drop out of the bidding he says "Pass" or "No." When the survivor is determined as between leader and middlehand, rearhand may if he wishes try to buy the privilege by the same procedure of bidding against the survivor.

If middlehand and rearhand pass without making any bid, leader may name his "game" (without bidding any specific number of points) or may pass. In the latter case, the hand must be played at Ramsch.

Each bid names merely a number of points, without specification of the intended trump or game. The lowest possible bid is 10. It is customary to bid up by increases of 2—10, 12, 14, and so on.

On conclusion of the bidding, the winning bidder, now called the Player, must declare his "game."

THE "GAMES"—Following is the list of the fifteen possible games that may be declared by the Player, together with the *base value* of each.

GAME	BASE VALUE

Tournee

with diamonds as trumps	5
with hearts as trumps	6
with spades as trumps	7
with clubs as trumps	8

Solo

with diamonds as trumps	9
with hearts as trumps	10
with spades as trumps	11
with clubs as trumps	12

Grand

tournee 12
guckser 16
solo 20
ouvert 24
ramsch 10

Null

simple 20
ouvert 40

Solo. On declaring Solo, the Player must also name the trump suit. The two skat cards (blind) are left face down and the hands are played out as dealt.

Tournee. On declaring Tournee, the Player picks up the top skat card. He may accept it as fixing the trump suit, in which case it must be shown to the others, or he may reject it without exposure (this privilege is called "passt mir nicht" —"It does not suit me"). When the first skat card is rejected, the second is turned face up and fixes the trump suit. The game is then known as "second turn."

If the card turned is a jack, the Player may select either the suit of the jack as trump, or may decide that only the jacks will be trumps, in which case the game becomes Grand Tournee.

Whether trump was fixed by the first or second card, the Player is entitled to put both skat cards in his hand and then discard any two cards face down.

Grand. In all Grand games, the only trumps are the jacks. Grand Solo is played without the use of the skat. On announcing Guckser, the Player picks up the skat cards without showing them, then discards face down any two cards to reduce his hand to ten. Grand Ouvert is a contract to win all of the tricks, with the Player's hand exposed on the table before the opening lead. Grand Tournee can arise only through the chance that a jack is turned up from the skat, following announcement of Tournee. The Player then has the option of declaring only jacks trumps, for a Grand Tournee.

Ramsch. Played only when all three participants refuse to make a bid or name another game. Ramsch is a Grand game, with only the jacks trumps. Each plays for himself and tries to take in as few points as possible.

Null. At Null, there are no trumps, and the cards in each suit rank: A (high), K, Q, J, 10, 9, 8, 7. Announcement of

Null is a contract not to win a single trick. The skat cards are set aside unused. At Null Ouvert the Player must expose his whole hand face up on the table before the opening lead.

THE SKAT—The two cards set aside from the play, whether they are the skat originally dealt or discards from the Player's hand, are added to the Player's tricks at the termination of play. Any counting cards found in the skat are reckoned in his score. At Ramsch, the skat is added to the winner of the last trick.

VALUES OF THE GAMES—The point value of each game has to be computed for scoring as well as bidding purposes. The point value of Null games is invariable, as given by the table under section The "Games." The point value of every other type of game is found by multiplying the base value, as given by the table, by the sum of all applicable *multipliers*. Following is the list of possible multipliers:

MULTIPLIERS

Matadors (each)	1
Game	1
Schneider	1
Schneider announced	1
Schwarz	1
Schwarz announced	1

Matadors. The term matadors refers to the holding of top trumps in unbroken sequence from the ♣ J down. A hand holding the ♣ J is said to be "with" a specified number of matadors. A hand lacking the ♣ J is said to be "against" as many matadors as there are trumps higher than the highest in the hand. *Examples:* A trump suit headed by ♣ J, ♠ J, ◇ J, is "with two," because the ♡ J is missing. A trump suit headed by ♡ J A 10 is "against three."

The first item in the total of multipliers applicable to a trump declaration is the number of matadors which the hand is either "with" or "against." The skat cards, whether used or not during play, are reckoned as part of the Player's hand in counting matadors. If the hand is "with," the skat may increase but cannot decrease the value of the Player's game. But is the hand is "against," a matador found in the skat may decrease the value. *Example:* Player has bid 30 and declares Heart Solo. His trumps are headed by ♡ J. Thus he is "against two," and expects to make contract through "Matadors 2, game 1, total multipliers 3; 3 times 10 is 30." But the ♣ J is found in the skat. The hand is thus "with one," the multipliers are reduced by one, and the Player is set unless in the play he manages to make schneider.

Game. In declaring any trump game, the Player contracts to win in tricks (plus whatever is in the skat) at least a majority of the 120 points in the pack, reckoned on this count:

Each ace counts	11
Each ten	10
Each king	4
Each queen	3
Each jack	2

(No count for lower cards.)

For gathering in tricks cards that total 61 points or more, the Player earns one multiplier, called the point for *game.*

Schneider. The Player strives to reach 61 points in cards, while the opponents strive to reach 60. Failure by either side to reach the half-total, i.e., 31 for Player, 30 for opponents, constitutes *schneider,* and adds one multiplier.

The Player may add one multiplier by predicting, before the opening lead, that he will make schneider, that is, gather at least 91 points in cards. Such announcement is allowed only in games where the skat cards are set aside untouched.

Schwarz. The winning of all ten tricks by one side constitutes *schwarz,* and it adds one multiplier. The Player may announce schwarz before the opening lead, i.e., he may contract to win every trick, and thereby gain one additional multiplier. Schwarz may be so announced only in games where the skat is not used.

COMPUTING THE GAME—The table of multipliers above shows the order in which the total must be computed, for all points beyond the count of matadors are cumulative. That is, having earned any of the subsequent multipliers the Player is entitled to all preceding it. *Example:* If he earns the point for schwarz, the Player also gets the points for schneider and schneider predicted.

The Player is not permitted to announce a game which cannot possibly score the value of his bid. That means that he may not declare Null if the bid is more than 20, nor Null Ouvert if the bid is more than 40.

THE PLAY—The opening lead is invariably made by the hand at the left of the dealer. Leader may lead any card he holds. Each other hand must follow suit to the lead, if able, remembering that at any trump declaration all four jacks are trumps. If unable to follow suit, a hand may trump or discard as he pleases. There is no compulsion to try to win tricks in any suit, if able. A trick is won by the highest trump played if it contains a trump, otherwise by the highest card of the suit led. The winner of each trick leads to the next.

OBJECT OF PLAY—At all trump declarations, the primary object of play is to win counting cards to the total of 61, the secondary objects are to win 91 points or win all the tricks. If the game is Null or schwarz announced, the object of the Player is to lose or to win all the tricks. At Ramsch the object is to gather as few counting cards as possible.

It must be emphasized that the Player cannot score at all, but loses the value of his game, if he fails to take in tricks the minimum number of points guaranteed by that game— 61, 91, all the tricks, or none of the tricks, as the case may be.

SCORING—The score sheet contains one column for each participant in the game. At the end of a hand, the value of the game is computed, as described by the foregoing sections. This value is entered as a plus quantity in the column of the Player, provided that it is at least as large as his winning bid, and provided that he has taken the minimum of points or tricks called for by his game. If the Player fails in either respect, the value of his game is entered in his column as a minus quantity. But the loss is doubled if the game was Guckser or second turn in a Tournee.

The multipliers for game, schneider, schwarz are duly applied to determine the value of the game, even when the Player fails to catch 61 points. In this case, the multipliers are deemed to accrue to the opponents. Therefore, on catching 60 points the opponents need not cease play, but may demand that it continue so that they may try to earn the multipliers for schneider or schwarz.

The value of the game may fall short of the bid by reason of an unlucky skat when the Player is "against." But the amount of his loss must be at least equal to his bid. In this case, his debit is the lowest multiple of the base value of his game that equals or exceeds his bid. *Example:* Player bid 24 and announced Spade Solo. He was originally "against two," but skat held ♠ J. Although Player made 61 points in cards, his game was worth only $2 \times 11 = 22$. His loss is 33, the lowest multiple of the base value 11 that exceeds 24.

SCORING OF RAMSCH—Ramsch is the only game in which each plays for himself. The player who gathers the least points in tricks is credited with 10 for winning the game, or 20 if he takes no tricks at all, the others scoring nothing. If all three tie in points taken in tricks, the leader is deemed the winner and scores 10 points. If two players tie for low score, the one who did not take the last trick as between these two is deemed the winner and scores 10. If one player takes all the tricks, he is considered to have lost the game and has 30 points subtracted from his score.

SETTLEMENT—The scoring column is kept as a running total of the points scored (or lost) by each player. When play terminates and settlement is to be made, each participant pays or receives according to the amount by which his final score falls below or above the average of all the scores. Example:

Final scores:

W	X	Y	Z
28	−75	137	82

It is convenient first to eliminate the minus signs by adding to all scores the numerical value of the largest minus score. Add 75 to each score above:

W	X	Y	Z
103	0	212	157

The total of the scores is now 472. Divide by 4, the number of players, to find the average, 118. Then the differences from average are:

W	X	Y	Z
−15	−118	+94	+39

The final pluses and minuses must of course balance.

IRREGULARITIES—See official rules, page 239.

Rauber Skat

In this variant, the Tournee game is eliminated, and the Player has the option of *handplay*—playing without the skat —or of picking up the skat and then naming his game. In either case he has a choice between naming a suit or only the jacks as trumps.

The increased use of the skat leads to livelier bidding and to some spectacular possibilities. Suppose that forehand wins the bid, picks up the skat, and then holds:

♣ - - - -
♦ A 9 8 7
♡ A 10 8 7
♦ A 10 8 7

If he wishes to risk the chance of finding a void in the hand of an opponent, the Player may try for maximum score by declaring clubs trumps. He lays away the two red aces, then leads his remaining ace and the two tens. If he can win these three tricks, he must catch at least 7 additional points in spades and 3 each in the red suits. The opponents catch only 54 points. The Player, being "against eleven," scores 12×12 or 144 points.

Expectancy of Finding Desired Cards in the Skat

The bidder's chance of finding at least *one* helpful card in the skat is shown in the following table.

TO FIND	PROBABILITY FOR	PERCENTAGE FOR	APPROXIMATE ODDS
Any one card	1/11	9%	10-1 against
Either of 2 cards	41/231	18%	5-1 against
Any one of 3 cards	20/77	26%	3-1 against
Any one of 4 cards	26/77	34%	2-1 against
Any one of 5 cards	95/231	41%	3-2 against
Any one of 6 cards	37/77	48%	even
Any one of 7 cards	6/11	55%	6-5 for
Any one of 8 cards	20/33	60%	3-2 for
Any one of 9 cards	153/231	66%	2-1 for

Official Rules of the North American Skat League

(Edition of Jan. 1, 1945. Reprinted by permission. Notes and commentary, enclosed in brackets in the rules, are by Joseph P. Wergin of Madison, Wis.)

These rules are designed for tournament play and assume certain customs in recording scores (as, a "won" and "lost" column for each player, and encirclement of certain penalty scores) which are not customary in home or club games.

1. CLASSES AND VALUES OF GAMES—*Section 1 Solos.* The Player declares any suit or jacks to be trump without the aid of the skat.

MULTIPLIERS

Each matador 1
Game 1
Schneider 1
Schneider announced (Solos only) 1
Schwarz 1
Schwarz announced (Solos only) . 1

SOLO BASE VALUES

Diamonds	9 points
Hearts	10 points
Spades	11 points
Clubs	12 points
Grand	20 points
Grand Ouvert	24 points

Section 2. Tournees and Guckser.

MULTIPLIERS

Each Matador	1
Game	1
Schneider	1
Schwarz	1

Section 3. Tournee. The player turns one card of the skat, thereby declaring the suit of this card to be trump except when he has turned one of the jacks, in which case he may either declare the suit of his jack to be trump or play a Grand Tournee. He must, however, decide before seeing the second card of the skat.

TOURNEE BASE VALUES

Diamonds	5 points
Hearts	6 points
Spades	7 points
Clubs	8 points
Grand	12 points

Section 4. Second Turn in a Tournee. The Player has the right to look at one of the skat cards; should this not suit him, he must show the second card, which shall be trump. Should the second card be a jack, the Player may name the suit of this card or Grand as trump. This play counts same as Tournee if won, but if the second card has been turned, the play, if lost, counts double. The Player need not show the first card if he decides to turn the second card, but he must show the second card before he places it with the other cards in his hand, otherwise he shall be charged with a lost play valued at 100 points.

Section 5. Guckser. The Player takes up both cards of the skat, thereby declaring jacks only to be trump. Should he win, the value is 16; losing 32. Every matador (with or against) counts 16 more, losing 32.

Any player attempting a Guckser should announce his play before picking up the skat cards.

[*Approved Ruling:* When, in playing a Guckser hand, the Player has bid 33, holding the heart matador; later finds one black matador in the skat, continues to play the hand and does not get schneider, he loses 96 points. This same principle also applies to a Tournee hand.]

2. NULL: 20 POINTS—The player announcing a Null wins his game by not making a trick.

3. NULL OUVERT; 40 POINTS—*Section 1.* The Player announcing Null Ouvert must expose his cards and play them openly. He wins his game by not making a trick.

Section 2. Null Ouvert and Grand Ouvert must be declared and the cards of the Player must be exposed before a card is played.

[*Approved Ruling:* No player may announce a Null after bidding more than 20, nor a Null Ouvert after bidding more than 40.]

4. RAMSCH—*Section 1.* When all pass, the lead or forehand has the option to announce and play Ramsch.

Section 2. A Ramsch shall be considered a game won to the player receiving the least points.

Section 3. Ramsch must be played when all participants have passed or failed to bid.

Section 4. The player receiving the least points will count 10 points as a game won; should he not take a trick, count 20 points as a game won.

Section 5. In case of a tie of all three players, the leader who announced the game is the winner of 10 points.

Section 6. If two players should be tied for low points, the player who does not take the last trick of the two is the winner of the game. Count 10 points.

Section 7. In case one player receives all the tricks, this should be considered a game lost, and the said player loses 30 points.

Section 8. The skat, or two cards commonly called the blind, shall be counted for the player taking the last trick.

Section 9. Any player misleading or neglecting to follow suit in Ramsch shall be eliminated from scoring, and the game shall continue as though no error had been made, each player making the error to be charged with the points made with a circle around the same in lost column.

5. DEALING—*Section 1.* The cards after they have been properly shuffled by the dealer, must be cut once (by the player to his right, taking off three or more, so as to leave at least 3 cards in each packet), and dealt in the following

order: 3-skat-4-3. The full deck of 32 cards must be taken up and dealt.

Section 2. If all cards are dealt, and bidding has commenced, the game must be played, even if the dealing was done out of turn; in such case the next deal must be made by the one who should have dealt before and then proceed as if no misdeal had been made, omitting, however, the one who had dealt out of his turn; thus each player deals but once during one round.

Section 3. In case a card is served face up, a new deal must be made.

Section 4. A dealer misdealing, and also, when turning a card face up, must deal again. If in the course of a game it develops that cards had been misdealt, i.e., that one or more players had either too many or not enough cards, then the Player loses the game if he did not have the right number of cards, even if the same thing occurred with one of the opponents. But if the Player had the right number of cards and one or both of the opponents had too many or not enough, then the Player wins, even if he would have lost the game otherwise. Each player should make sure before beginning the game that he has 10 cards, neither more nor less. (The dealer is no longer fined 10 points for misdealing.)

Section 5. The dealer has the right, and it is his duty, to call attention to any error in the play.

6. BIDDING—*Section 1.* Bids must be made only in numbers, the value of which occur in some possible game.

Section 2. He who bids and is awarded the play must play some hand that will score an equal amount of his bid or more.

7. OVERBIDDING—*Section 1.* If a Player has overbid his hand, the next higher value of the respective game is counted and charged against the Player; except in second turn and Guckser, where the charge is doubled.

The meaning of Rule 7, referring to the next higher value in an overbid hand, is that if a Player bids over the multiple, as for instance he bids 40, having diamonds jack in a Heart Solo and makes 61 points or more, he loses only 40 points if a black jack is in the blind.

Section 2. If the Player has overbid his game and one of the opponents makes an error, he wins the value of the game, being the amount he might have lost had no error occurred and the same value shall be charged against the opponent making such error. Both scored within a circle.

8. THE SKAT—*Section 1*. If before a game is announced, it is discovered that one or both of the skat cards are in the hand or amongst the cards of any participant, the dealer shall draw out of the hand of the person having the skat cards, or any of them, sufficient cards to leave said player 10 cards, after which the bidding shall proceed as if no mistake had been made, but the player causing this proceeding shall be fined 25 points and is forbidden to participate in the bidding and denied the opportunity to play any game during this particular deal.

Section 2. If any player by mistake has looked at either of the skat cards, he shall be barred from playing and fined 10 points. If he exposed one or both skat cards to another player, dealer shall mix the two skat cards, and he who plays a Tournee must turn the top card (second turn is barred), or he can play any other play.

Section 3. A dealer looking at the skat during play is charged with 100 points (encircled). Reason for penalty entered in "Remarks" column.

Section 4. If a player, when turning, accidentally sees both cards without having announced Second Turn, he shall be compelled to turn the top card and loses the right to play Second Turn or Grand.

Section 5. The skat must not be looked at by any participant before the end of the game, except by the Player when playing a game with the aid of the skat. The two skat cards, except when the Player plays a hand with the aid of the skat cards, shall remain with the dealer until the end of the game —and then turned face up on the table.

Section 6. If the Player who plays a Solo looks at the skat, he loses his game, but opponents may insist on his continuing for the purpose of increasing his loss.

Section 7. If either opponent examines the skat, the Player wins. He has the same privilege as in Section 6 and the one who looks at the skat loses the number of points the Player wins.

Section 8. Whoever discards more or less than two cards loses his game.

9. TRICKS—*Section 1*. All participants must keep their respective tricks in the order in which the cards were played so that each trick can be traced at the end of the game.

Section 2. The Player has the privilege to throw his game after the first trick and claim schneider. He loses this privilege after two cards of the second trick are on the table.

Section 3. Participants have the privilege to examine the last trick made. This must, however, be done before the next card is played.

Section 4. Examining tricks taken, except the last, or recounting is not permitted. Should this be done the opposing side may claim the game.

Section 5. If a player throws down his cards and declares his game won, he cannot claim another trick.

10. SCHNEIDER AND SCHWARZ—*Section 1.* In order to win game the Player must have at least 61; to make schneider he must have at least 91; to make schwarz he must take every trick.

Section 2. The Player to be out of schneider must have at least 31 points, the opponents 30.

Section 3. Schneider or schwarz cannot be announced in any game in which the aid of the skat was required.

Section 4. A player announcing a Solo has the privilege before a card is played of increasing the Solo or announcing Grand, schneider or schwarz.

11. REVOKES AND MISPLAYS—*Section 1.* If the Player misleads or neglects to follow suit, he loses the game, even though he already has 61 or more points. Any one of the opponents, however, has the privilege to have such error corrected and proceed with the game to its end for the purpose of increasing the Player's loss. If, then, one of the opponents makes one of these errors, the Player wins his game, and the full value scored by the Player is charged, within a circle, against the opponent making the error.

Section 2. If either of the opponents leads wrongly, plays out of turn or neglects to follow suit, the error must immediately be corrected if possible. The play then must proceed to the end. If the Player then makes one of the errors above mentioned, he loses the game and the first error is fully condoned. If the game proceeds at the insistence of either of the opponents, and again one of the opponents makes one of the errors referred to above, all previous errors are condoned. The Player must get 61 or more points to enable him to get a bona fide game. [The meaning of this section is that no player can win a bona fide hand on a misplay by an opponent. In such case the hand must be played to the end to determine if the Player could win his hand, or had a possible chance had the misplay by an opponent not occurred. The Skatmeister must be called to decide if the Player had a possible chance to win, and if so, he may so rule. He must okay the play if won. If the Skatmeister rules that the Player could not win, he then, nevertheless, receives credit for points, within a circle. The one making the error also loses the full value of the hand, within a circle.]

Section 3. If, during the progress of a game, the Player places his cards upon the table or exposes them, this shall be construed as his claiming the remaining tricks, and if he fails to make them all, he loses the full value of the game unless he already has 61.

Section 4. If, during the progress of the game, any one of the opponents places his cards upon the table or exposes them, this shall be construed as his declaring thereby to have defeated the Player's game, all the remaining cards belong to the Player, and should this made 61 or more points for the Player, he wins and the opponent who erred shall be charged with the full value of the game with a circle.

Section 5. Three-handed Tables. In a three-handed table the first card only, if played out of turn by the person who believes himself the one to lead, shall not be considered a misplay; nor shall any participant who may play out of turn on the last trick be in any manner penalized.

Schafskopf
(Schafkopf, or Sheepshead)

Schafskopf is at least 200 years old, being one of the precursors of Skat. Beside the principal variants here described, there are many local variants—for four actual players, or six actual players; with only the black queens ranking as trumps, or with no queens ranking as permanent trumps; with no trumps other than jacks, or jacks and queens, or with bidding to determine the right to name the trump suit; with a double pack of 48 cards, or a double pack of 64 cards. But the rules of play and the point values of the cards are the same in all these variants.

NUMBER OF PLAYERS—Three, four, or five, but only three play at a time.

RANK OF CARDS—All queens, jacks, and diamonds are trumps, ranking in order: ♣ Q (high), ♠ Q, ♡ Q, ◇ Q, ♣ J, ♠ J, ♡ J, ◇ J, ◇ A, ◇ 10, ◇ K, ◇ 9, ◇ 8, ◇ 7.

In each of the three side suits the cards rank: A (high), 10, K, 9, 8, 7.

THE DEAL—The draw, shuffle, cut and deal are as in Skat (page 232). Dealer gives three cards at a time to each of the three players, then two cards face down for the blind, then a round of four at a time, finally a round of three at a time. Each player thus receives ten cards.

DETERMINING THE PLAYER—Eldest hand has first right to pick up the blind. If he refuses, the privilege passes to the two others in turn. Whoever picks up the blind assumes a contract to win a majority of the points for cards, and plays alone against the other two. The *Player* after picking up the blind must discard two cards face down to restore his hand to ten cards. If all three pass, the hand must be played at "least," as described below.

GAME—For purposes of determining game, the cards have point values as follows (whether trump or plain):

Each ace	11
Each ten	10
Each king	4
Each queen	3
Each jack	2

(No count for lower cards.)

The total points in the pack is 120, and the player wins *game* if he takes 61 or more in tricks won in play. If he gathers 91 points or more, he wins *schneider*, and if he takes all the tricks he wins *schwarz*.

LEAST—If all three players pass, the hand is played for "*least*." Each plays for himself, the object being to take as few of the points for cards as possible.

The blind is left untouched until play is completed, when it is added to the last trick and goes to the winner thereof.

THE PLAY—The hand at dealer's left invariably makes the opening lead. Winner of each trick leads for the next. Other hands must follow suit to the lead if able. If unable to follow suit, a hand may trump or discard at will. There is no compulsion to win any trick if able. The highest trump played, or the highest card of the suit led if no trump is played, wins the trick. It is important to remember that all queens, jacks and diamonds are of the same "suit."

SCORING—Individual accounts are kept, a running total of the items won or lost by each participant. If the blind is picked up, the scoring values are:

Game	2
Schneider	4
Schwarz	6

If the Player catches 61 points or more, he is credited with the appropriate figure. If he fails to make 61, he is debited the appropriate figure (4 if he fails to catch 31 points or 6 if he loses all the tricks.)

At the game *least,* the player who gathers the fewest points scores plus 2, or plus 4 if he wins no tricks at all. If one player takes all the tricks, he is debited 4. If two players tie for low, the winner is he who did not take the last trick as between these two, and he gets 2 points. If each player gets 40 points in cards (triple tie), the winner is the hand that passed third, and he scores 2.

IRREGULARITIES—*Misdeal.* If a card is dealt face up there must be a new deal. If the wrong player deals, and the error is not discovered before the deal is complete, the hand is played; the deal then reverts to the player whose rightful turn it was, and continues in rotation, except that the player who dealt out of turn is skipped at his next turn in rotation. If any hand is dealt the wrong number of cards, there must be a new deal if the error is discovered before the opening lead; if the error is discovered later, play ends and the player wins if his hand was correct, or loses if it was incorrect.

Wrong discard. If after the opening lead the Player is found to have discarded more or less than two cards, he loses.

Looking at the blind. No participant (including dealer) may look at the cards in the blind, except the Player. Penalty, 4 points.

Misplay. If either opponent leads or plays out of turn, fails to follow suit when able, exposes a card except in his rightful turn to play, indicates his holding of any card by word or act, or examines any quitted trick but the last, the Player wins and the opponent in error is charged with the full loss.

If the Player leads or plays out of turn, fails to follow suit when able, or examines any quitted trick but the last, he loses.

Claims and concessions. If either side claims to have won game, all remaining unplayed cards belong to the other side. An opponent who makes an erroneous claim is charged with the entire loss. If the Player concedes loss of game, the concession must stand.

Auction Sheepshead

This is a variant of Schafskopf for four players, two against two as partners. The cards are dealt out four at a time, each hand receiving eight cards. Eldest hand makes first bid or pass, and each other hand in turn is allowed one bid. Bidding is by the number of points over 60 that the bidder (with help of his partner) guarantees to win in play. The only permanent trumps are ♣ J (high), ♠ J, ♡ J, ◇ J. Winning bidder names the trump, and eldest hand makes the first lead. Rules of play are as in Schafskopf.

Six-bid Solo

Many local variants of Skat are played, under such names as Solo, Slough, Sluff. All have in common that the point value of the cards and the object of play are the same as in Skat. They differ mainly in the number and types of "games" or declarations that may be bid. One of the most popular variants is Six-bid Solo. (The name Solo has also been given to certain variants of Whist, Bridge, and to the modern version of Ombre, as described on page 250.)

NUMBER OF PLAYERS—Three or four, but only three play at a time.

THE PACK—36 cards.

RANK OF CARDS—The cards in each suit rank: A (high), 10, K, Q, J, 9, 8, 7, 6.

POINT VALUE OF CARDS—The point value of the high cards is as in Skat:

Each ace counts..................	11
Each ten counts..................	10
Each king counts.................	4
Each queen counts................	3
Each jack counts.................	2

(No count for lower cards)

THE DEAL—If four play, the dealer does not give cards to himself. The rule of the deal is "4-3-widow-4." That is, dealer first deals a round of four at a time, beginning with the player at his left; then a round of three at a time, then three cards face down for a widow or blind; finally a round of four at a time. Each hand thus receives eleven cards.

BIDDING—Eldest hand makes the first bid or pass. Each bid consists in naming one of the six games. If he bids and next hand bids more (names a higher-ranking game) these two first settle who can make the higher bid. Once a player passes, he is out of the bidding. Third player settles with survivor of first two as to which can make the higher bid. Player who wins the bidding is called the Bidder. If all pass, there is a new deal by the next dealer in turn.

THE GAMES (BIDS)—There are six possible bids, ranking as follows:

Call Solo (high)
Spread Misere
Guarantee Solo
Misere
Heart Solo
Solo

Solo. At simple solo, Bidder names any suit other than hearts as trumps. The widow is set aside untouched, but is added to Bidder's cards at the end of play. Bidder does not name his trump unless and until his bid proves to be the high one.

Heart Solo. Same as simple solo in all respects, but hearts are trumps.

Misere. There are no trumps, and Bidder undertakes to avoid taking any counting card. The widow is set aside and is not used during play or counted afterward.

Guarantee Solo. Bidder guarantees to win a certain minimum of the counting cards: 74 points if he names hearts as trumps, or 80 if he names another suit. The widow is not used during play but is added to Bidder's cards afterward.

Spread Misere. Same as misere with two additions: Bidder exposes his whole hand face up after the opening lead, and the opening lead is made by the player at left of Bidder.

Call Solo. Bidder undertakes to win all 120 points. The widow is not used in play but is added to Bidder's tricks at end. Before the opening lead, Bidder calls for any card not in his hand, and the holder of this card must give it to him in exchange for any that Bidder chooses to give in return. If the called card is in the widow, there is no exchange of cards.

THE PLAY—Except in spread misere, the opening lead is invariably made by the player at left of dealer. Each hand must follow suit to the lead, if able, and if unable to follow suit must trump, if able. But there is no compulsion to trump high or low. The object in play (if there is a trump) is to win counting cards. The object in both misere games is to avoid taking any cards that count. The two other players combine against the Bidder.

SCORING—It is most convenient to use counters or chips and settle after every deal. The Bidder, if he makes the required number of points in play, collects the value of his game from each of the other players; if he fails, he pays a like amount to each other player. If there are four players, all share in the gains or losses, except that if the Bidder makes simple solo or heart solo he collects only from the two other active players.

GAME	BIDDER MUST TAKE	VALUE IN CHIPS
Call Solo	120 points	
hearts trumps		150
another trump		100
Spread Misere	no points	60
Guarantee Solo		40
hearts trumps	74 points	
another trump	80 points	
Misere	no points	30
Heart Solo	60 points	3 for each point over or under 60
Simple Solo	60 points	2 for each point over or under 60

In simple solo and heart solo, if each side wins 60 points there is no score for the deal.

IRREGULARITIES—The rules of Skat (page 232) should be used to govern irregularities in play.

Frog

This variant of Solo, very popular in Mexico and the southern United States, makes an excellent introduction to Six-bid Solo and Skat.

Frog is in all essentials the same as Six-bid Solo, with the difference that there are only three possible bids:

Frog (lowest). Hearts are trumps. The bidder picks up the widow and then discards any three cards face down. He collects or pays for every point he takes in play over or under 60.

Chico has the same meaning as *simple solo* in Six-bid Solo.

Grand (highest) has the same meaning as *heart solo* in Six-bid Solo.

Solo (Ombre)

The game Ombre, or Hombre, once popular throughout the world, has survived in a form called Solo, not to be confused with the variants of Skat and Whist known by the same name. Solo (Ombre) is an easy fast-moving game free of the complexities of count and scoring that are found in the other varieties.

NUMBER OF PLAYERS—Four.

THE PACK—32 cards (A, K, Q, J, 10, 9, 8, 7 of each suit).

RANK OF CARDS—The black queens are permanent trumps. The ♣ Q, called *spadilla*, is the highest trump, and the ♦ Q, called *basta*, is the third-highest trump. The second-highest trump, called *manilla*, is the 7 of the trump suit. The cards in each suit, trump or plain, rank as follows: A (high), K, Q (in red suits), J, 10, 9, 8, 7 (unless promoted to *manilla*).

THE DRAW—Any player distributes cards face up, one at a time around the table, and the first player who receives a club becomes the first dealer.

THE SHUFFLE AND CUT—Dealer has the right to shuffle last. The pack is cut by the player at his right; the cut must leave at least five cards in each packet.

THE DEAL—The rule of the deal is "3-2-3," that is, dealer first gives a round of three cards at a time, then a round two at a time, finally another round three at a time. Each player thus receives eight cards.

OBJECT OF PLAY—To win at least five tricks, or to win all eight tricks, dependent on the bid.

THE COLOR—One suit is fixed as *the color* by agreement before play commences. In the absence of agreement, clubs is the color. (*Variant.* The play commences without a color, and the suit of the first game won becomes the color thereafter.)

A bid is *in color* when it names this prefixed suit as trump; a bid is *in suit* if it names any other suit. Bids in color rank higher than bids in suit.

THE "GAMES"—The possible games that may be declared rank in bidding precedence as follows:

> Tout in color (high)
> Tout in suit
> Solo in color
> Solo in suit
> Simple Game (Frog) in color
> Simple Game in suit

If all four players pass without a bid, the hand must be played at the game Spadilla.

Simple Game (Frog). Player names the trump suit and then calls an ace which he does not hold himself. The holder of the called ace becomes his partner, but must say nothing to reveal the fact. The partnerships become evident when the called ace is played. Player and his partner must win at least five tricks.

If a player holds both spadilla and basta (the black

queens), he may not allow the hand to be played at Simple Game. If no higher bid has been made ahead of him, he must declare Solo or Tout. (This compulsion is called Forcée.)

Solo. Player names the trump suit and then plays alone against the other three.

Tout. This game is a Solo in which the Player undertakes to win all eight tricks.

Spadilla. If all four players pass without a bid, the holder of spadilla (♣ Q) must announce it and must undertake a Simple Game.

THE BIDDING—Eldest hand has the first turn to bid. He first settles with the next hand as to which will bid higher; the survivor settles with third hand, and so on. Once a player has passed he is out of the bidding.

The winning bidder is entitled to hold to the bid that won, or to name any higher declaration. Each bidder therefore conceals his real intention so far as possible, bidding only high enough to overcall the previous bid.

Eldest hand has the first turn to bid, and if he does not pass he says "I ask" (German, *ich frage,* whence the term *frog*). This is equivalent to a bid of Simple Game. If the next hand wishes to overcall, he says "Is it in color?" If the answer is "yes," the other may continue, "Is it a solo?" and so on. When the bidder whose intentions are so asked passes, the questioner stands committed to play a game at least as good as the last he named.

The winning bidder becomes the Player, and must at once announce his game and the trump suit.

THE PLAY—The opening lead is invariably made by eldest hand (the player at dealer's left). Each other hand must follow suit to the lead if able; if unable, the hand may discard or trump at will. A trick is won by the highest card of the suit led, or by the highest trump if it contains a trump. Winner of a trick leads for the next.

SCORING—The basic values of the games are as follows:

Simple Game in suit.............	2
Simple Game in color............	4
Solo in suit....................	4
Solo in color...................	8
Tout in suit....................	16
Tout in color...................	32

At Simple Game, the Player and his partner each win 2 or

lose 2. (If settlement is by chips, 4 chips thus change hands.)

At Solo or Tout, the value of the game is paid by each opponent to, or collected by each opponent from, the Player.

(*Variant*. In addition to this settlement for each hand, dealer puts 2 chips into a pool, and the pool accumulates until it is won by the first player who makes a Solo in color or a Tout.)

IRREGULARITIES—A player who fails to follow suit when able loses the game and must pay the entire loss for his side. If an opponent of the Player leads or plays out of turn, or exposes a card, his side loses and the offender must pay the entire loss. No penalty against the Player for similar errors; the error must be corrected if possible and play continued. (*Variant*. Where there is a pool, if a penalizable error is made in a Simple Game the offender also pays a *bete* to the pool. The bete is 16 chips, or as many as are needed to double the amount already in the pool.)

VARIANTS—There are many of these, because Solo has been played in so many different countries and for so many generations. Among the principal variants still played are:

1. The Player may not call the ace of a suit of which he is void; or

2. The Player may not call the ace of a suit of which he is void unless he also puts a card face down on the table; that card must be played to the first trump lead but cannot win a trick.

3. In a declared Simple Game or Solo, either side may win a double (in suit) or quadruple (in color) game by taking 8 tricks; provided that if the side plays on after winning the first 5 tricks, and then loses a trick, it must pay the double or quadruple value of the game.

PIQUET

NUMBER OF PLAYERS—TWO.

THE PACK—32 cards; two packs are used alternately.

RANK OF CARDS—A (high), K, Q, J, 10, 9, 8, 7.

THE DRAW—Lower card has choice of seats and deals first. If equal cards are drawn, there must be a new draw.

THE SHUFFLE AND CUT—Each player shuffles the pack that he himself will deal, usually while his opponent is dealing. Non-dealer cuts the pack. The cut must leave at least two cards in each packet.

THE DEAL—Each player receives 12 cards, dealt two at a time. The remaining eight cards are spread face down on the table, forming the *stock*. (In former times, the first five cards of the stock were distinctly separated from the last three, but now that formality is usually omitted.)

DISCARDING—After picking up his hand, non-dealer must discard at least one card, and may discard up to five, then take an equal number of cards from the top of the stock. If he leaves any of the first five, he may look at them without showing them to dealer.

Dealer is entitled to take all of the stock left by non-dealer, after first discarding an equal number of cards. Dealer is not obliged to take any cards from the stock. If he chooses to leave any or all, he may decide whether they shall be turned up to view of both players or set aside unseen.

The object in discarding is to form certain scoring combinations, as below.

CARTE BLANCHE—A hand with no king, queen, or jack is *carte blanche*. If dealt such a hand, non-dealer may expose it before his discard and score 10 points. If dealer picks up carte blanche, he may wait until non-dealer has discarded, then show it and score 10. (English rules require either player holding carte blanche to announce it before non-dealer discards.)

POINT—The greatest number of cards in any suit scores for *point* as many cards as are held. As between two holdings of the same length, the one with the greater pip total scores, counting ace 11; king, queen, jack and ten at 10 each; lower cards at pip value. If the players tie in point, neither scores.

SEQUENCE—A *sequence* of three cards in the same suit (*tierce*) counts 3; a sequence of four (*quart*) counts 4; a sequence of five or more counts 10 plus the number of cards. Only the player holding the highest sequence can score in this class; having established that he has the best sequence, he may score for all additional sequences he holds. Any sequence is higher than one of lesser length; as between sequences of equal length, the one headed by the higher card scores. If the players tie for best sequence, neither scores in this class.

SETS—A *set* comprises three or four cards of the same rank, higher than 9. The player holding the highest set scores it and any additional sets he may hold. Four of a kind, counting 14, are higher than three of a kind, counting 3. As between sets of an equal number of cards, the set higher in rank of cards scores.

DECLARING—The discarding completed, the players declare their holdings to determine the scores for point, sequence, and sets, in that order. But the player who does *not* score in a class need give no more information than is necessary to establish the other's superiority. The declaration therefore proceeds as in the following example (non-dealer being obliged to make the first declaration for each class):

Non-dealer. Four. (Naming length of suit for point.)

Dealer. How much? (With five or more cards of a suit, dealer would state "Five," etc. With no suit as long as four, dealer would say "Good.")

Non-dealer. Thirty-seven.

Dealer. Not good. Thirty-nine. (Dealer scores 4 for point.)

Non-dealer. Sequence of three. (Or, "Tierce.")

Dealer. How high? (He also holds a tierce.)

Non-dealer. Ace.

Dealer. Good.

Non-dealer. And another tierce. I score 6. I have three kings.

Dealer. Not good. 14 tens. I start with 18.

Non-dealer. I start with 6.

PROVING—On demand, a player must show any combination

of cards for which he has scored. Proving of scores is usually unnecessary, the player being able to infer the suit of his opponent's point, etc.

SINKING—A player is not obliged to declare any combination. *Example:* Non-dealer may say "No set" although he holds three queens, believing that dealer holds three kings. But if a player thus *sinks* a combination, he may not later declare it when he finds that it would have been high.

THE PLAY—The declaring completed, non-dealer leads to the first trick. The other must follow suit to a lead when able. A trick is won by the higher card of the suit led. The winner of a trick leads to the next.

The player scores one point for each card he leads higher than a 9, and one point each time he wins his opponent's lead with a card higher than a 9. The winner of the last trick gets one extra point for it.

(In America it is usual to count one for each lead and one for each trick taken, regardless of the rank of cards.)

Each, as he plays his card, announces his cumulative score up to that juncture, including the initial count for combinations. To continue the preceding example: Non-dealer scored 6 for two sequences. On his first lead (an ace) he announces "Seven." Dealer scored 18 for combinations; on winning his first trick (with a king) he says "Nineteen."

TRICKS—The winner of seven or more of the twelve tricks scores 10. If the tricks are split 6-6, neither scores. If one player wins all twelve tricks, he scores 40 for *capot* (nothing extra for majority or for the last trick).

PIQUE AND REPIQUE—A player who reaches a score of 30 or more in declarations, before his opponent scores anything and before a card is led, adds 60 for *repique*. A player who reaches 30 or more in declarations and play, before his opponent scores anything, adds 30 for *pique*.

GAME—A game comprises six deals. (*Variant.* The game is four deals, the scores of the first and last being doubled.) The player with the higher cumulative score at the end of the game wins the *difference* of the totals plus 100 for game, provided that the loser reached at least 100. If the loser failed to reach 100, he is said to be *rubiconed*, and the winner scores the *sum* of the totals plus 100 for game. (The loser is rubiconed even if the winner, also, failed to reach 100.)

IRREGULARITIES—*New deal* (by the same dealer). Compulsory if a card is exposed in dealing; at option of non-dealer if either player receives the wrong number of cards.

Erroneous discard. If a player discards more or less cards than he intended, he may not change his discard after touching the stock. If there are not enough cards available to him in the stock to replace all his discards, he must play with a short hand.

Erroneous draw from stock. If a player draws too many cards from the stock, he may replace the excess if he has not looked at them and if the correct order of the cards is determinable; otherwise the following rules apply. If non-dealer draws more than five cards from the stock he loses the game. If he draws less than five he should so announce; if he fails to do so, dealer is entitled to draw all that are left, even should dealer discard three and then touch the stock. If dealer draws any card from the stock before non-dealer has made his draw, dealer loses the game.

Concession. Once a player concedes an adverse combination to be good he may not claim a superior combination.

False declaration. If a player claims and scores for a combination that he does not hold, he may announce his error before playing a card and the scoring in that class is corrected. Should a player play a card before announcing his error, he may not score at all in that deal; his opponent may declare and score all combinations he holds, even if they are inferior, and may score for all tricks he wins in play.

Wrong number of cards. If, after the opening lead, one hand is found to have an incorrect number of cards, play continues. A hand with too many cards may not score for play in that deal. A hand with too few cards may score for play, but cannot take the last trick. If both hands are incorrect the deal is abandoned and there is a new deal by the same dealer.

KLABERJASS

(Kalabrias, Klob, Klab, Clob, Clabber, Clobber, Clubby)

This is the famous two-hand game played by the Broadway characters in Damon Runyon's magazine and motion picture stories, and, under its several names, enjoys wide popularity in the United States.

NUMBER OF PLAYERS—Two.

THE PACK—32 cards.

RANK OF CARDS—In trumps, J, 9, A, 10, K, Q, 8, 7. In other suits, A, 10, K, Q, J, 9, 8, 7.

THE DRAW—Cut for deal; low deals. The turn to deal alternates.

THE SHUFFLE AND CUT—Both players may shuffle, the dealer last; dealer's opponent cuts, leaving at least three cards in each packet.

THE DEAL—Six cards to each player, three at a time, non-dealer first. The next card is turned up and the remainder of the pack is placed, face down, so as partly to cover it.

BIDDING—There may be one or two rounds of bidding. Non-dealer bids first. He may *take it* (accept the turned-up suit as trump); or *pass* (reject that suit); or *schmeiss* (offer either to play the turned-up suit or to throw the hand in, as his opponent may choose). If the opponent says "Yes" to a schmeiss, there is a new deal; if the opponent says "No" the turned-up suit becomes trump.

If non-dealer passes, dealer may take it, or pass, or schmeiss.

If both pass, there is a second round of bidding. Non-dealer may name one of the other three suits as trump; or may schmeiss (offering to name one of those suits, or to let the hand be thrown in, as the dealer chooses); or may pass again. If he passes again, dealer has the last turn and may name one of the other three suits as trump or may have a new deal.

As soon as either player accepts or names a trump, the bidding ends. The player who accepts or names the trump suit becomes the *maker*.

REDEALING—Dealer now gives three more cards to each player, one at a time, so that each has nine cards in his hand. Dealer then turns up the bottom card of the pack and places it on top of the pack; it is shown for the player's information only and has no part in the play.

Any player holding the 7 of trumps may exchange it for the card previously turned up, but does not score any points for so doing.

MELDING—Only sequences may be melded; in forming sequences the cards rank A, K, Q, J, 10, 9, 8, 7, and the ace may be used only in the sequence A-K-Q. A four-card sequence counts 50, and a three-card sequence 20.

Non-dealer starts by announcing the point value of the best sequence he holds—thus, with ♡ Q J 10 he would say "twenty." If dealer has no sequence as good, he says "Good." If he has a higher-ranking sequence, he says "No good." In either case the melding is ended, and non-dealer leads to the first trick.

When dealer has a sequence of the same length as non-dealer, his response to the announcement is "How high?" Non-dealer must then name the card heading his sequence; again dealer replies that it is good, or no good, or that he has a sequence headed by the same card. If the latter, then a trump sequence outranks a sequence in any other suit. If both sequences are in non-trump suits, neither is scored. (*Variant*. If the sequences are equal in every respect, non-dealer scores.)

THE PLAY—Non-dealer always leads first; he may lead any card. It is necessary to follow suit if able, to trump when unable to follow suit but when having a trump, and to win a trump lead if able. The higher trump played wins any trick containing a trump, and the higher card of the suit led wins any other trick. The winner of each trick leads to the next.

After both have played to the first trick, the player with the higher-ranking meld shows and scores all sequences in his hand, while his opponent may not count any sequence.

A player holding the king and queen of trumps may score 20 points for them by announcing, immediately upon playing the second of them to a trick, "Bella." Holding K Q J of trumps, a player may score for both sequence and Bella.

SCORING—Each player scores, for cards taken in tricks:

Trump jack (jasz)	20
Trump 9 (menel)	14
Each other jack	2
Each queen	3
Each king	4
Each ten	10
Each ace	11
Last trick	10

The maker, in melds and cards, must score more than his opponent scores in melds and cards. If he does, each player scores points whatever he makes; if the maker is tied, he scores nothing while his opponent scores whatever he made; if the maker has the lower score, he is *bete* and his opponent scores all points made by both players in that deal.

GAME—The first player to reach 500 wins the game. If both players go over 500 in the same deal, the higher score wins. (*Variant*. The maker's score is counted first, and when he reaches 500 he wins.)

IRREGULARITIES—(See also General Laws, page 14.)

Misdeal. Before bidding, non-dealer may either require a new deal or require correction if any of his cards is exposed in dealing, if a card is exposed in the pack, or if either player has the wrong number of cards. For correction, a hand with too many cards is offered face down to the opponent, who draws the excess; a short hand is supplied from the top of the pack.

Incorrect hand, if discovered after the bidding has started, must be corrected.

A revoke is: failure to follow suit, to trump, or to play over on a trump lead, when required by law to do so; announcing a meld not actually held (as, for example, by saying "How high?" when not holding a sequence of equal value); having too few or too many cards after leading or playing to the first trick. The non-offender receives all points for melds and cards on that deal.

A player may not exchange the dix for the turned-up card after playing to the first trick, nor score 20 for the trump king-queen if he does not announce "Bella."

Games Similar to Klaberjass

In each of these games, the rules are same as in Klaberjass, with the following exceptions:

BELOTTE—This is the most popular two-hand game of France. It is identical with Klaberjass, except: The "schmeiss" is called "valse" (waltz). The highest-ranking melds are four of a kind, counting 200 for four jacks and 100 for four nines, aces, tens, kings or queens, the groups ranking in that order. A five-card sequence is worth 50, a four-card sequence 40, a three-card sequence 20. The player having the highest-ranking group scores all groups in his hand; the player having the highest-ranking sequence scores all sequences in his hand. If the maker does not score more points than his opponent, he loses his own points but the opponent does not score the combined totals of both players.

DARDA—Two, three or four may play; if four play, the dealer scores against the maker. The rank of cards in trumps is Q, 9, A, 10, K, J, 8, 7, and the queen (not the jack as in Klaberjass) counts 20, the jack only 2. In non-trump suits the rank is A, 10, K, Q, J, 9, 8, 7. There is no schmeiss.

After trump has been named and three more cards have been dealt to each player, the undealt cards are turned face up, squared so that only the top card shows, becoming the widow. A player may exchange the trump 7 for the turned-up card (the trump 8 may be exchanged if the 7 was turned), then may successively take the exposed card of the widow as long as it is a trump, discarding a card from his hand each time.

The maker then leads. Each player announces his meld on his first play; thereafter it does not count, including trump K-Q (bele). After the first trick is completed, players with melds of the same length ask and decide which is highest.

Scoring. The maker succeeds if neither opponent has as high a score as his. If he succeeds, he scores 1 if his score is less than 100; 2 if it is 100-149; 3 if it is 150-199; 4 if it is 200 or more. Game is 10.

Four of a kind. If four of a kind are held, there is no play; the highest four of a kind wins the hand, scoring: 4 for four queens, 3 for four nines, 2 for four aces, kings, jacks or tens.

Irregularities. Any irregularity stops play, and every player except the offender scores 2.

CRIBBAGE

Cribbage is one of the best of two-hand games. It combines in sociable proportions the luck of the deal with opportunity for skill in discarding and play.

NUMBER OF PLAYERS—Two or three, or four as partners. Best two-hand.

THE PACK—52 cards.

RANK OF CARDS—K (high), Q, J, 10, 9, 8, 7, 6, 5, 4, 3, 2, A.

THE DRAW—Lowest card deals. Players drawing cards of the same rank must draw again.

THE SHUFFLE AND CUT—Dealer has the right to shuffle last. The player at his right cuts. The cut must leave not less than four cards in each packet.

THE DEAL (two-hand)—Each player receives six cards, dealt one at a time. Players deal alternately during the game. Loser of a game deals first for the next game.

THE CRIB—Each player looks at his six cards and *lays away* two of them to reduce his hand to four. The four cards laid away together constitute *the crib*, which belongs to the dealer but is not exposed or used until after the play.

THE STARTER—After the crib is laid away, non-dealer cuts the pack and dealer turns up the top card of the lower packet. This card, placed face up on the pack, is *the starter*. If the starter is a jack (called *his heels*) dealer *pegs* (scores) 2 points at once. The starter is not used in the play.

THE PLAY—After the starter is turned, non-dealer lays one of his cards face up on the table. Dealer similarily exposes a card, then non-dealer again, and so on—the hands are exposed card by card, alternately except for *go's* as noted below. Each player keeps his cards separate from those of his opponent.

As each plays, he announces the total of pips reached by the addition of his card to those previously played. (*Exam-*

ple: Non-dealer begins with a 4, saying "Four." Dealer plays a 9, saying "Thirteen.") The kings, queens and jacks count 10 each; every other card counts its pip value (ace being one).

THE GO—During the play, the running total of cards may never be carried beyond 31. If a player is unable to add another card without exceeding 31, he says "Go" and his opponent pegs 1. But the player gaining the go must first lay down any additional cards he can without exceeding 31. Besides the point for go, he is then entitled to any additional points he can make through pairs and runs. If a player reaches exactly 31, he pegs 2 instead of 1 for go.

The player who called "Go" must lead for the next series of play, the count starting at zero. The lead may not be combined with any cards previously played to form a scoring combination, the go having interrupted the sequence.

Playing the last card of all pegs 1 for go, plus 1 extra if it brings the count to exactly 31. The dealer is sure to peg at least 1 point in every hand, for he will have a go on the last card if not earlier.

PEGGING—The object in play is to score points by *pegging.* In addition to go, a player may score for the following combinations:

Fifteen. For adding a card that makes the total 15, peg 2.

Pair. For adding a card of the same rank as that played last previously, peg 6. (Note that face cards pair only by actual rank, jack with jack, but not jack with queen.)

Triplet (also called *Threes* or *Pair Royal*). For adding the third card of the same rank, peg 6.

Four (also called *Double Pair* or *Double Pair Royal*). For adding the fourth card of the same rank, peg 12.

Run (Sequence). For adding a card which forms, with those played last previously, a sequence of three or more, peg 1 for each card in the sequence. (Runs are independent of suits, but go strictly by rank, e.g., 9-10-J is a run but 9-10-Q is not.)

It is necessary to keep track of the order in which cards are played to determine whether what looks like a pegging formation is interrupted by a foreign card. *Examples:* Cards are played in this order: 8, 7, 7, 6. Dealer pegs 2 for fifteen, and opponent pegs 2 for pair, but dealer cannot peg for run because of the extra sevenspot. Again, cards are played in this order: 9, 6, 8, 7. Dealer pegs 2 for fifteen on his first play, and 4 for run on his second play. The cards were not played in sequential order, but form a true run with no foreign card.

COUNTING THE HANDS—When play ends, the three hands are counted in order: non-dealer (first), dealer's hand, crib. This order is important, for toward the end of a game the non-dealer may "count out" and win before dealer has a chance to count, even though the dealer's total would have exceeded that of his opponent.

The starter is considered to be a part of each hand, so that all hands in counting comprise five cards. Following are the basic formations of scoring value:

> *Fifteen.* Each combination of cards that totals 15 counts 2
>
> *Pair.* Each pair of cards of the same rank counts 2
>
> *Run.* Each combination of three or more cards in sequence counts ....1 for each card in the sequence
>
> *Flush.* Four cards of the same suit in hand (not crib, and not including starter) count 4
>
> Four cards in hand or crib of the same suit as starter count 5
>
> (No count for fourflush in crib not of same suit as starter.)
>
> *His Nobs.* Jack of same suit as starter counts 1

COMBINATIONS—In the above table, the word combination is used in the strict technical sense. Each and every combination of two cards that make a pair, of two or more cards that make 15, of three or more cards that make a run, count separately. *Example:* A hand (with starter) of 8, 7, 7, 6, 2 scores 8 points for four combinations that total 15; the 8 with one 7, and with the other 7; the 6-2 with each 7 in turn. It scores 2 for pair, and 6 for two runs of three —8-7-6 using each seven in turn. The total is 16. An experienced player computes the hand thus: "Fifteen 2, fifteen 4, fifteen 6, fifteen 8, and 8 for double run is 16."

Certain basic formulations should be learned to facilitate counting. For pairs and runs alone:

A triplet counts 6.

Four of a kind counts 12.

A run of three, with one card duplicated (*double run*), counts 8.

A run of four, with one card duplicated, counts 10.

A run of three, with one card triplicated *(triple run)*, counts 15.

A run of three, with two different cards duplicated, counts 16.

The following list includes many of the hands the beginner may find some difficulty in counting.

Cribbage Scores

1—	1—	2—	2—	3=16	
1—	2—	3—	3—	3=15	
1—	4—	4—	4—	10=12	
2—	3—	4—	4—	4=17	
2—	2—	3—	3—	4=16	
2—	3—	3—	3—	4=17	
3—	3—	4—	4—	5=20	
3—	4—	4—	4—	5=17	
3—	4—	4—	5—	5=16	
3—	6—	6—	6—	6=24	
4—	4—	5—	6—	6=24	
4—	5—	5—	6—	6=24	
4—	5—	6—	6—	6=21	
5—	N—	5—	5—	5=29	
5—	5—	5—	5—	10=28	
5—	5—	10—	J—	Q=17	
6—	6—	9—	9—	9=20	
6—	9—	9—	9—	9=20	
6—	6—	7—	7—	8=20	
7—	7—	7—	8—	9=21	
7—	7—	7—	8—	6=21	
7—	7—	7—	8—	8=20	
7—	8—	8—	8—	8=20	
7—	7—	8—	8—	9=24	
7—	8—	8—	9—	9=20	
5—	5—	N—	J—	J=21	

2—	6—	7—	7—	8=16	
6—	7—	8—	9—	9=16	
3—	3—	6—	6—	6=20	
3—	3—	3—	4—	5=21	
1—	1—	7—	7—	8=12	
3—	3—	3—	6—	6=18	
3—	3—	6—	6—	9=14	
5—	5—	5—	N—	J=23	
5—	5—	5—	10—	10=22	
1—	4—	4—	N—	4=13	
5—	5—	10—	N—	Q=18	
2—	2—	2—	2—	9=20	
3—	3—	3—	3—	9=24	
3—	3—	3—	3—	6=20	
4—	4—	4—	4—	7=24	
1—	7—	7—	7—	7=24	
4—	4—	4—	7—	7=20	
4—	4—	7—	7—	7=14	
3—	3—	4—	5—	5=20	
1—	1—	6—	7—	7=12	
2—	6—	6—	7—	7=12	
7—	7—	7—	1—	1=20	
3—	4—	4—	4—	4=20	
5—	5—	5—	4—	6=23	
1—	1—	6—	7—	8=13	

No hand can make a count of 19, 25, 26, or 27. N = His Nobs.

MUGGINS *(optional)*—Each player must count his hand (and crib) aloud and announce the total. Should he overlook any score, his opponent may say "Muggins" and then himself score the points overlooked.

GAME—Game may be fixed at either 61 points or 121 points. Play ends the moment either player reaches the agreed total, whether by pegging or counting his hand. If non-dealer "goes out" by count of his hand, dealer may not count either his hand or crib in the effort to escape lurch.

Each game counts one for the winner, but if the loser fails to pass the halfway mark (fails to reach 31 with game of 61, or 61 with game of 121) he is *lurched*, and the winner scores two games.

THE CRIBBAGE BOARD—Scoring by pencil and paper is very inconvenient in Cribbage. A special device is therefore used, the *cribbage board* (see illustration). This is a wooden or composition tablet with four rows of 30 holes each, divided into two pairs of rows by a central panel. There are usually four or two additional holes near one end, called *game holes*. With the board come four pegs, usually in two contrasting colors.

The board is placed between the two players, and each takes two pegs of the same color. (The game holes are provided to contain the pegs before the start of a game.) Each time a player scores, he advances a peg along a row on his side of the board, counting one hole per point. Two pegs are used so that the rearmost can be jumped ahead of the foremost, its distance from the latter showing the increment in score. The custom is to "go down" (away from the game holes) on the outer rows and "come up" on the inner rows. The game of 61 is "once around" and 121 is "twice around."

If a cribbage board is not available, each player may use a piece of paper or cardboard, marked thus:

Units ... 1 2 3 4 5 6 7 8 9 10
Tens 1   2   3   4   5   6

Two small markers are used (as small coins or buttons) for counting in each row.

IRREGULARITIES—*Misdeal*. There must be a new deal by the same dealer if the cards are not dealt one at a time, if any hand receives the wrong number of cards, if a card is found faced in the pack, if a card is exposed in dealing, or if the pack be found imperfect.

Wrong number of cards. If one hand (not crib) is found to have the wrong number of cards after laying away for the crib, the other hand and crib being correct, the opponent may either demand a new deal or may peg 2 and rectify the hand by drawing out excess cards or dealing additional cards from the pack to supply a deficiency. If the crib is incorrect, both hands being correct, non-dealer pegs 2 and the crib is corrected by drawing out excess cards or dealing added cards from the pack. If more than one hand (including crib) is found incorrect, there must be a new deal, and if either player held the correct number in his hand he pegs 2.

Erroneous announcement. There is no penalty for announcing a wrong total of cards or a wrong count, but the error must be corrected on demand. If an error in announcing the total is not noticed until the next card is played, it stands as announced. If an error in counting a hand is not noticed until the opponent commences counting, or until the cut for the next deal, it stands.

No player is entitled to help from another or from a bystander in counting his hand. Scores overlooked may not be taken by the opponent unless there has been previous agreement to enforce *muggins*.

Erroneous play. A player who calls "go" when able to play may not correct his error after the next card is played. A player who gains a go and fails to play additional cards when able may not correct his error after the next card is played. In either case, the card or cards erroneously withheld are dead as soon as seen by the opponent, and the offender may not play them nor peg with them, and the opponent of the offender pegs 2 for the error.

Error in pegging. If a player places a peg short of the amount to which he is entitled, he may not correct his error after he has played the next card or after the cut for the next deal. If he pegs more than his announced score, the error must be corrected on demand at any time before the cut for the next deal and his opponent pegs 2.

Three-hand Cribbage

Draw for first deal, thereafter the deal rotates to the left.

Deal five cards to each player, one at a time, and one card to the crib. Each player lays away one card to the crib, which belongs to dealer. Eldest hand cuts for the starter.

When a player calls "go" the next hand must continue play if able, and if he does play, the remaining hand must then play if able. If the first hand after the go cannot play, the second hand does not play. In any case, the point for go is won by the hand that played the last card.

All other rules of play and scoring are as in two-hand Cribbage. The hands are counted in order to the left, beginning with eldest hand and ending with the crib. Game is usually fixed at 61.

Four-hand Cribbage

Draw for partners and first deal. Deal five cards to each player, one at a time. Each player lays away one card to the crib, which belongs to the dealer. Rules of play are as at three-hand Cribbage.

Scores made by partners are amalgamated in a running total. One player for each side should be appointed to keep the score. Game is 121.

CASSINO

NUMBER OF PLAYERS—Two, three or four. Four usually play as partners, two against two, partners facing each other across the table.

THE PACK—52 cards.

VALUES OF CARDS—Face cards have no numerical value; an ace counts 1, any other card its pip value.

THE DRAW—Players draw or cut for first deal; low deals. When two play, the winner of each hand deals the next; when three or four play, the turn to deal passes to the left.

THE SHUFFLE AND CUT—The dealer shuffles and the player nearest his right cuts.

THE DEAL—Beginning with the opponent nearest his left, dealer gives two cards at a time, face down, to each opponent; then two cards face up to the table in front of him; then two cards face down to himself. This is repeated, so that each player has four cards and there are four face-up cards on the table, which completes the first round of dealing. The remainder of the deck is set aside to be used in redealing. The dealer may deal the cards one at a time if he prefers.

OBJECT OF PLAY—To take in cards, which score points as follows:

Greatest number of cards taken in.... 3
Greatest number of spades taken in... 1
Big Cassino ($\diamond$ 10)................. 2
Little Cassino ($\spadesuit$ 2)............... 1
Each ace 1
Each sweep (not always played in
　　two-hand games) 1

A sweep consists of taking in all cards on the table.

In partnership play, cards, spades and counting cards taken in by both partners are counted together.

When there is a tie for cards or spades, the points do not count. *Example:* If each side has 26 cards, the 3 points are not scored. If in three-handed play two players have five spades each, the point for spades is not scored.

THE PLAY—Each player in turn, beginning with eldest hand, must play one card. He has the following choice of plays:

Taking in. A player may take in and pile on the table in front of him, face down, the card he plays plus any card or combination of cards on the table which pair with it. *Example:* With a six he may take in any six on the table, or a four and a two, or a six and a four and a two, or two or three sixes, etc.

Building. A player may add a card from his hand to a card or cards on the table, to form any combination which at his next turn he will be able to take in. He must announce what he is building. *Example:* Having a six and two in his hand, he may add the two to a four on the table, announcing "building six." With two fours in his hand and four on the table, he may place a four from his hand on a table four and announce, "building fours." Builds must be left face up on the table and may be taken by any other player in turn who has the appropriate card.

Face cards may not be combined in any way; with two jacks on the table, a player holding a jack may take in one of them but not both. He may not build jacks, queens or kings.

Increasing a build. A player may add a card from his hand to a build already standing on the table, provided he will be able to take in the increased build on the next turn. *Example:* Opponent has built a seven with six and ace; player holding nine and two may place a two on the six and ace, building nine; opponent in turn may place an ace on the build, increasing it to ten. A player may increase his own build as well as his opponent's or partner's.

A single combination may be increased; a multiple combination may not be. *Example:* When a player has built fours with a four, a three and an ace, the build may not be increased to nine by adding an ace. It may be taken only by a four.

A build may be increased only with a card from the hand, not with any card from the table. If a five has been built, a deuce is on the table and the player olds an ace and an eight, he may not take his ace plus the deuce on the table plus the cards built and increase the build to eight.

Adding to a build. A player may add a card from his hand to a build already on the table, and combine a card from his hand with a card on the table to add to that build. *Example:* There is a build of nine on the table, and a six on the table; a player may take a three from his hand and the six on the table to add to the build of nine. If the build was made by another player, he need not have a nine in his hand to do this; that is, in partnership play a partner may add to his partner's build without being able to take in the build.

At the time of taking in a build, the player may also take in any card or combination on the table which pairs with his card; for example, he is taking in a build of seven and at the time there are a four and a three on the table; even though these are not part of the build, he may take them in.

A card once taken in and turned may not be examined by the player or side taking it, and may be examined by an opponent only before the next time he plays.

Trailing. A player who does not wish to make any other play must "trail" by playing a card face up on the table; but he is not permitted to trail while any build he made is standing on the table.

REDEALING—When each player has played all four of his cards, the dealer picks up the remainder of the pack and deals four more cards to each player, but this time does not deal any cards to the table. When these have been played, he deals four more cards to each player, and so on until the pack has been exhausted. Before dealing the final round, dealer must announce the fact that it is the last. Failure to make this announcement is subject to penalty (see Irregularities).

Cards untaken prior to any new round of dealing remain on the table. After the pack is exhausted, the player who last takes in a card gets all the cards remaining on the table at the end, but these do not constitute a sweep unless they are all paired with the last card played.

GAME—When play ends, each player or side turns up the cards it has taken in and counts the points to which it is entitled. A sweep is identified at the time it is taken in by leaving one card face up in the pile, so the cards representing sweeps will be facing the other way and may be picked out easily.

There are several ways to decide the winner, including:

(a) In two-handed play, each complete deal usually represents a game. Sweeps do not count, and the majority of the

11 points wins (except that the game may end in a tie if each player scores 4 points and gets 26 cards).

(b) 11 points constitute the game; if a player or side scores 11 points in two deals, its score is doubled, and if it scores 11 points in one deal its score is multiplied by four. In any event the loser's score is deducted from the winner's score to determine the margin of victory. If both sides reach 11 points on the same deal, the higher score wins, and if both have the same score the game ends in a tie.

(c) 21 points constitute the game. If both sides reach 21 on the same deal, the points are counted in this order to determine the winner: cards, spades, big cassino, little cassino, ♤ A, ♧ A, ♡ A, ◇ A, and sweeps.

IRREGULARITIE:—(See also General Laws, page 14).

In two-hand play, when each deal constitutes a game, any irregularity loses the game.

Misdeal. If the dealer deals with an unshuffled or uncut pack, his opponent may call it a misdeal before making his first play, and may decide whether the dealer shall deal again or lose his deal. If the dealer fails to announce the final round, his opponent may call the deal off or let it stand.

Irregularities in dealing. If the dealer gives any player too few cards, he must supply the deficiency from the top of the pack. If any card is exposed in dealing before the first four cards are dealt to the table, that card goes to the table and is replaced from the top of the pack. If a card is exposed in dealing after the table has its four cards, dealer must take the exposed card and give the opponent another card; if the dealer has already looked at his own four cards, he supplies the opponent from the top of the pack, the exposed card goes to the table, and on the next round the dealer plays with fewer cards than the opponent. If dealer gives any player too many cards, and it is discovered before that player looks at his hand, the excess may be drawn from the hand and restored at the top of the pack; if the player has looked at his hand, he may put the excess among the cards on the table, choosing the cards he will put there, and on the next round of dealing the dealer plays with fewer cards than his opponent.

If on the final round there are not enough cards to give every player four, the dealer receives fewer cards than the opponents (unless the pack is shown to be imperfect, in which event the entire deal is void).

Taking in wrong cards. If a player takes in a card to which he is not entitled, it must be restored to the table upon demand at any time before an opponent next plays a card; after that, the error may not be corrected.

Counting or looking back at cards. If a player counts or looks back at any cards taken in and turned, except at cards taken in since he last played, his opponent may either add one point to his own score or deduct one point from the offender's score.

Not taking in builds. If a player trails when he has a build standing on the table, he must on demand take in the build; but the card with which he trailed remains on the table, and he does not play in his next turn. If a player has not the appropriate card with which to take in a build he made, his opponent may add one point to his own score or deduct one point from the offender's score.

Play out of turn. A card played out of turn must remain on the table, as though the offender had trailed with it, and the offender does not play in his next turn; in partnership play, his partner may not take in that card.

Exposed card. If two or three hands play, no penalty. In partnership play, the card exposed is immediately placed upon the table and the offender does not play in his next turn. The offender's partner may not take in the card which was exposed.

Royal Cassino

Jacks count 11, queens 12, kings 13, aces either one or 14 as the holder wishes; there is no restriction on combining or pairing face cards. Play is exactly as in regular Cassino, and 21 points constitute the game. The game may also be played with a 60-card pack including 11s and 12s (see page 14).

Draw Cassino

After the first round of dealing, the undealt cards are placed upon the table to form a stock. Each player, after playing, draws a card from the stock to restore his hand to four cards. Otherwise the rules of either regular Cassino or Royal Cassino apply, as the players prefer.

Spade Cassino

Either regular or Royal Cassino is played, but (in addition to the count for cards, spades, big cassino and aces) the ace, jack and deuce of spades count 2 points each and other spades count one point each; 26 points may be scored in each deal, exclusive of sweeps, if played. Game is 61 points and the margin of victory is the difference between the winning score and the losing score; this is doubled if the losing score is less than 31. Spade Cassino can most conveniently be scored on a cribbage board (see page 266) with every point being recorded as the card is taken in.

CHILDREN'S AND FAMILY GAMES

I Doubt It

This game is excellent for children, for adults or for mixed groups; may be played haphazardly or scientifically; is easy to learn and lends itself to hilarity; and is especially good when eight or ten players all wish to play in the same game.

NUMBER OF PLAYERS—Any number up to twelve or thirteen.

THE PACK—Five or fewer players should use a single 52-card deck; five players may use either a single or a double pack; six or more players should use a double pack, two 52-card packs shuffled together.

THE SHUFFLE AND CUT—The first dealer is decided by lot in any way; anyone may shuffle, and it does not matter whether the cards are cut or not.

THE DEAL—Two or three cards at a time to each player in rotation beginning at the dealer's left, until, on the last round of dealing, they are dealt out one at a time as far as they will go.

OBJECT OF THE GAME—To get rid of all one's cards.

RANK OF CARDS—A (high), K, Q, J, 10, 9, 8, 7, 6, 5, 4, 3, 2.

THE PLAY—The player at dealer's left must place on the table in front of him, face down, any number of cards from one to four; as he puts them down, he must announce that he is putting down as many aces as the number of cards. Thus, he may put down three cards, saying, "Three aces." But the cards need not be aces; the player is not compelled to tell the truth.

Any player at the table may then say "I doubt it," in which event the cards are turned up. If the player's statement was true (if, in the case cited, the three cards were actually aces) the doubter must take them and all other cards which have been played on the table into his hand; if the announcement

275

was false in any respect, the player himself must take all the cards on the table, including his own, into his hand. If two or more players doubt the announcement, the one who speaks first is the official doubter; if two players doubt simultaneously, the one nearer the player's left is the official doubter.

When an announcement is not doubted, the cards played remain on the table in front of the player until, by the rules of the game, some player is compelled to pick them up and add them to his hand.

When the first player's announcement has been doubted or not, the player on his left must put down one to four cards and announce that he is putting down so many kings; next, the player at his left must put down and announce so many queens; and so on around the table, so that when a player in turn has announced deuces the next player must start with aces again.

When the double pack is being used, the player is permitted to put down any number of cards from one to eight. The principle is that a player must be permitted to put down every card of a group if he holds it; four of a kind with a single pack, eight of a kind with a double pack.

GAME—When a player puts his last card down on the table and either is not doubted, or, upon being doubted, is shown to have announced correctly, the game ends and each other player pays his one point (one chip). *Variant.* Some play that each other player must give him one chip for every card remaining in his hand.

IRREGULARITIES—If a player doubts any player's announcement before it is made, his doubt is void and he may not doubt that player's announcement when it is made.

There is no misdeal; any irregularity in dealing must be corrected as well as possible, by adjusting the cards in the respective hands even if the players have looked at them.

It is quite ethical to make false statements, such as saying, when in turn to play sevens, "I haven't any sevens," when in fact the player has one or more sevens in his hand.

Three-card I Doubt It

In one popular variant of I Doubt It, the cards are dealt around only as far as they will go equally and any remaining cards are put face down in the center o fthe table. Each player in turn puts down exactly three cards in front of him, and the first player may choose what denomination of cards he will announce; that is, he may say "three sevens," or "three kings," or anything else he chooses. Each player in turn thereafter, in putting down his three cards, must name the next higher denomination than the player preceding him. When a player has only one or two cards left, he must draw enough cards from the stock in the center of the table to be able to put down three cards. The game ends when a player gets rid of his last three cards.

War

For the youngest age group—with parent, brother, or sister.

NUMBER OF PLAYERS—Two.

CARDS AND DEAL—One 52-card pack, king ranking high and ace low. Count out 26 cards for each player.

OBJECT OF THE GAME—To win all the cards.

THE PLAY—Each player has his stack of cards in front of him, face down. Each turns up a card and the higher card wins, the winner putting both cards face down on the bottom of his stack. If the cards are the same rank, each player covers his card with one face-down card and then turns up another card and the higher card takes all six cards. If the turned cards are again the same, each take another face-down card and another face-up card and the winner takes all ten cards; and so on.

Go Fish

(Fish, Go Fishing, Authors)

For the earliest card players, ages 6 to 9.

NUMBER OF PLAYERS—Two to five.

THE PACK—52 cards.

THE DRAW—Any player deals one card face up to each player, and low deals, the cards ranking from A (high) to a 2 (low).

THE SHUFFLE AND CUT—Dealer shuffles the cards and the player at his right cuts them.

THE DEAL—Cards are dealt one at a time to the left, beginning with eldest hand. With two or three, each player receives seven cards; with four or five, each receives five. The remainder of the pack is placed face down on the table to form the stock.

THE PLAY—Eldest hand begins by saying "(John), give me

your kings," addressing by name any of the other players, and naming any rank provided he himself holds at least one card of that rank. The player addressed must hand over all the cards asked for, but if he has none, he says, "Go fish!" and the asker draws the top card of the stock.

When a player has had to fish, without making a catch, the turn to ask passes to his left.

The object in play is to form *books*. A book is any four of a kind, as four kings. On getting the fourth card of a book, the player shows all four, places them on the table before himself, and plays again.

If the asker gets one or more cards of the named rank from the player addressed, he asks again. He may address the same or any other player and name the same or any other rank. So long as he is successful in getting cards, his turn continues. Also, if when told to fish he gets the fourth card of the book in the rank named, he shows the book and his turn continues. (*Variant*. Some like to play that the turn continues when the fisher gets the card named from the stock, even though it does not complete a book.)

The game ends when the ownership of all thirteen books has been decided. If one player is left without cards, he may in turn draw from the stock and ask for cards of that rank, but if the stock is gone he is out of the play.

Authors

Authors is similar to Go Fish, but is often played more seriously. It is best for four or five players. The whole pack is dealt out, as nearly evenly as possible. Each player in turn must call for a single card by rank and suit, as, "(John), give me the queen of diamonds." His turn continues so long as the player asked has the card named, but passes to the left upon his first failure.

The following remedies for irregularities apply to both Go Fish and Authors.

SCORING—Every time a player makes and shows four of a kind, every other player in the game pays him one chip (or, if a score is being kept, he wins one point from every other player).

IRREGULARITIES—*Misdeal*. There must be a new deal by the same dealer if any card is exposed in dealing, or if any player has too few cards and calls attention to it before he has looked at his hand.

Exposed card. When a player drops or otherwise exposes his possession of a card, he merely restores it to his hand. If a player exposes another player's possession of any card except by legally asking for and receiving it, he must pay one chip to each other player in the game.

Playing out of turn. If a player asks for cards when it is not his turn, he may not thereafter score a book in that rank.

Failure to show a book. Unless a player shows a book before the end of the turn in which he makes it, he may no longer score for it.

Illegal call. If a player asks for a rank when holding no card of that rank (or, in Authors, asks for a card which he already holds), he must pay one chip to each other player in the game. In Go Fish, he must also return cards surrendered in response to his illegal call to the previous owner, whenever the error is discovered.

Failure to give up card. If a player fails to hand over a card he has when properly asked for it, he pays a chip to each other player in the game and may not score a book in that rank.

Pig

A very hilarious game for children or for adults who want to relax.

NUMBER OF PLAYERS—Three to thirteen.

THE PACK—Four cards representing any one denomination, for each player in the game; thus, four players would use a 16-card pack consisting of four aces, four kings, four queens and four jacks.

THE SHUFFLE AND DEAL—Any player shuffles the pack thoroughly and deals four cards, one at a time, to each player.

OBJECT OF THE GAME—To make a group of four of a kind in your hand, or not to be the last to notice when someone else does so.

THE PLAY—The players look at their hands; then every player passes one card to the player at his left and picks up the card passed by the player at his right. When any player has in his hand four cards of one denomination, as four kings, he stops passing or picking up cards and puts his finger to his nose. The other players must immediately stop passing and each must put his finger to his nose. The last to do this is the Pig.

Old Maid

This game is a perennial favorite with children.

NUMBER OF PLAYERS—Any number from two up, each playing for himself.

THE PACK—51 cards (a 52-card pack with one of the four queens discarded).

THE DEAL—Any player shuffles the pack and deals them around, one at a time to each player, as far as they will go; they do not have to come out even.

OBJECT OF THE GAME—To form and discard pairs of cards, and not to be left with the odd card at the end.

THE PLAY—Each player removes from his hand, in twos, all pairs of cards (with three sixes a player may remove only two of them). The dealer then offers his hand, spread out face down, to the player at his left, who draws one card from it. This player discards any pair which may have been formed by the card drawn, then offers his own hand to the player at his left. Play proceeds in this way until all cards have been paired but one—the odd queen, which cannot be paired—and the player holding that card is the Old Maid.

IRREGULARITIES—If any player discards two cards which are not a pair, causing three unpaired cards instead of one to remain at the end, the player who committed the irregularity is the Old Maid.

Slapjack

For the youngest children, who play it by themselves.

NUMBER OF PLAYERS—Three to eight, each for himself.

THE PACK—52 cards.

THE DEAL—Any player may deal first. The cards are shuffled and dealt out, one at a time to each player in rotation, until all have been dealt; they do not have to come out even. Each player, without looking at any of his cards, squares up his hand into a neat pile in front of him, face down.

OBJECT OF THE GAME—To win all the cards, by being first to slap each jack as it is played to the center.

THE PLAY—Each player in turn, beginning at the dealer's left, must lift one card from the pile in front of him and place it face up in the center of the table; in doing this, he must turn up the card away from him, not toward him, so that he may not see it any sooner than any other player. Accordingly, he should try to make the play with a very quick movement so that other players may not see the denomination of the card before he does.

When the card played to the center is a jack, the first player to slap his hand down on it takes it, and, with it, all cards below it in the center of the table. The player winning these cards turns them face down and shuffles them with the cards in his hand still remaining on the table in front of him, to form his new hand.

When more than one player slaps at a jack, the one whose hand is lowest (directly on top of the jack) wins the pile.

When a player has no more cards left, he remains in the game until a jack is next turned, and may slap at the jack in an effort to get a new hand; if he fails to win, he is out of the game.

Play proceeds until one player has all the cards. That player is the winner.

IRREGULARITIES—If a card is exposed in dealing, that player's cards must be shuffled before he places them face down in front of him and plays.

If a player slaps at any card in the center other than a jack, he must give one card, face down, to the player of that card.

Concentration (Memory)

This is an excellent game for any number of players of any type—serious players, casual players, even people who have never played cards before.

NUMBER OF PLAYERS—Any number from two up.

THE PACK—52 cards.

THE DEAL—Any player shuffles the pack and lays all the cards out face down, one at a time, so that no two cards touch or overlap at the corners. The entire surface of the table is usually necessary to make room for all the cards.

OBJECT OF THE GAME—To take in pairs of cards of the same denomination, as two sixes or two queens.

THE PLAY—The first player may be decided in any way. Each player in turn must turn up any two cards on the table, leaving the first face up until he has turned the second. If the two cards form a pair, he takes them and turns up two more cards. Whenever the two cards he turns up do not form a pair, he turns both cards face down again, leaving them in exactly the same position on the table that they were in when he first turned them. The turn to play then passes to the player at his left.

SCORING—There are alternative methods:

(a) The player who takes in the greatest number of pairs receives one counter, or chip, or point, from each other player in the game; if two players tie for the highest number of tricks, they split the winnings.

(b) Each player collects one counter from each other player for every pair he has taken in.

Go Boom

A game to please serious young players.

NUMBER OF PLAYERS—Any number from two up.

THE PACK—Up to six players use the 52-card pack; seven or eight players may use the 62-card pack (see page 14) or a double pack (two 52-card packs shuffled together); more than eight players should use the double pack.

RANK OF CARDS—A (high), K, Q, J, 10, 9, 8, 7, 6, 5, 4, 3, 2. If the 62-card pack is used, the 13, 12 and 11 rank next under the jack.

THE DRAW—Low deals, ace being low in the draw.

THE SHUFFLE AND CUT—Dealer shuffles and the player on his right cuts.

THE DEAL—Seven cards to each player, dealt one at a time in rotation; the remainder of the pack is placed face down in the center of the table, and is the *stock*.

OBJECT OF THE GAME—To be the first to have played all his cards.

THE PLAY—Eldest hand leads; he may lead any card. Each player in turn thereafter must follow suit or play a card of the same denomination as the card led; thus, if the ◇ J is led each player in turn must play any diamond or any jack. A player who cannot so play must draw from the stock until he can, and when the stock is exhausted and he cannot so play he simply does not play to the trick. The highest card of the suit led wins each trick; as between cards of identical rank, the one played first outranks the other. The winner of each trick leads to the next.

SCORING—The first player to get rid of all his cards wins the game. He collects from each other player the pip value of the cards remaining in that player's hand, aces counting one each and face cards ten each, other cards their pip value.

GAME—Each deal may constitute a game; play may continue until one player has scored 200 points; or, after each deal, each player may be charged with the points remaining in his hand and play may continue until one player is minus 100, at which point the lowest score is the winner of the game.

IRREGULARITIES—There is no penalty for failure to play when able. See also General Laws, page 14.

Pounce

This belongs to the Solitaire family, but is rather a hilarious game for large groups.

NUMBER OF PLAYERS—As many as can sit at the table and each have room to play a game of Canfield (page 305). Best for six or more.

CARDS—One 52-card pack for each player; no two packs should be the same in color.

PLAY—Each player shuffles his pack and plays a game of Canfield. Whenever any player has an ace, he must play it to the center to begin a foundation pile; only aces can begin the foundation piles. Any player may play to any foundation pile in the center, and when two or more try to play to the same pile, the card played is the one that gets there first. Players run through their hands, three cards at a time, over and over until the game ends.

OBJECT OF THE GAME—The first player to get rid of his *stock* (original pile of thirteen cards) wins the game, regardless of how many cards he or any one else has played to the foundations. The cards are then separated into the original packs for a new game.

STOPS FAMILY

Michigan

(Boodle, Newmarket, Chicago, Saratoga, Stops)

Michigan, the most popular member of the Stops family, is ideal for groups in which there is no acceptable game known to all members; for a novice can play the game after a brief explanation.

NUMBER OF PLAYERS—From three to eight.

THE PACK—52 cards, plus the four boodle cards (see "Layout," below) from another pack.

RANK OF CARDS—The cards in each suit rank: A (high), K, Q, J, 10, 9, 8, 7, 6, 5, 4, 3, 2.

THE DRAW—Players may take seats at random. Any player distributes the cards one at a time around the table; the player who receives the first jack deals first.

THE LAYOUT—From another pack are taken ♡ A, ♣ K, ◇ Q, ♠ J. These four cards, called *boodle* or *money* cards, are placed in the center of the table and remain throughout the game.

THE ANTE—Before the deal, each player other than dealer places one chip on each boodle card; the dealer, two chips on each. *Variant.* Each player antes a fixed number of chips, placing them where he wishes on the layout.

THE SHUFFLE AND CUT—Dealer has the right to shuffle last. The player at his right cuts. The cut must leave at least five cards in each packet.

THE DEAL—The cards are dealt one at a time to the left. One more hand is dealt than the number of players, the extra hand being immediately to left of the dealer. The cards are dealt out as far as they will go, even though all hands may not receive the same number of cards. (*Variant.* Dealer has the right either to exchange the extra hand for his own, or to sell the extra hand to the highest bidder.) No player may see the extra hand except the player, if any, who exchanges his hand for it.

THE PLAY—Each card as played is placed face up before the owner, separate from all other hands, and the player names its rank and suit.

Eldest hand plays first. He may play any suit, but must play the lowest card he holds in the suit. The player holding the next higher card in sequence in the same suit plays it, and so on, the sequence in the suit being continued until it is *stopped* by a card in the dead hand or by the ace. The hand that played last before the *stop* makes the next play; he must play a new suit and his lowest card in that suit. If he has no other suit, the turn to play passes to his left. (*Variant.* In some games he is permitted to continue the same suit whenever he has no other suit in his hand.)

Any time that a player is able to play a card that duplicates a money card, he takes all the chips from that card. Any chips remaining on the layout after termination of the play remain there until won in a subsequent deal.

OBJECT OF PLAY—The object in play is twofold: (1) to get rid of all one's cards; (2) to play a money card and collect from the layout.

SETTLEMENT—Play ends as soon as any player plays his last card. He collects one chip from each other player for every card remaining in that player's hand. (*Variant.* In some games the suit must always be changed, and if no player can change suits after a stop play ends and there is no payment for the deal.)

IRREGULARITIES—Should a player start a suit with a card not the lowest he holds in the suit, he must pay one chip to each other player and he may not collect for any money cards he plays subsequent to his error.

Should a player cause a stop by failing to play a card when able, play continues as usual, even though the card withheld may later enable the offender to get a stop. But the offender may not collect for any money cards he plays subsequent to the error; if at the end of the hand the chips are still on the money card of the suit of the card erroneously withheld, the offender must pay an equal amount to the player (if any) who held the duplicate; if the offender is first to get

rid of his cards, he does not collect, but play continues to
determine the winner.

Fan Tan

(Parliament, Sevens, Card Dominoes, Stops)

NUMBER OF PLAYERS—From three to eight.

THE PACK—52 cards.

RANK OF CARDS—The cards in each suit rank: K (high), Q,
J, 10, 9, 8, 7, 6, 5, 4, 3, 2, A.

THE DRAW—Players may take seats at random. Any player
distributes the cards one at a time around the table; the
player who receives the first jack deals first.

THE SHUFFLE AND CUT—Dealer has the right to shuffle last.
The player at his right cuts. The cut must leave at least five
cards in each packet.

THE ANTE—Each player puts one chip in a pool, before each
deal.

THE DEAL—The cards are dealt one at a time to the left. All
are dealt out, so that some players may receive fewer cards

On each eight,
build up; nine,
ten, jack, queen
and king—fol-
lowing suit.

On each six, build
down; five, four,
three, two and
ace — following
suit.

than others. It is usual for each player dealt the lesser number of cards to ante one extra chip into the pool.

THE PLAY—Each player in turn, commencing with eldest hand, must play a card if possible. The plays that may be made are: (1) any seven; (2) any card in suit and sequence with a card previously played. The sevens as played are placed in a row in the center of the table. The sixes are placed in another row on one side, and the eights on the other side, of the sevens of their respective suits. The fives and lower cards in sequence are piled on the sixes, while the nines and higher cards in sequence are piled on the eights.

Each must play in his turn if possible; if he cannot play he puts one chip in the pool and the turn passes to his left neighbor.

OBJECT OF PLAY—To get rid of all cards in the hand. When one player succeeds, play ends. Each other places as many chips in the pool as he holds cards remaining, and the winner then takes the pool.

IRREGULARITIES—If a player passes when he could play, he must pay three chips into the pool. If he passed when able to play a seven, he must in addition pay five chips to the holders of the six and eight of the same suit.

Fan Tan Variants

Five or Nine. The first player able to play at all has choice of playing either a five or a nine. Whichever he chooses sets the denomination of the foundations, which are then built up on one side and down on the other as in Fan Tan.

Snip Snap Snorem (*Earl of Coventry*). First player may play any card. Whatever he plays calls for the other three cards of the same rank. The opportunity to play rotates in turn to the left. The hand that plays the fourth card then plays any card for the next series. Each pass costs the player one chip. If a player fails to play when able, the error is rectified without penalty.

Play or Pay. First player may play any card. The sequence in the suit must be built up until all thirteen cards are played. The sequence in the suit is continuous: J, Q, K, A, 2, and so on. The opportunity to play rotates to the left, and if unable to play in turn the player puts one chip in the pool. Whoever plays the thirteenth card of a suit may play any card for the next series. First to get rid of his cards takes the pool.

Eights

(Crazy Eights, Crazy Jacks, or Swedish Rummy)

The game of Eights offers more opportunity than any other member of the Stops family to overcome poor cards by skilful play.

NUMBER OF PLAYERS—From two to eight; best for two, three or four with partnerships.

THE PACK—52 cards. With six or more players, use two packs shuffled together.

THE DRAW—Players may take seats at random. Any player distributes the cards one at a time around the table; the player who receives the first spade deals first.

THE SHUFFLE AND CUT—Dealer has the right to shuffle last. The pack is cut by the player on his right. The cut must leave at least five cards in each packet.

THE DEAL—The cards are dealt one at a time to the left, beginning with eldest hand. With two players, deal seven cards to each. With more players, deal five to each. The balance of the pack, placed face down in the center of the table, forms the *stock*. After all hands are dealt, dealer turns up the top card of the stock and places it in a separate pile. This card is the *starter*. If an eight is turned, it must be buried in the middle of the pack and the next card turned.

THE PLAY—Beginning with eldest hand, each player in turn must place one card face up on the starter pile. If unable to play, a player must draw cards from the top of the stock until he can, or until the stock is exhausted. If unable to play when the stock is exhausted, a player passes his turn. A player may draw from the stock if he wishes, even though able to play.

Each card played (other than an eight) must match the card showing on the starter pile, either in suit or in denomination. Thus, any club may be played on any club; any queen on any queen. The eights are *wild;* that is, an eight may be played at any time in turn, and the player specifies a *suit* for which it calls (never a denomination). The following player must play either a card of the specified suit or an eight. (Some prefer to play with jacks, or some other rank, wild.)

Object of Play—To get rid of all cards in the hand. The player who first succeeds wins the game, and collects from each other player the value of his remaining cards computed on this count:

Each eight........................ 50
Each king, queeen, jack or ten...... 10
Each ace........................ 1
Each other card.............pip value

If the game ends in a block, no hand being able to play and the stock being exhausted, the player with the lowest count in his remaining cards collects from each other player the difference of the counts. Players who tie divide the winnings.

A four-handed partnership game does not end until both partners on a side go out. When the first hand goes out, the other three continue to play. If the game ends in a block, the total counts of the two sides are compared to determine the winner.

Irregularities—If the dealer gives any hand more than the correct number of cards, any other player draws the excess cards from the hand and restores them to the middle of the pack. If the dealer gives a player less than the correct number of cards, this player must draw a sufficient number of additional cards from the top of the stock. After the stock is exhausted, a player who passes when able to play may be forced to play by demand of any other player. If the score of a game ending in a block has been agreed upon, it stands even though the discovery is made that a hand could have continued play.

Hollywood Eights

This variant is two-hand Eights with scoring like that of Gin Rummy. The cards count: each eight, 20; ace, 15; face cards, 10; lower cards, pip value. The player who first amasses 100 points wins a game. The score sheet is set up for three simultaneous games. The first hand won by each player is scored only in Game 1. The second hand won is scored in Games 1 and 2. The third and all subsequent wins are scored in all three games. When any of these games ends, Game 4 may be opened up, and so on.

RED DOG (HIGH CARD POOL)

NUMBER OF PLAYERS—Any number from two to ten.

THE PACK—52 cards. Poker chips or suitable counters of any sort should be used.

RANK OF CARDS—A (high), K, Q, J, 10, 9, 8, 7, 6, 5, 4, 3, 2.

THE ANTE—A pool is formed by each player putting in one chip.

THE DRAW—Any player deals the cards one at a time, face up, to the players in turn until a jack shows, designating the first dealer.

THE SHUFFLE AND CUT—Any player may shuffle, the dealer last. The player at dealer's right cuts the cards, leaving at least four cards in each packet.

THE DEAL—Dealer gives five cards, one at a time, face down, to each player in turn, beginning with the player on his left. (*Variant.* Some deal only four cards to a player; with more than eight in the game, this is necessary.)

THE BETTING—The player at dealer's left, after looking at his cards, may bet any portion of the number of chips in the pool at the time. A player who does not wish to bet may pay one chip to the pool; however, he could if he wished bet one chip against the pool. No bet may exceed the number of chips in the pool at the time.

When the player has placed his bet, the dealer turns up the top card remaining in the pack. If the bettor has a card of the same suit and of higher rank, he shows the card and takes back the amount of his bet plus an equivalent amount from the pool. If he has no card which will beat the card shown, he must show his entire hand and the amount of his bet is added to the pool. The next player in turn then places a bet, another card is turned, and the same procedure is followed until all players including the dealer have bet.

If at any time the pool has no more chips in it (because

some player has "bet the pot" and won), each player again puts up one chip to restore the pool.

When every player has had his turn to bet, the turn to deal passes to the player at the dealer's left.

(*Variant.* In some games, the dealer does not turn up the top card of the pack; he removes or "burns" this card, face down, and turns up the next card. If five cards are dealt to each player, this procedure is possible only when there are no more than seven in the game.

IRREGULARITIES—If a player is dealt too few cards, he does not have to play if he does not wish to; but he may bet if he wishes. If no hand is dealt to a player, he is out of the play for that deal and there is no penalty on the dealer. A player dealt too many cards is out of the deal, and there is no penalty on the dealer.

Money once put in the pot may not be removed.

A player's bet is final when, in turn, he names the amount he is betting.

BLACK JACK

(Twenty-One or Vingt-et-Un)

Black Jack traditionally rivals Poker for popularity in the United States Army, and is one of the most widely played games in homes and clubs. It has two main forms: *With a permanent bank*, the same player always deals and all bets are placed against this player; *with a changing bank*, every player in the game has a chance to be dealer. The latter form is the one most often played in homes.

Black Jack with a Permanent Bank

NUMBER OF PLAYERS—As many as can sit at the table; but usually seats are provided for no more than seven or eight players besides the dealer.

THE PACK—104 cards (two 52-card packs shuffled together). In addition, the dealer uses a joker or blank card which is never dealt, but is faced up at the bottom of the pack to mark the location of the last of the shuffled cards.

THE SHUFFLE AND CUT—Dealer and any other player who wishes to may shuffle portions of the pack until all cards have been shuffled and combined. Any player may cut the pack. The extra card is placed face up at the bottom.

BETTING—Before the deal begins, each player places a bet, in chips, in front of him on the table; usually minimum and maximum limits are placed upon betting, so that, for example, no player may bet less than one chip nor more than ten.

THE DEAL—When all players have placed their bets, dealer gives one card face down to each other player in rotation; then one card face up to himself; then another card face down to each player including himself. Thus each player except the dealer receives two cards face down, and dealer receives one card face up and one card face down.

OBJECT OF THE GAME—Counting any ace as 1 or 11, as he

wishes, any face card as 10, and any other card at its pip value, each player attempts to get a count of 21, or as near to 21 as possible, without going over 21.

NATURALS—If a player's first two cards are an ace and a face card or ten, giving him a count of 21 in two cards, he has a *natural* or *black jack*. If any player has a natural and dealer does not have a natural, dealer immediately pays that player one and one-half times the amount of his bet. If dealer has a natural, he immediately collects the bets of all players who do not have naturals, but no player need pay any more than he bet originally. If dealer and any other player both have naturals, the bet of that player is a stand-off (he takes back his chips, and neither pays nor collects).

If dealer's face-up card is a ten, face card or ace, he may look at his face-down card to see if he has a natural; if his face-up card is anything else, he may not look at his face-down card until his turn comes to draw.

DRAWING—If dealer did not have a natural, when he has settled all bets involving naturals he turns to the player nearest his left. That player may *stand* on the two cards originally dealt him, or may require the dealer to give him additional cards, one at a time, until after receiving any such card he stands on the total already dealt to him if it is 21 or under; or *busts* (goes over 21), in which case he immediately pays the amount of his bet to the dealer. Dealer then turns to the next player in turn to his left and serves him in the same manner.

When dealer has thus served every player, he turns up his own face-down card. If his total is 17 or more he must stand. If his total is 16 or under, he must take a card and must continue to take cards until his total is 17 or more, at which point he must stand. If dealer has an ace, and counting it as 11 would bring his total to 17 or more (but not over 21, he must count the ace as 11 and stand.

SETTLEMENT—A bet once paid and collected is never returned. If dealer goes over 21, he pays to each player who has stood the amount of that player's bet. If dealer stands at 21 or less, he pays the bet of any player having a higher total; collects the bet of any player having a lower total; and is at a stand-off with any player having the same total.

RESHUFFLING—As each player's bet is settled, dealer gathers in that player's cards and places them face up on the bottom of the pack. Dealer continues to use the originally shuffled

pack until he comes to the face-up blank card, which signifies the end of the shuffled cards. At this point he interrupts
the deal, shuffles all cards not in play, has them cut by any
player or players, again places the blank card face up on the
bottom, and continues the deal. Before any deal, if the dealer
does not think there are enough cards to go around in the
next deal, he may gather up all cards for a new shuffle and
cut.

SPLITTING PAIRS—If a player's two first cards are of the same
denomination—as, two jacks, or two sixes—he may choose
to treat them as two separate hands. The amount of his
original bet then goes on one of the cards, and he must place
an equal amount as a bet on the other card. When this player's turn to draw comes, dealer first gives him one card face
up to each. The player may then require dealer to give an
additional card or cards to either hand, in whatever order
he wishes, until he has gone over or stood on both hands.
The two hands are treated separately, dealer settling with
each on its own merits.

IRREGULARITIES—If a player is dealt too many cards, he
may keep any two and discard the surplus, face up. If a
player is dealt a card he did not ask for, or if the next card
to be dealt is faced in the pack, he may accept it or reject
it; if he rejects it, the next player who draws a card may
accept it or reject it, and if that player rejects it, it goes in
the discard. If a player is dealt only one card, he may withdraw his bet or may have the card supplied when his turn
comes, but not before; if the dealer has a natural, the player
withdraws his bet. If a player is dealt no card, he withdraws
his bet. If a player is dealt a card face up that should have
been face down, he may accept it or withdraw his bet.

If the dealer has a natural but does not announce it before
he has offered a card to the first player in turn, he is deemed
to have a count of 21 as though made with three or more
cards.

Black Jack with a Changing Bank

NUMBER OF PLAYERS—Two to fourteen.

THE PACK—52 cards.

VALUES OF CARDS—Ace 1 or 11 (at holder's option); any
face card, 10; any other card, its pip value.

DETERMINING THE FIRST BANKER—Any player picks up the
pack and deals the cards in rotation, face up, until a black

jack (spades or clubs) falls to any player. That player is the first dealer.

THE SHUFFLE AND CUT—Dealer shuffles the pack and any other player may cut. Dealer then turns up the top card of the pack, shows it to all players, and places it, face up, at the bottom of the pack; this is called *burning* a card, and when that card is reached in the deal there must be a new shuffle and cut before dealing continues, in the manner described on page 293.

FIRST ROUND OF DEALING—Dealer gives one card face down to each player in rotation, including himself.

BETTING—After looking at his card, each player places a bet, which may not be less than one chip nor more than the betting limit established for the game, usually not more than three chips. After all players other than the dealer have bet, dealer may require that all bets be doubled. Any player may then redouble his bet. *Example.* A player bets two chips. Dealer doubles, requiring that player to put up two more chips. The player redoubles, putting up four more chips and making his total bet eight chips.

COMPLETION OF THE DEAL—Dealer then gives one card face up to each player in rotation, including himself.

NATURALS—If a dealer has a natural (ace, and face card or ten) every player pays him double the amount of his bet, except that another player having a natural pays the dealer only the amount of his bet. If any other player has a natural and the dealer has not, the dealer pays that player double the amount of his bet.

DRAWING CARDS—If the dealer does not have a natural, he starts with the player nearest his left and gives each player in turn as many cards as that player requests, one at a time, until that player goes over 21 and pays, or stands.

When all players have gone over or have stood, dealer turns up his face-down card and may draw cards until he wishes to stand. Dealer is not bound by rules to stand on or draw to any total. If dealer goes over 21, he pays all players who have stood; if dealer stands on a total of 21 or less, he pays all players who stood with a higher total, and collects from all players who stood with the same or a lower total—"ties pay the dealer."

A player against dealer may split a pair (see page 294).

BONUS PAYMENTS—Any player who forms one of the following combinations collects immediately from the dealer, and cannot later lose his bet even if the dealer has a higher total:

If a player has five cards and his total is 21 or under, he collects double his bet; with six cards totaling 21 or under, four times his bet; and so on, doubling for each additional card.

A player who makes 21 with three sevens receives triple the amount of his bet.

A player who makes 21 with eight, seven and six receives double the amount of his bet.

The dealer does not collect more than the amount of the players' bets for making any one of these combinations, nor does he necessarily win if he has five or more cards with a total under 21.

CHANGING THE BANK—Dealer continues as dealer until another player is dealt a natural and dealer has no natural; in this case, after all bets in the current deal have been settled, the player who had the natural becomes the next dealer. If two or more players have naturals and the dealer has none, the one nearest the dealer's left becomes the next dealer. A player entitled to deal may, if he wishes, sell the privilege to another player.

IRREGULARITIES—If dealer fails to burn a card, he must, on demand, shuffle the remainder of the pack and burn a card before continuing the deal.

If dealer fails to give any player a card on the first round of dealing, he must on demand supply that player from the top of the pack unless attention is called to the error after dealer begins the second round of dealing, in which case the player lacking a card stays out for that deal.

If dealer gives any player his first card face up, that player must still make his bet, but dealer must give him his next card face down. If dealer fails to give him his next card face down, the player may withdraw his bet and drop out for that deal.

Any player who stands must expose his face-down card as soon as dealer has stood or gone over. If that player has in fact a total of more than 21, he must pay dealer double the amount of his bet even if dealer has gone over.

If the dealer gives a player two cards on the first round of dealing, that player may choose which card to keep and which to discard; or may keep both cards, play two hands, and place a bet on each. He may not, however, play both cards as belonging to the same hand.

If dealer gives a player two cards on the second round of dealing, the player may choose which to keep.

If a card is found faced in the pack, the player to whom it would fall may accept it or refuse it.

If dealer gives a card to a player who did not ask for it, that player may keep the card if he chooses, or may refuse it, in which case it is a discard and is placed face up at the bottom of the pack. The next player in turn may not claim it.

CHEMIN DE FER

Chemin de Fer is a variant of the game of Baccarat,
which is a favorite game in the famous casinos on the French
Riviera. It is also called Chemmy, Shimmy, and by similar
diminutives.

NUMBER OF PLAYERS—Any number from two up to thirty or
more.

THE PACK—Six 52-card packs shuffled together and dealt
from a dealing box, called a *shoe*, which releases one card at
a time, face down.

THE SHUFFLE AND CUT—Any player takes a portion of the
six packs, shuffles it, and offers it to any other player to cut.
The cards so shuffled and cut are placed in the shoe until all
six packs are there.

THE DEAL—There is usually a croupier who does not participate in the game except to assist the players in making and
settling their bets, and to advise them on the proper procedure of the game and to quote to them the mathematical
advisability of alternate plays. When there is such a croupier,
the right to deal first is put up at auction; the player bidding
the highest number of chips as the amount of his bank becomes the first dealer.

Before dealing, the dealer must announce the amount of
his bank—that is, the number of chips he places at stake.
Other players, in order or precedence to the left, may then
bet against him all or any portion of his bank, but the dealer
is never responsible for the payment of bets exceeding the
amount of the bank.

If any player calls "Banco" it means that he accepts the
dealer's entire bank as a wager, and all smaller bets must be
withdrawn. If two or more players banco, the one nearest the
dealer's left makes the bet.

When all bets are placed, or when the bets are equivalent
to the dealer's entire bank, the dealer deals one card face

down to the player who made the largest bet against him; then one card face down to himself; then another card face down to the player against him, then another card face down to himself.

OBJECT OF THE GAME—To form, in two or three cards, a combination counting as nearly 9 as possible. Face cards and tens count 10 (or 0), aces 1, other cards their pip value; but the tens are disregarded in the total. Thus, a five and a six total 11, count merely as 1.

If either player has a count of 8 or 9 in his first two cards, he has a *natural* and shows his hand immediately. If dealer alone has a natural, dealer wins all bets. If the opponent alone has a natural, dealer pays all bets. A natural 9 beats a natural 8; two naturals of the same number are a stand-off, cards are tossed in, all bets are withdrawn, and players place their bets for the next deal (called a *coup*).

If neither dealer nor his opponent has a natural, the opponent may on demand draw one card, which is dealt face up. Dealer may then, if he wishes, draw one card face up. Either player may, if he prefers, stand on his original two cards.

When both players have stood or drawn, all cards are shown; if dealer is nearer 9 than his opponent, he collects all bets; if his opponent is nearer 9, dealer pays all bets; and if they have the same total, all bets are a stand-off and are withdrawn.

RULES OF DRAWING—The rules of most Chemin de Fer games require that each player decide to stand or draw on the grounds of mathematical advisability, in accordance with the following rules.

Player against dealer must draw to 4 or under; must stand on 6 or 7; and has the option of drawing or standing if his number is 5.

The dealer, if his opponent stands, must stand on 6 or 7, and must draw to 5 or under. If dealer's opponent draws, and the card he draws is an ace, face card or ten, dealer must stand on 4 and must draw to anything lower; a nine, dealer must stand on 4, has the option on 3, must draw to anything lower; if the opponent draws an eight, dealer must stand on 3, must draw to anything lower; if the opponent draws a seven or six, dealer must stand on 7, must draw to anything lower; if the opponent draws a five or four, dealer must stand on 6, must draw to anything lower; if the opponent draws a three or two, dealers must stand on 5, must draw to anything lower.

(*Variant.* In some games, the dealer and any player who bancos are allowed to use their own judgment as to whether or not to draw, regardless of mathematical advisability.)

CHANGING THE BANK—The dealer remains the dealer so long as he wins or has a stand-off on every coup. When he loses a coup, the next player in turn to his left becomes the dealer.

The new dealer announces the amount of his bank and bets are placed and the deal continues as before; the cards are not removed from the shoe and reshuffled until at least five-sixths of the original quantity of cards have been dealt, and usually dealing continues from the shoe until only a few cards are left in it.

Baccarat

Baccarat is identical with Chemin de Fer except:

The dealer retains the deal until the total amount of his original bank has been lost, or until he voluntarily retires.

In each coup, the dealer deals three hands—one to his right, one to his left, and one to himself. Players may bet either on the right or on the left hand against the dealer, or may bet a *cheval*—meaning that they win only if dealer loses to both hands against him, and lose only if dealer beats both hands against him. Dealer plays separately against each of the two hands he has dealt against him as in Chemin de Fer, the object being to achieve a total as close to 9 as possible.

STUSS, FARO

Stuss is identical in principal with Faro, which was once the most popular game with a fixed banker played in the United States, but which has almost vanished now except in Nevada.

NUMBER OF PLAYERS—Any number can play. All bets are placed against the dealer (banker). The banker is usually selected by auction, being the player who agrees to put up the largest stake as the amount of his bank.

THE PACK—52 cards.

THE LAYOUT—A complete spade suit, pasted to a board or enameled on felt, is placed on a table; players signify their bets by placing chips on any card shown on the layout. The spade suit is selected arbitrarily; actually all suits are equivalent, the ranks of the cards being all that count.

THE DEAL—The cards are shuffled by any player or players, and cut by any player. After bets have been placed (as described below), dealer turns up the top card of the pack and places it at his left; this card is called *soda* and has no bearing on bets. The dealer then turns the next card and places it face up on his right. He then turns the next card and places it on top of soda, at his left. The dealing of these two cards constitutes a *turn*.

BETTING—The first card turned up in any turn (except soda) always *loses;* the second card *wins.* Before any turn, players may place bets on cards in the layout; chips placed on any card signify a bet that such card will win, unless a *copper* (penny or similar disc) is put on top of the chips, in which case the player is betting that the card will lose. Any such bet is settled the next time that a card of the indicated rank is turned up. *Example:* A player puts a chip on the ♠ 6 in the layout. Dealer turns up two cards, neither of which is a six, so the player's bet remains on the layout, unsettled. But in the next turn the first card turned by dealer is the ♡ 6;

this means that the six "loses," and the dealer takes the player's bet. If the player had bet on the six to lose (by *coppering* his bet), the dealer would have paid him; or if the ♡ 6 had been the second card in that turn, instead of the first, the player would have won his bet and dealer would have paid him.

After each turn, all bets settled by that turn are paid and collected; other bets remain on the layout, new bets may be placed, and unsettled bets may be withdrawn.

As the deal progresses, all cards that lose form one pile, and all cards that win form another pile.

SPLITS—If two cards of the same rank come up on the same turn, so that a bet on that rank both wins and loses, it is called a *split;* dealer takes all bets on that rank (this is the dealer's sole advantage in the game). Bets on other ranks are not affected. [In Faro, the dealer takes only half the amount of bets on cards on which a split occurs.]

CALLING THE TURN—A record of all cards turned is kept, so that the cards remaining undealt are always known. When only three cards remain, a player may bet on the exact order in which those cards will come up and the dealer pays him four to one if he is correct (this is *calling the turn*). There are six ways in which the cards may come up, so the actual odds against the player are five to one. If two of the last three cards are a pair, it is a *cat-hop* and the dealer pays only two to one; for there is no distinction among the suits, and if for example ♠ J and ◇ J remain, the player is not invited to bet on the order in which these two cards will show.

Faro

Faro (originally Pharoah) is played with a permanent banker, who deals the cards from a *dealing box;* many elaborate combinations of bets are permitted, and the dealer takes only one-half of the bets when a split occurs.

Monte Bank

NUMBER OF PLAYERS—Any number can play, one being selected as banker. The banker places upon the table the full amount that he proposes risking on the game.

THE PACK—40 cards, leaving out the 10s, 9s and 8s of each suit.

THE PLAY—The banker takes the pack and shuffles it thoroughly, offering it to the players to cut. Holding the pack face down, he draws two cards from the bottom and places them face up on the table. This is known as the "bottom layout." He then takes two cards from the top of the pack, still holding it face down, for the "top layout."

The players bet on either layout any amount they please up to the limit of the bank. The remainder of the pack is then turned face up and the card that shows is known as the "gate." If it is the same suit as either of the cards in the top layout, the banker pays all bets on that layout. If there is a card of the same suit as the gate in the bottom layout the banker pays that also. The banker wins all bets on a layout which has no card of the same suit as the gate.

All bets settled, the two layouts are thrown aside, the pack is turned face down, the old gate discarded, and two fresh layouts are made and bet upon. A new gate is shown, and this process is continued until the pack is exhausted.

SOLITAIRE (PATIENCE)

How Solitaire Games Are Played

All solitaire games are played with one or more full packs of 52 cards each. Most of them proceed in the following way:

Some or all of the cards are distributed face up in some distinctive array, forming the tableau. The tableau together with any other cards dealt at the outset are often called the *layout*.

The initial array may be changed by *building*. Certain cards of the tableau are immediately available for play, while others may not be played until certain blocking cards are removed.

The first objective is to release and play into position certain cards called *foundations*. The ultimate objective is to build up the whole pack onto the foundations, and if that can be done the solitaire is "won."

If not all of the pack is laid out in the tableau at the beginning, the remainder of the pack forms the *stock*, from which additional cards are brought into play according to the rule of the game. Cards from the stock which can find no place in the tableau or on foundations are laid face up in a separate pile called the *talon* or *waste pile*.

In some games, the layout includes a special packet of cards called the *stock;* any remainder of the pack not dealt out at the beginning is then called the *hand*.

In many games a vacancy in the tableau created by the removal of cards elsewhere, called a *space*, is of capital value in manipulating the tableau.

The *rank of cards* in solitaire games is: K (high), Q, J, 10, 9, 8, 7, 6, 5, 4, 3, 2, A.

Solitaire games are often played on playing areas smaller than a card table; and some solitaire games would require more playing area than even a card table affords, if regulation-size cards were used. For these occasions, miniature "Patience" playing cards are available.

Almost any solitaire game is often humorously called "Idiot's Delight."

Accordion

CARDS—One pack.

TABLEAU—Lay out the cards one by one, face up, in a row from left to right.

OBJECT—To get all the cards in one pile, by building.

BUILDING—Any card may be placed on top of the next card at its left, or the third card at its left, if the cards are of the same suit or of the same rank. *Example.* Four cards, from left to right, are: ♡ 6 ♡ J ♣ 9 ♡ 9. The ♡ 9 may be placed either on the ♣ 9 or on the ♡ 6.

When the movement of one or more cards has formed a pile, the entire pile is moved with the top card. In the example above, when the ♡ 9 is put on the ♣ 9, the two may be put on the ♡ J and then the whole on the ♡ 6.

Dealing to the tableau may be interrupted at any time to make moves. It is not obligatory to make any move.

Canfield

CARDS—One pack.

THE LAYOUT—Count off 13 cards, face down, square them up, then place them face up to the left. This is the *stock*. Turn up the next (14th) card as the first foundation and place it above the stock, to the right. Beside the stock deal a row of four cards face up, to the right, forming the tableau.

FOUNDATIONS—The other three cards of the same rank as the first foundation must be played up in a row with it immediately they become available. Build up on each foundation in suit and sequence, going "around the corner." *Example:* If a queen is the first foundation, each other queen forms a foundation and is built up; as, ◇ Q, ◇ K , ◇ A, ◇ 2, ◇ 3 and so on, up to ◇ J.

OBJECT—To build all four foundations up to the thirteenth card of each.

HAND—The rest of the pack after the layout is dealt forms the *hand*. Turn over three cards at a time from the hand; the top card of each such packet is available for building, and the lower cards are available once the upper are played.

LAYOUT FOR CANFIELD

TALON—Place each packet of three cards, as turned up from the hand, on a talon pile below the layout. The top card of the talon is always available for building. When all the hand is played onto the talon, turn the talon face down to make a new hand, and go through it by threes again.

BUILDING—An entire pile of the tableau must be moved as a unit. (*Variant.* The top card of a pile may be moved alone). Any movable card or cards (from tableau, stock or hand) may be placed only on a card next-higher in rank than the bottom card of the unit, and of opposite color. *Example:* ♡ 8 may be placed on ♣9 or ♠ 9.

SPACES—A space in the tableau must be filled by the upper-most card of the stock. The stock must at all times be kept squared up so that only the uppermost card can be identified. When the stock is exhausted, spaces may be filled from the hand and talon.

The hand may be run through any number of times until play comes to a standstill or the game is won.

Napoleon at St. Helena

(Big Forty, Forty Thieves)

CARDS—Two packs shuffled together.

TABLEAU—Ten piles of four cards each, dealt by rows, all face up. Cards should overlap so that the player can see them all.

FOUNDATIONS—All aces, placed above the tableau as each is released from it or turned from the stock.

BUILDING—Only the uppermost card of a pile may be moved. Removal of a card releases the one below. A card may be

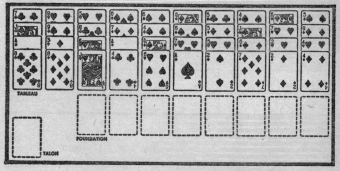

LAYOUT FOR NAPOLEON AT ST. HELENA

placed only on another of the same suit and next-higher rank. *Example:* ♠ 7 may be placed only on ♠ 8. A king may not be built on an ace; aces must be placed as foundations as soon as possible. Foundations are built up in suit and sequence, from ace to king.

OBJECT—To get all eight foundations built up to the king.
SPACES—When any of the ten tableau piles is entirely cleared away, any movable card may be placed in the space.
STOCK—Cards are turned up one at a time from the top of the stock and may be built on tableau or foundations.
TALON—Stock cards which cannot be built are placed face up in a pile below the tableau. The top card of the talon is always available for building onto the tableau or foundation. It is best to overlap the talon cards so that all may be seen.

Klondike

CARDS—One pack.

TABLEAU—28 cards in 7 piles. The first pile, one card; the
second, two cards; and so on up to seven. The top card of
each pile is face up; all others are face down.

Deal from left to right by rows; first row: one card face
up and six face down; second row: a card face up on the
second pile, and one face down on each other pile; and so on.

FOUNDATIONS—
The four aces.
Each ace, as it
becomes avail-
able, must be
played to a row
above the tableau.
Foundations are
built up in suit
and sequence.

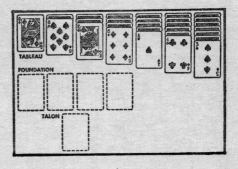

OBJECT—To get
the four suits
built onto the
foundations up to
the kings.

LAYOUT FOR KLONDIKE

BUILDING—Any movable card (from tableau, stock or talon)
may be placed only on a card next-higher in rank than bottom card of the unit, and of opposite color. If more than
one card is face up on a tableau pile, all such cards must be
moved as a unit. *Example:* ◇ 3, ♣ 4, ♡ 5 may be moved as
a unit onto ♠ 6 or ♣ 6. When there is no face-up card left
on a pile, the next card below is turned face up and becomes
available.

SPACES—May be filled only by kings.

STOCK—The rest of the pack after the tableau is dealt forms
the stock. Turn up cards from the top of the stock one by
one, and build each if able. The stock may be run through
only once. (*Variant.* Go through the stock by threes, as in
Canfield, without limit.)

TALON—Place unusable stock cards face up on a talon pile.
The uppermost card of the talon is always available for play,
provided the next card of the stock has not been turned.

Double Solitaire

Two play, seated across a card table from each other, each with his own pack of cards (the two packs must be of different colors or designs). All foundations may be played on by either, but a player cannot play to his opponent's tableau. The first player is determined by the low card on the one-card piles; if these cards are the same, the two-card piles decide, and so on. A player's turn ends when he puts a card face up on his wastepile, and his opponent's turn begins. A player's turn ends also if he makes any other play when able to start a foundation pile with an ace, if his opponent stops him. The winner is the player who has played the most cards to the foundations, when the game becomes blocked (or if either player goes out).

Spider

Cards—Two packs shuffled together.

Tableau—Ten piles of five cards each, dealt by rows. The first four cards of each pile are dealt face down, the top cards face up. All play is made on the tableau; there are no foundations and no talon.

Building—The top card of a pile may be moved, together with all below it which follow it in ascending suit and sequence. A sequence of available cards may be broken at any point and some left behind. *Example:* Pile from top down shows ♡ 4, ♡ 5, ♡ 6, ♣ 7; the first one, two, or three cards may be moved as a unit, but ♣ 7 may not be moved until the covering three cards are removed.

When all face-up cards on a pile are removed, the next card below is turned face up and becomes available.

A movable unit of cards may be placed either in a space or on a card of rank next-higher than the bottom card of the unit, regardless of color or suit. *Example:* ♢ J may be moved onto any one of the four queens. A king can be moved only into a space.

Object—To assemble thirteen cards of a suit, in ascending sequence from top down (ace to king) on top of a pile. Whenever a suit is so assembled, lift it off and discard it from the game. The solitaire is won if all eight suits are so cast out.

Space—May be filled with any movable unit.

STOCK—When all possible or desired moves on the tableau come to a standstill, deal another row of ten cards face up on the tableau piles. Before such a deal may be made, all spaces in the tableau must be filled. The final deal comprises only four cards, which are placed on the first four piles from the left. (*Variant.* The four extra cards are added face down to these piles in laying out the tableau.)

Streets and Alleys

CARDS—One pack.

THE LAYOUT—Deal a column of four cards to left center of the table, then a column to right center, leaving room between these two columns for another. All cards are dealt face up. Continue dealing the cards in columns of four alternately at left and right, overlapping outward from the center with those already down. Deal out the whole pack, whereupon each row at the left will contain seven cards and each row at the right, six. This array forms the tableau.

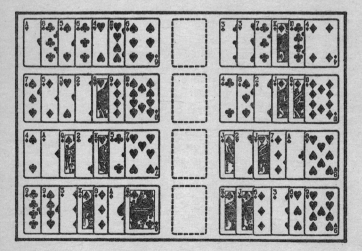

LAYOUT FOR STREETS AND ALLEYS

FOUNDATIONS—The four aces. As each ace is released, move it into the center between the wings of the tableau. Build up on the foundations in suit and sequence.

BUILDING—Only the outermost card of each row is available for transfer. A card may be moved onto the outer end of a row, provided that it is in descending sequence with the card there, regardless of suit. *Example:* ◇ 5 may be placed on ◇ 6, ♡ 6, ♣ 6, or ♤ 6.

SPACES—Any available card may be placed in a space.

OBJECT—To get all cards built onto the foundations.

The Beleaguered Castle

Same as Streets and Alleys except that the four aces are removed from the pack first and placed in the center column. Each row of the tableau is then six cards.

Poker Solitaire

CARDS—One pack.

TABLEAU—Turn up the first 25 cards one by one, placing them in a square array five cards wide and five deep. Each card as turned may be placed anywhere with reference to those previously placed, so long as all remain within the 5x5 limits. Once placed, a card may not be moved.

OBJECT—To score as high a count as possible in the ten Poker hands formed by the five rows and five columns of the tableau.

SCORING—There are several systems of scoring, of which the two below are the most popular. The American system follows the ranking of hands in the game of Poker, while the English system is based on the actual difficulty of forming the hands in Poker Solitaire.

HAND	AMERICAN SCORE	ENGLISH SCORE
Royal Flush	100	30
Straight Flush	75	30
Four of a Kind............	50	16
Full House	25	10
Flush	20	5
Straight	15	12
Three of a Kind...........	10	6
Two Pair	5	3
One Pair	2	1

Variant No. 1. Each card must be played vertically, laterally, or diagonally adjacent to a card previously placed.

Variant No. 2. Spread 25 cards face up and make the best possible tableau, knowing all the cards in play.

Poker Squares

Poker Solitaire lends itself to a contest of skill among a large number of players.

NUMBER OF PLAYERS—Any number.

CARDS—One pack for each participant.

PRELIMINARIES—One player is appointed *caller* in each round. The turn to call may rotate around the table. The caller shuffles his pack; each other player sorts his own pack into suits so as to be able to locate any named card quickly.

THE PLAY—The caller turns up the first 25 cards from the top of his pack, one by one, calling aloud the suit and rank of each card. Each player, including the caller (unless he be a non-playing referee), takes the called card from his pack and places it in his own tableau.

SCORING—When all tableaux are complete, each is counted according to the agreed system, and the highest score wins the round. Or an agreed number of rounds may be played and the winner is the player with the highest cumulative score. The scoring tables used in Poker Solitaire may be adopted.

Calculation

CARDS—One pack.

FOUNDATIONS—Remove from the pack and lay in a row any ace, any two, any three, and any four.

OBJECT—To build twelve cards on each foundation in arithmetical sequence (regardless of suit). The sequences on the four piles must be:

> A, 2, 3, 4, 5, 6, 7, 8, 9, 10, J, Q, K.
> 2, 4, 6, 8, 10, Q, A, 3, 5, 7, 9, J, K.
> 3, 6, 9, Q, 2, 5, 8, J, A, 4, 7, 10, K.
> 4, 8, Q, 3, 7, J, 2, 6, 10, A, 5, 9, K.

STOCK—The 48 remaining cards of the pack are the stock. Turn up cards one by one from the stock and play each either on a foundation or a waste pile.

WASTE PILES—Stock cards may be placed on any of four waste piles below the foundations. The top card of a waste pile is always available for play on a foundation, but may not otherwise be moved once it is placed.

RUSSIAN BANK

(Crapette)

This is one of the most popular of all two-hand games. It is essentially a form of double Solitaire and follows the general principles given on page 304.

NUMBER OF PLAYERS—Two.

CARDS—Two full packs of 52 cards each, with different backs.

RANK OF CARDS—K (high), Q, J, 10, 9, 8, 7, 6, 5, 4, 3, 2, A.

THE DRAW—One pack is spread face down and each player draws a card. Lower card has choice of packs and seats, and plays first. (*Variant.* The player whose tableau card nearest him is the lower in rank plays first; if these two cards are equivalent, the next-nearest cards decide, and so on. There is no rank of suits.)

THE SHUFFLE—Each player shuffles the pack to be used by his opponent.

THE LAYOUT—Each player cuts his pack and deals twelve cards face down in a pile at his right, forming his *stock.* Next he deals four cards face up, in a column above his stock extending toward his opponent. The eight cards so dealt form the *tableau.* Sufficient space must be left between the two columns of the tableau to accommodate two additional columns of cards. The player finally leaves the remainder of his pack face down below the tableau column at his left, forming his *hand.* (*Variant.* Some deal thirteen cards as the stock pile.)

FOUNDATIONS—The eight aces are the foundations. Each ace as it becomes available must be immediately placed in one of the reserved spaces between the columns of the tableau. The foundations are built up in a suit and sequence. *Example:* on ◊ A must be played ◊ 2, ◊ 3 and so on to ◊ K. A card once played on a foundation may not thereafter be moved.

OBJECT OF PLAY—To be the first to get rid of all cards in stock and hand.

METHOD OF PLAY—Each in turn makes as many moves as he can or will, under the rules below. A turn ends when (a) the player is unable to, or fails to, play a card turned from his hand; or (b) he makes an error in order of play, whereupon his opponent says "Stop!" (See *Order of Play*.)

AVAILABLE CARDS—Only one card at a time may be moved. The cards available to be transferred elsewhere are (a) top cards of tableau piles, (b) top cards of the stock, (c) the card turned up from the hand. (In rules on *stops*, a card is not deemed available merely because it can be made available by the transfer of covering cards.)

MOVES IN TABLEAU—A card may be placed on a tableau pile if it is in descending sequence and opposite color with the top card thereof. *Example:* ♠ 7 may be placed on ◇ 8 or ♡ 8. *A space* in the tableau may be filled by any available card.

MOVES ONTO ADVERSE STOCK AND TALON—A card may be placed on the opponent's stock or opponent's talon if it matches in suit and is in sequence; the sequence can be up or down or both. *Example:* If opponent's stock shows ♠ J, player may load it with ♠ Q or ♠ 10; having added ♠ Q, the player may continue with ♠ K or with the other ♠ J.

A player may never play from the tableau onto *his own* stock or talon, nor from the *adverse* stock or talon onto the tableau or foundations.

ORDER OF PLAY—Under penalty of being stopped and losing his turn, a player must observe the following rules:

Rule 1. Whenever a card becomes available that can be played on a foundation pile, it must be so played immediately.

At his first turn to play, each player must make all possible plays onto foundations; only then may he turn the top card of his stock. But at any later stage, if he plays from stock to foundation the last face-up card, he may turn up the next card of the stock, even though cards from the tableau may be playable on foundations. In other words, once he has dipped into his stock, he is entitled to sight of a top card of his stock to guide his choices in play on the foundations.

Rule 2. With choice of cards playable on foundations,

cards from the stock must be played before cards from the tableau.

Having satisfied the foundations, the player may then build on the tableau as he pleases. The top card of his stock is turned face up, and if this is played off the next is turned up. There is no compulsion to play a card from stock to tableau if able, but

Rule 3. No card may be turned up from the hand while a space exists in the tableau that can be filled from the stock.

Rule 4. Cards are turned up from the hand one by one, and so long as each can be and is played the player's turn continues. On turning an unplayable card, the player must put it, face up, on a talon pile between his hand and stock, and his turn ends.

Having played a card from his hand, the player may complete whatever additional moves the play makes possible, from stock and in tableau, before turning the next hand card. He must beware of delaying such additional moves, for should he look at the next hand card, and should this be unplayable, his turn is over.

When the stock is exhausted, spaces in the tableau may be filled from the hand.

Rule 5. It is a violation of the rules of order to touch one available card when another must, under the rules, be played before it.

In some circles the severity of this rule is relaxed; the player is not subject to a stop until he completes a wrong play by removing his hand.

A player may touch any cards at any time for purpose of arranging, provided that he states this purpose.

THE TALON—Unplayed cards turned from the hand are laid face up in a talon pile. The talon cards are not available for transfer elsewhere, but the opponent can load the talon from tableau, his stock, or his hand. A player may examine his talon by spreading the cards without disarranging them, in which case his opponent is entitled to see them also. But a player may not spread his opponent's talon pile. When the hand is exhausted, the talon is turned face down, forming a new hand.

STOPS—When a player violates a rule of order, his opponent may say "Stop!" and on demonstration of the error may take over the turn to play. If the error was the turning of a card from stock or hand, the card must be turned down. If the error was in moving a card, the play must be retracted.

SCORING—The player who first plays all of his stock, hand, and talon onto the tableau, foundations, etc., is the winner. He scores one point for each card left in the adverse hand and talon, 2 points for each card left in the adverse stock, plus 30 points for game.

IRREGULARITIES—If a player attempts an incorrect build, as ♤ J on ♧ J, there is no penalty, but the play must be retracted on demand. It is not permitted to look at any card in stock or hand until it is regularly turned up; if a player inadvertently turns up and sees a card not in due order, his turn ends as soon as he completes his current play. *Example:* A player turns up two cards together from his stock. He may play off the top card, if able, but then loses his turn. A stop may not be called if the player has been allowed to complete a move after his erroneous move.

One-Pack Russian Bank

NUMBER OF PLAYERS—Two.

CARDS—Full pack of 52 cards.

RANK OF CARDS—Continuous sequence: A, 2, 3, 4, 5, 6, 7, 8, 9, 10, J, Q, K, A, 2, etc.

THE DEAL—Each player receives 26 cards, dealt in one round of two at a time and eight rounds of three at a time. The player squares his cards face down in a pile at his left.

THE PLAY—The first player deals from his hand four cards face up, in a row. He builds as he can according to the rules below. When he can no longer play, the second player deals a row of four cards and makes what plays he can. Thereafter, each player in turn faces the top card of his hand and plays as he can. When he turns an unplayable card, he places it face up on a talon pile at his right.

BUILDING—All building is in suit and sequence. In making a build on the tableau (the eight cards originally dealt face up), or in loading his opponent's talon, the player may start the sequence up or down, as he pleases; thereafter the sequence must be continued in the same direction.

SPACES—On creating a space in the tableau, the player may use it to make shifts in the tableau, since any card may be placed in the space. It is permissible to use spaces to reverse the order of sequence in a tableau pile. Before closing his turn, the player must fill all spaces with cards turned from his hand.

LOADING THE ADVERSE TALON—A card turned from the hand may be played onto the opponent's talon, if it fits in suit and sequence, even though it could also be played onto the tableau. But a card from the tableau may not be played onto the talon.

THE TALON—Cards may not be played off the talon. When the hand is exhausted, the talon is turned face down to form a new hand.

OBJECT OF PLAY—To get rid of all cards in hand and talon, into the tableau.

(NOTE: *In contrast with two-pack Russian Bank, there is no stock pile, there are no foundations, and a player may not be stopped for an oversight.*)

Technical Terms

NOTE: For technical terms that are the same as the names of games, see the Index beginning on Page v.

ABOVE THE LINE—*Bridge*. The place on score sheet where premiums are scored.

ADVERSARY—Any opponent; one playing against the highest bidder.

ADVERTISE — *Poker*. Make a bluff intended to be exposed.

AGAINST — *Skat*. Same as WITHOUT.

AGE — 1. Same as ELDEST HAND. 2. *Poker*. The right to bet last after the draw.

ALONE—*Euchre family*. A bid to play without help of partner.

ALTERNATE STRAIGHT—Same as SKIP STRAIGHT.

ANCHOR—*Duplicate Bridge*. In pivot or progressive play, one who retains his seat throughout the contest.

ANNOUNCE — 1. Name the trump suit. 2. Show melds. 3. Predict schneider or schwarz.

ANTE—1. A bet made before the deal or before drawing cards. 2. Contribution to a pot which, at the start, belongs equally to all players.

ASK—1. *Whist*. Signal partner to lead trumps. 2. *Skat family*. Inquiry by eldest hand whether the next hand wishes to compete in the bidding.

ASSIST—1. *Euchre*. Order partner to take up trump. 2. *Bridge*. Same as RAISE (2).

AUCTION — The period of the bidding.

AUTHORIZED OPPONENT — *Bridge*. One solely entitled to assess a penalty.

AVAILABLE CARD — *Solitaire*. One which may be transferred elsewhere in the layout.

AVONDALE SCHEDULE—The recommended table for scoring of Five Hundred.

BACK DOOR — *Bezique*. A sequence in a plain suit.

BACK IN—*Poker*. Come into the betting after checking.

BACK TO BACK — *Stud Poker*. Said of the hole card and first upcard when they are a pair.

BAIT—1. *Rummy family*. A discard intended to influence an opponent's later discard. 2. Same as BETE.

BALANCED HAND—A hand with no void, singleton, or very long suit.

BALKING CARDS — *Cribbage*. Cards unlikely to produce a score, given to the opponent's crib.

318

BANCO — *Chemin-de-fer*. A bet equal to the entire bank.

BANK—Gambling house; dealer in a gambling game.

BANKER — 1. Dealer against whom all others bet. 2. *Poker*. The player who keeps the supply of chips.

BARRED — Estopped from bidding by a legal penalty.

BASE—*Canasta*. The number of natural cards required in a canasta.

BASTO, OR BASTA—The queen of spades.

BATE—Same as BETE.

BEG—*All Fours*. A proposal by eldest hand to dealer that three additional cards be dealt to each hand and that a new card be turned up for trump.

BELA, OR BELLA — *Klaberjass*. The king and queen of trumps.

BELOW THE LINE—*Bridge*. The place on the score sheet where the trick score is entered.

BEST (*as third-best*)—Highest-ranking.

BEST BOWER—The joker, when it is the highest trump.

BET BLIND—Bet without looking at the hand.

BETE (pronounced *bate*) — 1. Beaten. 2. A forfeit paid by a loser or by a transgressor of a rule of correct procedure.

BET THE POT — Bet as many chips as there are in the pot at the moment.

BETTING INTERVAL — *Poker*. Period in which each player may bet or drop out.

BICYCLE—The lowest hand at Lowball.

BID—An offer to contract to win a certain number of tricks or points in play; to make a bid.

BIDDER — 1. Any player who makes a bid. 2. The player who makes the highest bid and assumes the contract.

BID OVER—Overcall; bid higher than the last previous bid.

BIG CASSINO—The ten of diamonds.

BIG DOG—*Poker*. A hand consisting of ace-high and nine-low but no pair.

BIG TIGER — *Poker*. A hand consisting of king-high and eight-low but no pair.

BLACK JACK—Ace and any 10-point card.

BLACK LADY — The queen of spades.

BLACKWOOD CONVENTION — *Contract Bridge*. A system of cue-bidding to reach slams, invented by Easley Blackwood.

BLANK—1. Void; holding no cards of (a suit). 2. To discard all cards of (a suit) or all low cards from (a high card).

BLAZE—*Poker*. A hand composed entirely of face cards.

BLIND—1. A compulsory bet or ANTE (2) made before the cards are dealt. 2. The WIDOW, as in Skat.

BLIND LEAD—One made before certain cards are disclosed.

BLITZ—Same as SHUTOUT.

BLOCK—A situation in which the player in turn is unable to play, or no player is able to play.

BLOCKING A SUIT—So playing that a partner with the longer of two partnership holdings in a suit cannot obtain the lead in that suit.

BLUE PETER—*Whist*. The signal for a trump lead.

BLUFF—*Poker*. A bet on a hand

that the player actually does not believe is best.

BOARD—1. *Stud Poker*. The exposed cards of all active players. 2. A deal, in Duplicate Bridge.

BOBTAIL — *Poker*. A FOUR FLUSH or DOUBLE-ENDED STRAIGHT.

BONUS—A score given for holding certain cards or completing a high contract.

BOOBY PRIZE—Prize for lowest score.

BOOBY TABLE—In progressive play, the table of highest number, to which losers move from table No. 1.

BOODLE CARD — *Stops family*. Extra cards placed in a layout on which bets are laid.

BOOK—*Whist family*. The number of tricks a side must win before it can score by winning subsequent tricks; usually, six tricks.

BOWER — See LEFT BOWER, RIGHT BOWER.

BOX—1. *Gin Rummy*. The score for winning a deal. 2. An apparatus from which cards are dealt, as in Faro.

BREAK—1. To divide in a specified way, as evenly or unevenly—said of the cards held by one's opponents. 2. *Rummy*. The point at which the stock contains too few cards for everyone to have another draw. 3. *Rummy*. The act of making the first meld.

BREAKS—1. Luck. 2. Distribution of the adverse cards between the two hands.

BRIDGE—*Euchre*. A score of 4 when opponents have not more than 2.

BRISQUE—*Bezique*. Any ace or ten.

BUCK—*Poker*. A token used as a reminder of the order of precedence in dealing, exercising any privilege or duty, etc.

BUCK THE TIGER — *Faro*. Play against the bank.

BUG—*Poker*. The joker, when it may be used only as an ace or as a wild card in filling a flush, a straight, or a low hand.

BUILD — 1. *Cassino*. Combine two or more cards to be taken in later. 2. *Solitaire*. Transfer cards among the tableau cards and foundations.

BULL—Ace.

BUNCH—1. Abandon the deal; gather cards preparatory to shuffling. 2. *Auction Pitch*. An offer to play a contract of 2 or to have a new deal, at the opponent's option.

BURN A CARD—Expose and bury it, or place it on the bottom of the pack.

BURY A CARD—1. Place it in the middle of the pack or among the discards, so that it cannot be readily located. 2. *Pinochle*. Lay aside, for future counting.

BUSINESS DOUBLE—*Bridge*. One made for the purpose of exacting increased penalties.

BUST — 1. A hand devoid of trick-taking possibilities. 2. *Black Jack*. Draw cards totaling more than 21.

BUY—Draw from the widow or stock; cards so received.

BUY-IN—Same as STACK (2).

BY ME—A declaration meaning "Pass."

CALL—1. Declare; bid or pass; *Bridge*. Any pass, double, redouble or bid. 2. *Poker*. Make a bet exactly equal to the last previous bet.

CARDS—*Cassino*. The score of 3

for winning a majority of the cards.

CARTE BLANCHE—A hand without a face card.

CASE CARD—The last card of a rank remaining in play.

CASH—Lead and win tricks with established cards.

CASH POINTS — *Cassino*. The scores for big and little cassino and aces.

CAT—See BIG TIGER, LITTLE TIGER.

CATCH—Find valuable cards in the widow or draw from the stock.

CAT-HOP—*Faro*. Two cards of the same rank among the last three.

CENTER—*Solitaire*. The foundation piles.

CHECK—1. Counter; chip. 2. *Poker*. A nominal bet; usually one which does not require that any chip be put in the pot.

CHICANE—Void of trumps.

CHIP—A token used in place of money; place chips in the pot.

CHOUETTE—A method by which three or more players can participate in a two-hand game.

CINCH—*Cinch*. Play a trump higher than the five, to prevent an opponent from winning with a pedro.

CINCH HAND—One that is sure to win.

CLEAR—1. *Hearts*. Having taken in tricks no counting cards. 2. To establish (a suit); to draw (trumps).

CLOSE CARDS—Same as NEAR CARDS.

COFFEE HOUSING — Attempting to mislead opponents as to one's cards by speech and manner.

COLD HANDS — *Poker*. Hands dealt face up, as for the determination of the winner of extra chips in dividing the pot.

COLOR—Suit; also, red or black.

COLUMN—*Solitaire*. A line of cards extending away from the player.

COME IN—Enter the betting.

COME-ON—*Bridge*. A signal to partner to continue leading a suit; echo.

COMMAND—The best card of a suit; master card; control.

COMMOQUER—*Panguingue*. Any card but an ace or king.

CONDITION—A meld that has extra value, as in Panguingue.

CONDONE—Waive penalty for an irregularity.

CONTRACT — The obligation to win a certain minimum number of tricks or points.

CONTRACTOR—The high bidder.

CONVENTIONS—Advance agreement between partners on how to exchange information by bids and plays.

COPPER—*Faro*. A token placed on a bet indicating that it is a bet on a card to lose.

COUNTER—1. Chip; a token used in place of money. 2. A card that has scoring value when won in a trick.

COUNT OUT—Go game, especially by accumulation of points during play of a hand.

COUP—1. A brilliant play. 2. A winning play or bet.

COURT CARD—Same as FACE CARD.

COVER—Play a card higher than the highest previously played to the trick.

CRIB—*Cribbage*. The extra hand formed by the players' discards, belonging to the dealer.

CRIBBAGE BOARD—A device for scoring.

CROSS-RUFF—*Whist family*. Alternate trumping of each other's plain-suit leads by the two hands of a partnership.

CROSS THE SUIT—*Euchre*. Name as trump a suit of color opposite from that of the rejected turn-up card.

CUE-BID—*Contract Bridge*. One that systematically shows control of a suit, especially by possession of the ace or a void.

CURSE OF SCOTLAND—The nine of diamonds.

CUT—1. Divide the pack into two packets and reverse their order. 2. Same as DRAW (1).

CUTTHROAT—Three-handed; applied also to any game in which each plays for himself.

CUT THE POT—Take a percentage from the pot.

DEAD CARD—One which cannot be used in play.

DEAD HAND—One barred from further participation.

DEAD MAN'S HAND—A poker hand, two aces and two eights, said to have been held by Wild Bill Hickok when he was shot and killed.

DEADWOOD—1. *Poker*. The discard pile. 2. *Rummy*. Unmatched cards in a hand.

DEAL—1. Distribute cards to the players; the turn to deal. 2. The period from one deal to the next, including all incidents of making the trump, bidding, melding, discarding, playing, showing, and scoring. 3. The cards dealt to the players respectively; a layout of the hands of all players.

DEALER—1. The player who distributes the cards in preparation for play. 2. Banker.

DEAL OFF—Make the first deal in the last round after which the session ends.

DEAL OUT—Omit giving a card or cards to a hand in regular turn during the deal.

DECK—Pack.

DECLARATION—Call; bid; naming of a trump suit or game; the trump suit or game as named in a bid.

DECLARE—1. Call; bid; name the trump. 2. Announce; meld.

DECLARE OUT — Same as COUNT OUT.

DECLARER—1. *Bridge*. The player who plays both his hand and the dummy. 2. Same as BIDDER (2).

DEFENDER — Contract Bridge. An opponent of declarer.

DEFENSE—*Bridge*. The opponents of the opening bidder, during the auction, or of the declarer, during the play; their acts and tactics.

DEMAND BID—Forcing bid.

DENIAL BID—*Bridge*. One showing lack of support for partner's declaration.

DENOMINATION — 1. Rank. 2. *Contract Bridge*. The suit or no-trump as named in a bid.

DEUCE—Any two-spot.

DEVIL'S BED POSTS—The four of clubs.

DIS — *Pinochle*. The lowest trump. Also, *dix*.

DISCARD—1. Lay aside excess cards in exchange for others from the stock or the widow; a discarded card or cards. 2. Play a plain-suit card not of the same suit as the lead.

DISCARD PILE—1. *Rummy*. Cards previously discarded. 2. *Solitaire*. Same as TALON.

DISTRIBUTION—Division of cards among the hands, especially as to the number of each suit held by each hand.

DIX—Same as DIS.

DOG—See BIG DOG, LITTLE DOG.

DOUBLE—*Bridge*. A call which has the effect of increasing the trick values and penalties in case the last preceding bid becomes the contract.

DOUBLE BETE—*Pinochle*. The penalty suffered by a bidder who has elected to play the hand and has lost.

DOUBLE DUMMY—*Whist family*. A game or situation in which a player knows the location of all cards.

DOUBLE-ENDED STRAIGHT—*Poker*. Four cards in sequence that can be filled to a straight by the draw of a card of next-higher or next-lower rank.

DOUBLE PAIR ROYAL—Four of a kind.

DOUBLE RUN—*Cribbage*. A hand comprising a run of three cards with one rank duplicated.

DOUBLETON—*Whist family*. An original holding of two cards in a suit.

DOWN—Defeated; having failed to make a contract; set back.

DRAW—1. Pull cards from a pack spread face down to determine seats, first deal, etc. 2. Receive cards from the stock to replace discards.

DROP—Withdraw from current deal or pot.

DUCK—*Bridge*. Fail to COVER when able.

DUMMY—*Bridge*. Declarer's partner; the hand laid down by him and played by declarer.

DUPLICATE—A form of Bridge or Whist play in which all contestants play the same series of deals, which are kept in orig-inal form by use of *duplicate boards*.

DUTCH STRAIGHT—Same as SKIP STRAIGHT.

EAGLES—The United States name of the fifth suit, green in color, at one time added to the standard deck.

EASY ACES—*Auction Bridge*. The condition when each side holds two aces.

ECHO—*Whist family*. The play, for signaling purposes, of a higher card before a lower card of the same suit.

EDGE—Same as AGE.

ELDEST HAND—The player at the left of the dealer.

ENDHAND—*Skat family*. The active player who is third in order of bidding.

END PLAY—Any of several strat-egems (especially, THROW-IN) that can usually be executed only in the last few tricks of the play.

ENTRY—A card with which a hand can eventually win a trick and so gain the lead.

ESTABLISH—Same as CLEAR (a suit).

EUCHRE—*Euchre*. Failure of the maker to win the number of tricks contracted for.

EXIT—Get out of the lead; compel another hand to win a trick.

EXPOSED CARD—One played in error, inadvertently dropped, or otherwise shown not in a legitimate manner, and there-fore (in most games) subject to penalty.

FACE CARD—Any king, queen, or jack. (The ace is not a face card.)

FACED—Lying with its face exposed.

FALSE CARD—One selected for

play, when there is a choice, to mislead opponents as to the contents of the hand.

FATTEN—1. *Poker*. Same as SWEETEN. 2. *Pinochle*. Same as SMEAR.

FIFTEEN—*Cribbage*. A combination of cards totaling 15 in pip values; the score of 2 for such a combination.

FILL—*Poker*. Draw cards that improve the original holding.

FINESSE—*Whist family*. An attempt to make a card serve as an equal to a higher-ranking card held by an opponent.

FIRST HAND—1. The leader to a trick. 2. The first player in turn to CALL.

FISH—Draw cards from the stock.

FIVE FINGERS — The five of trumps.

FLAG FLYING—*Bridge*. Assuming a losing contract to prevent the opponents from winning a game.

FLASH—Expose a card, as in dealing.

FLUSH—1. *Poker, Cribbage*. A hand with all cards of one suit. 2. *Pinochle*. A meld of the A, K, Q, J, 10 of trumps.

FOLD—*Stud Poker*. Withdraw from the current deal, as signified by turning one's cards face down.

FOLLOW SUIT—Play a card of the same suit as the lead.

FORCE—1. Compel a player to trump if he wishes to win the trick. 2. *Contract Bridge*. By a coventional call, demand that partner bid. 3. *Rummy*. Discard a card that the next player is required to take.

FOREHAND — *Skat family*. The active player who is first in order of bidding; eldest hand.

FOUL HAND — *Poker*. One of more or less than the legal number of cards.

FOUNDATION—*Solitaire*. A card on which a whole suit or sequence must be built up.

FOURFLUSH—*Poker*. Four cards of the same suit.

FOUR OF A KIND—Four cards of the same rank, as, four aces.

FOURTH-BEST — *Whist family*. The fourth-highest card of a suit held by a hand.

FREAK—1. *Bridge*. A hand of extraordinary pattern. 2. *Poker*. A wild card.

FREE BID—*Bridge*. One made voluntarily, not under any systematic compulsion.

FREE DOUBLE — *Bridge*. The double of an adverse contract which is sufficient for game if made undoubled.

FREE RIDE—*Poker*. Playing in a pot without having to ante or bet.

FREEZE — *Canasta*. Discard a wild card, making it more difficult to take the discard pile.

FREEZEOUT—Any variant of a game in which a player must drop out when his original stake is exhausted.

FROG—*Skat family*. The bid of lowest value. Also, *frage*.

FULL HAND — Same as FULL HOUSE.

FULL HOUSE — *Poker*. A hand comprising three of a kind and a pair.

GAME—1. A pastime, in the general sense, as Bridge, Poker. 2. The specific number of points that determines the winner of a contest, as 121 points in Cribbage. 3. The specific number of tricks or points that must be won in play to fulfill contract, as 61 or more in Skat.

4. A declaration, as in Skat. **5.** A variant of the basic game named by the dealer to be played in that deal, as in Dealer's Choice Poker. **6.** A certain card, as the ten of trumps in some variants of all Fours. **7.** A system of play.

GATE—The pay-off card, as in Monte Bank.

GIFT — *All Fours.* The point scored by eldest hand when he begs and dealer rejects.

GIN — *Gin Rummy.* A hand completely formed in sets, with no deadwood.

GO—*Cribbage.* A call signifying that the player cannot play another card without exceeding 31; the score of 1 point to opponent when go is called.

GO DOWN—*Rummy.* Meld, especially when the act terminates play.

GO OUT—**1.** Get rid of all cards in the hand, as in Rummy, Michigan. **2.** Reach the cumulative total of points necessary for game, as in All Fours, Cribbage; count out.

GO OVER—Bid higher.

GOULASH—*Bridge.* A deal of unshuffled cards, three or more at a time, to produce unusual hands.

GRAND—*Skat family.* A declaration in which only the jacks are trumps. Also, *grando.*

GRAND COUP—*Bridge.* A stratagem of play, the trumping of partner's winning plain card in order to shorten a trump holding to advantage.

GRAND SLAM — *Whist family.* The winning of all 13 tricks by one side.

GROUP—*Rummy.* A meld of cards of the same rank.

GUARDED — *Bridge.* Accompanied by as many small cards of the same suit as there are higher cards outstanding, as Q, x, x.

GUCKSER—*Skat.* A declaration in which jacks are trumps and the bidder picks up the skat. Also, *gucki.*

HAND—**1.** The cards dealt to or held by any player; any player. **2.** Same as DEAL (2). **3.** *Solitaire.* An undealt remainder of the pack after the tableau is laid out.

HANDPLAY—Playing without use of the widow.

HIGH—*All Fours family.* The ace of trumps, or the highest trump dealt; the score for holding such card.

HIGH-LOW—**1.** *Bridge.* Same as ECHO. **2.** *Poker.* Designating a pot that the high and low hands divide.

HINTERHAND — Same as END-HAND.

HIS HEELS—*Cribbage.* A jack turned as starter; the score of 2 to the dealer for this turn-up.

HIS NOBS—*Cribbage.* A jack of the same suit as the starter, in hand or crib; the score of 1 point for such jack.

HIT ME—*Black Jack.* Player's request for an additional card.

HOC—The last card in a deal of Faro. Also, *hock, hockelty.*

HOLDING—The cards in one's hand.

HOLD UP—*Bridge.* Refuse to win a trick with.

HOLE CARD—*Stud Poker.* The first card received by a player, which is dealt face down.

HONORS—High cards, especially if they have scoring value. *Bridge.* The five highest trumps, or, if there is no trump, the four aces.

HONOR-TRICKS — *Bridge.* High cards, in hand evaluation.

IMMORTAL HAND — Same as CINCH HAND.

IMPROVE—Draw cards that increase the value of the hand.

INDEX—The small number and suit symbol printed near the corner of a card, used to read the card when it is held in a fan with others. The *index value* of a card its its number, face cards counting 10 each.

INFORMATORY DOUBLE—*Bridge.* A systematic double made primarily to give information to partner.

INITIAL BID—Same as OPENING BID.

INSIDE STRAIGHT—*Poker.* Four cards needing a card of interior rank to make a straight, as 9, 8, 6, 5.

INSUFFICIENT BID—One that is not legally high enough to overcall the last previous bid.

INTERMEDIATES—*Bridge.* Cards such as nines and tens, not high enough to be valued but affecting the strength of the hand.

IN THE HOLE—Minus score, so-called from the practice (as in Euchre) of marking a score as minus by drawing a ring around it.

IRREGULARITY — Any departure from a law of correct procedure.

JACK—1. *All Fours family.* The score for winning the jack of trumps in play. 2. *Hearts.* A pool not won because no hand is clear, and therefore held intact for the next deal.

JACKPOTS — *Poker.* A deal in which everyone antes; usually, in such a deal a pair of jacks or better is required to open.

JAMBONE—*Railroad Euchre.* A

bid to play alone and with the entire hand faced on the table.

JAMBOREE—*Railroad Euchre.* A hand holding the five highest trumps, which is shown and scored without play.

JASS, JASZ—The jack of trumps, in Klaberjass.

JINK IT—*Spoil Five.* Play for all five tricks.

JOKER—An extra card furnished with the standard pack, and used in some games as the highest trump or as a wild card. See also BUG.

JUMP BID—*Bridge.* A bid of more tricks than are legally necessary to overcall.

JUNIOR—Same as YOUNGER.

KIBITZER—A non-playing spectator.

KICKER—*Draw Poker.* An extra card kept with a pair for a two-card draw.

KILTER—*Poker.* A hand nine-high with no pair, straight or flush.

KITTY—A percentage taken out of the stakes to defray expenses or pay admission fees; a pool to which betes are paid and from which royalties are collected; incorrectly used to mean WIDOW.

KNAVE—The jack of a suit.

KNOCK — 1. *Rummy family.* Signify termination of play by laying down one's hand. 2. *Poker.* Signify disinclination to cut the pack, or to bet, by rapping on the table.

LAPS—The carrying forward of excess points from one game to the next.

LAST—Points scored for winning the last trick, as in Pinochle.

LAY AWAY—1. *Pinochle.* Same

as BURY (2). **2.** *Cribbage.* Give cards to the crib.

LAY-DOWN—Same as CINCH HAND.

LAY OFF—*Rummy.* Get rid of cards on an opponent's meld.

LAYOUT—*Solitaire.* The array of cards first dealt out, comprising the tableau and possibly a stock and foundations.

LEAD—Play first to a trick; the card so played.

LEAST—*Schafskopf.* The game played if all players pass, the object being to take as few counting cards as possible.

LEFT BOWER—*Euchre.* The other jack of same color as the jack of the trump suit.

L. H. O.—*Bridge.* Left-hand opponent.

LIGHT—In debt to the pot.

LIMIT—*Poker.* The maximum amount by which a player may increase a previous bet.

LINE—*Gin Rummy.* Same as BOX.

LITTLE CASSINO—The two of spades.

LITTLE DOG—*Poker.* A special hand, consisting of seven-high and deuce-low but no pair.

LITTLE SLAM—Same as SMALL SLAM.

LITTLE TIGER—*Poker.* A special hand, consisting of eight-high and three-low but no pair.

LIVE CARD—One still in the hands or stock or otherwise available; one that is not DEAD.

LOCK—A sure thing; cinch.

LONE PLAYER—One who elects to play without help of his partner's hand; solo player.

LONG CARD—One left in a hand after all opponents are exhausted of the suit.

LONG GAME—A game in which

all cards are dealt originally, as Bridge.

LONG SUIT—*Whist family.* A holding of more than four cards in a suit; the longest holding in any suit in a hand.

LOOK—Same as CALL (2).

LOSING CARD—One that cannot be expected to win a trick. Also, *loser.*

LOVE—Score of zero.

LOW—*All Fours family.* The two of trumps, or the lowest trump dealt; the score for holding or winning such card.

LURCH—The winning of a game when the opponent has not yet passed the half-way mark.

MAKE—The contract; the trump suit; to name the trump suit or game.

MAKE GOOD — *Poker.* Add enough chips to meet the previous bet.

MAKER—Player who names the trump suit or game.

MAKE UP—Gather and shuffle the pack for the next deal.

MANILLE, OR MANILLA — The lowest card of the trump suit, when it ranks as the second-best trump.

MARCH—*Euchre.* The winning of all five tricks by one player or one side; the score for winning all the tricks.

MARRIAGE—*Bezique family.* A meld of the king and queen of a suit.

MASTER CARD — The highest card of a suit remaining live or unplayed.

MATADOR—Any of an unbroken sequence of trumps from the highest down; any high trump.

MATCHED SET—*Rummy family.* Same as SET (1).

MATCH-POINT SCORING—*Bridge.*

A method of scoring in duplicate play.

MEET A BET—*Poker*. CALL (2); add enough chips so as to make a total contribution equal to the maximum made by any previous player.

MELD—A combination, set, or group of cards of value in scoring or in getting rid of one's cards; to show or announce such a combination.

MENEL—*Klaberjass*. The nine of trumps.

MIDDLEHAND—*Skat family*. The active player who is second in order of bidding.

MILKING—A method of shuffling, by drawing cards simultaneously from top and bottom of the pack and piling them on the table.

MISDEAL—Any departure from the laws of correct procedure in dealing.

MISERE OR MISERY—Same as NULLO.

MIXED PAIR — In tournament play, a partnership of a man and a woman.

MOUTH BET — A bet offered without actually putting chips in the pot.

MUGGINS—*Cribbage*. The right of a player to take points overlooked by his opponent.

MULTIPLIERS—*Skat*. Factors by which the base value of the trump suit is multiplied to determine the value of a game.

NATURAL—1. Without any wild card. 2. A combination which wins without further play and without contest except from another natural.

NEAR CARD—*Cribbage*. A card consecutive with another card, or nearly so.

NEGATIVE DOUBLE — Same as INFORMATORY DOUBLE.

NEXT—*Euchre*. The other suit of the same color as the rejected turn-up card.

NO-TRUMP—A declaration that offers to play the hand without a trump suit.

NULLO—A declaration in which the object of play to avoid winning tricks or points.

ODD TRICK—*Bridge*. Any won by declarer in excess of six.

OFF, OFFSIDE—*Bridge*. Not in position to be captured by a finesse.

OFFICIAL —*Pinochle*. Validated by the winning of a trick—said of the score for a meld.

ONE-ENDER—*Poker*. A, K, Q, J or A, 2, 3, 4.

OPEN—1. Make the first declaration or the first bid. 2. *Poker*. Make the first bet, especially in jackpots. 3. A declation that offers to play with the entire hand faced on the table. 4. *Stud Poker*. Face up on the table. 5. Make the first lead of a suit.

OPEN-ENDER—*Poker*. Same as DOUBLE-ENDED STRAIGHT.

OPENERS — *Poker*. A holding that entitles a player to open the pot.

OPENING BID—The first bid of the auction.

ORDER UP—*Euchre*. A declaration by an opponent of dealer, accepting the turn-up card for trump.

ORIGINAL BID—Same as OPENING BID.

OUVERT—Same as OPEN (3).

OVERBID—1. Overcall. 2. A bid that cannot be expected to be fulfilled.

OVERCALL—Make a bid legally

sufficient to supersede the last previous bid.

OVERHAND SHUFFLE—A shuffle executed by holding the pack in one hand and dropping packets from the top into the other hand.

OVERTRICK—*Bridge.* Any won by declarer in excess of his contract.

PACK—Deck; the aggregation of all cards used in a game. See page 14.

PACKET—A portion of the pack, especially in shuffling and cutting.

PAINT — 1. *Hearts.* Discard a heart on a trick won by another player. 2. *Low Poker.* Deal a face card to a player drawing to low cards.

PAIR—1. Two cards of the same rank. 2. A partnership of two players.

PAIR ROYAL—*Cribbage.* Three of a kind.

PAM—The jack of clubs.

PART-SCORE — *Bridge.* A trick-score total of less than game. Also, *partial.*

PASS—1. A declaration signifying that a player does not wish to bid or bet, or that he withdraws from the current deal. 2. *Hearts family.* Cards exchanged among the original hands after the deal.

PASS OUT A DEAL—Abandon the deal after all players pass.

PASST MIR NICHT—*Skat.* The second turn.

PAT HAND—*Draw Poker.* One which makes no discard and no draw; a player who draws no cards.

PATTERN — *Whist family.* A group of four integers, as 4-4-3-2, expressing the way in which a given suit is divided

among the four hands or a given hand is divided into suits.

PEDRO — *Cinch.* The five of trumps, or the other five of the same color.

PEG—*Cribbage.* A marker used for scoring on a cribbage board; win points, especially during the play.

PENALTY CARD — *Contract Bridge.* An exposed card that must be played at first legal opportunity.

PENALTY DOUBLE — *Same as* BUSINESS DOUBLE.

PENNY ANTE—*Poker.* A game in which the ante or limit is one cent.

PIANOLA—*Bridge.* A lay-down hand.

PICTURE CARD—Same as FACE CARD.

PIGEON—*Poker.* A card drawn that geatly improves the hand.

PINOCHLE—*Pinochle.* A meld of the queen of spades and jack of diamonds.

PIP—Any of the large suit symbols ♠, ♡, ♢, ♣ printed on the face of a card (excluding index marks). *Pip value* is the numerical or index value of the card.

PIQUE—*Piquet.* The winning of 30 points before opponent scores a point; the bonus of 30 points therefor. Also, *pic.*

PITCH — *Auction Pitch.* The opening lead, which fixes the trump suit.

PIVOT — A schedule for four players whereby each plays with every other as his partner; the player who remains in the same seat while the others progress.

PLACES OPEN—*Pinochle.* Outstanding cards that will improve a hand.

PLAIN SUIT—Any that is not trumps.

PLAYER—1. A participant in a game. 2. *Skat.* The highest bidder, who then plays alone against the two others in partnership. 3. A card that can legally be played.

PLAYING TO THE SCORE—Modifying normal strategy of bidding or play when one side is close to game.

PLAY OFF—*Cribbage.* Play a card of rank far enough from that of previous cards so that opponent cannot make a run.

PLAY ON — *Cribbage.* Play a card that may enable opponent to make a run.

POINT—1. A unit of scoring. 2. *Piquet.* A scoring combination, the holding in a suit that totals the greatest number of pips; the score therefor.

POINT COUNT—*Bridge.* A method of evaluating one's hand by assigning a relative number of points to each high card held.

PONE—The player at dealer's right; in two-hand play, the non-dealer.

POOL—Same as POT.

POST-MORTEM — Discussion of the merits of the bidding and play of a deal.

POT—The aggregate of chips or money at stake in a deal, consisting usually of contributions from each active player.

PREDICT—*Skat.* Same as ANNOUNCE (3).

PREËMPTIVE BID — *Bridge.* A high opening bid, made to shut out adverse competition.

PREMIUMS—1. Same as ROYALTIES. 2. *Bridge.* All scores other than for odd tricks.

PROGRESSION — Movement of players or of boards from table to table in Progressive or Duplicate Bridge.

PSYCHIC BID—*Bridge.* One made without the cards to support it, for the purpose of misleading the opponents.

PUNTER — One who plays against the bank.

PUPPY-FOOT—The ace of clubs; any club.

PURE CANASTA—Natural Canasta.

QUART—*Piquet.* A sequence of four cards in the same suit.

QUATORZE—*Piquet.* Four of a kind (tens or higher), counting 14.

QUICK TRICKS—Same as HONOR-TRICKS.

QUINT—*Piquet.* A sequence of five cards in the same suit.

QUITTED TRICK—One that has been turned face down.

RAISE — 1. *Poker.* Put more chips in the pot than are necessary to meet the previous bet. 2. *Bridge.* Bid an increased number of tricks in a declaration previously bid by partner.

RAKE-OFF—The percentage of the stakes taken by the house or club, usually by means of a kitty.

RAMSCH—*Skat.* A Nullo game which is played if all players pass.

RANGDOODLES—Variant of ROODLES.

RANK—The ordinal position of a card in its suit.

REARHAND — Same as ENDHAND.

REBID—*Bridge.* A bid made by a player who has previously bid.

RENEGE—Same as REVOKE.

RENOUNCE—Play a card not of the suit led.

REPIQUE—*Piquet.* The winning

of 30 points in hand, without play, before the opponent scores a point; the bonus of 60 points therefor. Also, *repic*.

RESPONSE—*Bridge*. A bid made in reply to a bid by partner.

REVOKE — Fail to follow suit when able; fail to play a card as required by a law of correct procedure or by a proper penalty.

RIFFLE—A manner of shuffling (see page 17).

RIGHT BOWER — *Euchre*. The jack of the trump suit.

ROBBING—Exchanging a card in the hand for the card turned up for trump.

ROB THE PACK—*Cinch*. Select any desired cards from the stock (the privilege of the dealer).

ROODLES—*Poker*. Any special pot with increased ante or stakes.

ROTATION—Progression of the turn to deal, to receive cards, to bid, or to play; in the United States, the rotation is usually clockwise, the turn passing from each player to the player nearest his left.

ROUGH—*Poker*. Relatively bad.

ROUND — Any division of the dealing, bidding or play, in which each hand participates once, e.g., the series of deals from one player's turn to his next turn; the series of bids from one player's turn to the next; a trick.

ROUND GAME—One in which there are no partnerships.

ROUND HOUSE — *Pinochle*. A meld comprising a king and a queen of each suit. Also, *round trip*.

ROUND-THE-CORNER — Circular

sequence of rank, the highest card being deemed adjacent to the lowest, as, Q, K, A, 2, 3, a round-the-corner straight in Poker.

ROYAL FLUSH—*Poker*. An ace-high straight flush.

ROYAL MARRIAGE — *Bezique family*. A meld of the king and queen of trumps.

ROYAL SEQUENCE — *Pinochle*. Same as FLUSH.

ROYALTIES—Payments collected by a player who holds any of certain high hands, in addition to whatever he wins in regular play.

RUBBER—The winning of the first two out of three games by one side, or of a series of deals in Four-Suit Bridge.

RUBBER BRIDGE — *Bridge*. A form of play in which rubbers are scored (as opposed to duplicate play).

RUBICON — *Piquet*. Failure of the loser of a game to reach 100 points.

RUFF—Play a trump on a plain-suit lead.

RULE OF ELEVEN—*Bridge*. The fact that when a player leads his fourth-best card in a suit, the number of that card subtracted from 11 will reveal the number of higher-ranking cards in the other three hands.

RUMMY—*Rummy family*. Get rid of the last card in the hand; lay down a hand completely formed in sets; also, call attention to a play overlooked by an opponent.

RUN—A sequence of three or more cards of the same suit, as in Cribbage, Rummy.

RUN THE CARDS — *All Fours*. Deal additional cards and

make a new turn-up, when a beg is accepted.

SACRIFICE BID — *Bridge.* One made without the expectation that the contract will be fulfilled, for the purpose of saving greater loss.

SANDBAGGING—Withholding action on a good hand in order to trap an opponent into greater loss.

SCHMEISS—*Klaberjass.* A declaration which is a proposal to accept the turn-up card for trump or abandon the deal.

SCHMIER—Same as SMEAR.

SCHNEIDER — 1. *Skat family.* Failure of one side to win 31 or more points in a play. 2. *Gin Rummy.* Same as SHUT-OUT.

SCHWARTZ—*Skat family.* The winning of all the tricks by one player or one side.

SCORE—1. The counting value of specific cards or tricks. 2. The accumulated total of points won by a player or a side. 3. Score sheet.

SECOND HAND—Second in turn to call or play.

SECOND TURN—*Skat.* Turn-up of the second skat card for trump.

SEE—*Poker.* Meet a bet. CALL (2).

SENIOR—Eldest hand.

SEQUENCE—Two or more cards of adjacent rank, as 8, 9, 10; in Rummy, such cards in the same suit.

SERVE—Deal, especially in giving additional cards at Draw Poker.

SET—1. A combination of melding or scoring value, as in Rummy. 2. Defeat the contract, as in Bridge.

SET BACK—A deduction from a player's accumulated score; a variant name for certain games, as Cutthroat Euchre.

SEXTETTE—*Piquet.* A sequence of six cards in the same suit.

SHOE—A dealing box used in Chemin de Fer.

SHORT GAME—Any in which not all the cards of the pack are put into play during a deal.

SHORT SUIT—*Whist family.* A holding of fewer than four cards in a suit.

SHOW—1. Meld; expose. 2. *Cribbage.* Count the hand.

SHOWDOWN—*Poker.* The facing of all active hands to determine the winner of a pot.

SHUFFLE—Mix the cards in the pack preparatory to dealing.

SHUTOUT—1. *Gin Rummy.* The winning of a game when opponent has not scored a point. 2. *Bridge.* A preëmptive bid.

SHY—Short, as said of a pot to which additional antes are due, or of a player who owes chips to the pot.

SIDE CARD—1. Any of a plain suit. 2. *Poker.* The highest card in the hand outside of a pair or two pairs, referred to in deciding higher hand between two that hold one or two pairs of the same rank.

SIDE MONEY—A bet in a side pot.

SIDE POT—*Table Stakes Poker.* One separate from the main pot, made by continued betting after one player has put all his chips in the main pot.

SIDE STRENGTH—High cards in plain suits.

SIDE SUIT—Same as PLAIN SUIT.

SIGHT—The right to compete

for the main pot in the show-down.

SIGNAL—*Whist family.* Any convention of play whereby one partner properly informs the other of his holdings or desires.

SIMPLE GAME — *Skat family.* The lowest declaration that may be bid.

SIMPLE HONORS — *Auction Bridge.* The holding of three honors by one side; the score therefor.

SIGN-OFF—A bid that asks partner to pass.

SINGLETON—*Whist family.* An original holding of one card in a suit.

SINK—*Piquet.* Omit announcement of a scoring combination (for possible advantage in play).

SKAT—*Skat family.* The widow.

SKEET—*Poker.* A special hand, consisting of 2, 5, 9 and two other cards lower than 9, but no pair.

SKIP BID—Same as JUMP BID.

SKIP STRAIGHT—*Poker.* A special hand, consisting of a sequence of odd or even cards, as J, 9, 7, 5, 3.

SKUNKED—Beaten without having scored a point.

SLAM—The winning of all the tricks by one side.

SLUFF or SLOUGH — Same as DISCARD (2).

SMALL SLAM — *Whist family.* The winning of twelve tricks by one side.

SMEAR—Discard a counting card on a trick won by partner. Also schmier.

SMOKE OUT — *Hearts family.* Force out the queen of spades by repeated leads of the suit.

SMOOTH — *Poker.* Relatively good.

SMUDGE—*Auction Pitch.* A bid to win all four points.

SNEAK—*Whist family.* A plain-suit singleton.

SODA—*Faro.* The first card.

SOLO—A bid to play without using the widow.

SPACE—*Solitaire.* A vacancy in the tableau created by the removal of all cards of one pile.

SPADILLE or SPADILLA — The queen of clubs.

SPLIT—1. *Faro.* The appearance of two cards of the same rank in one turn. 2. Same as BREAK. 3. *Bridge.* To play one of equal honors.

SPLITTING OPENERS—*Poker.* In a jackpot, discarding part of the combination that qualified the hand to open (in an effort to better the chances of improvement).

SPOT CARD—Any of rank 10, 9, 8, 7, 6, 5, 4, 3, 2.

SPREAD — 1. Open; show. 2. Meld. 3. A contract that can be fulfilled without playing.

SQUEEZE—1. Look at one's cards by slightly separating them at one corner to see the indexes. 2. *Bridge.* Compel other hands to discard; an end-play dependent upon compelling adverse discards.

STACK—Pile of chips; quota of chips assigned to each player.

STAND—1. *All Fours.* A declaration by eldest hand that he is satisfied with the turn-up card for trump. 2. Decline to draw additional cards.

STAND-OFF—A tie or draw.

STAND PAT—Decline to draw additional cards; play with one's original hand.

STARTER—*Cribbage*. The card cut by non-dealer and turned up by dealer, prior to the play.

STAY—*Poker*. Remain in the pot without raising; meet a bet; call; see.

STIFF CARD—Same as LONG CARD.

STILL PACK—The one not dealt or to be dealt, when two packs are used alternately.

STOCK—An undealt portion of the pack, which may be used later in the same deal.

STOP—1. *Stops family*. Interruption of play caused by absence of the next card in sequence; the card so missing. 2. *Russian Bank*. A call upon opponent to cease play because of an irregularity in order of play.

STOP CARD—*Canasta*. A card, such as a black three, that cannot be taken as the top discard.

STOPPER—A holding by which a hand can eventually win a trick in a suit led by an adversary.

STRADDLE—*Poker*. Raise the previous player's BLIND (1) or the previous player's straddle, by doubling it.

STRAIGHT—*Poker*. A hand of five cards in sequence, but not all in the same suit.

STRAIGHT FLUSH—*Poker*. A hand of five cards in sequence in the same suit.

STRINGER—SEQUENCE.

STRIP—1. Remove low cards from (the deck) to reduce the number of cards in it. 2. *Bridge*. Play so as to render opponent(s) void in a suit, preparatory to an end-play.

SUPPORT — RAISE (2); cards that are of assistance to partner.

SWEEP—*Cassino*. The taking in of all cards on the table; the score of 1 point therefor.

SWEEPSTAKE—*Hearts*. A method of settlement; the pot is won only by a player who is clear.

SWEETEN—*Poker*. Ante again to a jackpot not opened on the previous deal.

SYSTEM—*Bridge*. An agreement between partners on the requirements for various bids and tactical procedure in various situations.

TABLEAU—*Solitaire*. That part of the layout, excluding foundations, on which builds are made. In some games, the entire layout.

TABLE STAKES—*Poker*. A method of placing a limit on betting.

TAKE-ALL—*Hearts*. The winning of all the counting cards by one player.

TAKE IN—Gather cards from the table, as in Cassino.

TAKEOUT — 1. *Bridge*. A bid, over partner's bid, in a different denomination. 2. *Poker*. Same as STACK (2).

TAKE THE LEAD—*Stud Poker*. Make the first bet in a round.

TAKE UP—*Euchre*. Accept the turn-up card for trump (by dealer).

TALLY—Score sheet, especially as used in progressive play.

TALON — *Solitaire*. Waste pile; cards laid aside as unplayable on being turned up from the stock or hand.

TAP — *Poker*. Bet the whole amount of chips in front of a player.

TENACE—*Whist family*. A holding of two cards in a suit, lacking one or more cards of intervening rank, as A, J. Perfect tenace lacks one intervening card; imperfect tenace lacks two or more. Major tenace is A, Q; minor tenace is K, J.

TENTH CARD—Any of pip value 10, as a face card at Cribbage.

THIRD HAND—Third in turn to call or play.

THREE OF A KIND—Three cards of the same rank, as three aces.

THREES—Same as THREE OF A KIND.

THROW-IN — An end-play dependent on compelling an opponent to win a trick and then lead to his disadvantage.

THROW OFF—Discard; smear.

TIERCE—*Piquet*. A sequence of three cards of the same suit.

TIGER—See BIG TIGER, LITTLE TIGER. Also: *Blind Tiger*, blind opening (Poker); *Buck the Tiger*, play Faro.

-TIMER, as EIGHT-TIMER—*Draw Poker*. A hand that will be improved by the draw of any of the specified number of outstanding cards.

TOPS—Highest cards of a suit.

TOTAL-POINT SCORING—*Bridge*. A method of scoring in duplicate play.

TOUCHING—Adjacent in rank.

TOURNEE—*Skat*. A declaration which offers to turn up a card from the skat to fix the trump suit.

TRAIL—*Cassino*. Play a card to the table without building or taking in.

TREY—Any threespot.

TRICK—A round of cards during the play, one card being contributed by each active hand; the packet of such cards when gathered.

TRICK SCORE — *Bridge*. Points made by declarer for odd tricks; the part of the score sheet where such points are entered.

TRIPLETS—Three of a kind.

TRUMP CARD — Any of the trump suit, or one arbitrarily designated as a trump by the rules of the game.

TRUMP SUIT—One selected under the rules of the game to have the special privilege that every card in this suit ranks higher than any non-trump card in trick-winning.

TURN—1. A player's opportunity, in due rotation, to deal, declare, play, etc. 2. *Faro, etc.* A play that decides how certain bets shall be settled.

TURN IT DOWN—*Euchre*. Reject the turn-up card as trump.

TURN-UP—A card turned face up, after the deal, to fix or propose the trump.

TWO-SUITER—*Bridge*. A hand containing five or more cards in each of two suits.

UNBLOCK—*Bridge*. Avoid or resolve a blocked suit, by cashing or discarding high cards.

UNDERCUT—*Gin Rummy*. Show a hand that counts the same or less than opponent's, after he has knocked.

UNDER THE GUNS—*Poker*. Said of the first player in turn to bet.

UNDERTRICK—*Bridge*. Any by which declarer falls short of making his contract.

UNLIMITED POKER—Agreement that there will be no limit on the size of a bet and the number of raises.

UNLOAD—Get rid of the dangerous cards in one's hand.

UNMATCHED CARD—*Rummy family*. Any that is not part of a set; deadwood.

UP—*Poker*. A term used as in "aces up" to designate the higher pair in a two-pair hand.

UPCARD—1. *Stud Poker*. One properly dealt face up. 2. *Gin Rummy*. The first card turned up from the stock after the deal; the uppermost card of the discard pile.

UPPERCUT—*Bridge*. Play a high trump to force out a higher trump in an opponent's hand.

VIGORISH—The fee or percentage accruing to the banker of a game.

VOID—Same as BLANK SUIT.

VULNERABLE—*Contract Bridge*. Said of a side that has won a game toward rubber.

WASTE PILE—Talon; a pile of discards; cards laid aside as unwanted or as unplayable.

WHANGDOODLES—Variant of ROODLES.

WHEEL—Same as BICYCLE.

WHIPSAWED — *Faro*. Condition of one who loses two bets on the same turn.

WIDE CARDS — *Cribbage*. Two cards separated in rank by two or more cards.

WIDOW—Extra cards dealt at the same time as the hands, and which usually become the property of the highest bidder. Also called the blind, the skat.

WILD CARD—One that may be specified by the holder to be of any rank and suit.

WITH, as WITH THREE—*Skat*. Holding the specified number of top trumps in unbroken sequence from the jack of clubs down.

WITHOUT—*Bridge*. A call meaning "No trumps."

WITHOUT, as WITHOUT TWO—*Skat*. Lacking the specified number of top trumps, all higher than the best held in the hand.

x—A symbol representing any card lower than the lowest specified card of the same suit, as ♡ J-x (♡ J and any heart lower than the jack).

YARBOROUGH—*Whist family*. A hand containing no card higher than a nine.

YOUNGER HAND—In two-hand play, the one who does not make the opening lead.